Poverty
and
Public Policy

Recent Titles in
Studies in Social Welfare Policies and Programs

Social Planning and Human Service Delivery in the Voluntary
Sector
Gary A. Tobin, editor

Using Computers to Combat Welfare Fraud: The Operation and
Effectiveness of Wage Matching
David Greenberg and Douglas A. Wolf

POVERTY AND PUBLIC POLICY

An Analysis of Federal Intervention Efforts

MICHAEL MORRIS
AND
JOHN B. WILLIAMSON

STUDIES IN SOCIAL WELFARE POLICIES AND
PROGRAMS, NUMBER 3

Greenwood Press
New York • Westport, Connecticut • London

Library of Congress Cataloging-in-Publication Data

Morris, Michael, 1949-
  Poverty and public policy.

  (Studies in social welfare policies and programs,
ISSN 8755-5360 ; no. 3)
  Bibliography: p.
  Includes index.
  1. Public welfare—United States. 2. United States—
Social policy. 3. Poor—United States. I. Williamson,
John B. II. Title. III. Series.
HV95.M67   1986   361.6'1'0973   86-398
ISBN 0-313-24942-3 (lib. bdg. : alk. paper)

Library of Congress Catalog Card Number: 86-398
ISBN: 0-313-24942-3
ISSN: 8755-5360

First published in 1986

Greenwood Press, Inc.
88 Post Road West, Westport, Connecticut 06881

Printed in the United States of America

The paper used in the book complies with the
Permanent Paper Standard issued by the National
Information Standards Organization (Z39.48-1984).

10 9 8 7 6 5 4 3 2 1

Copyright Acknowledgment

For permission to use materials, we gratefully acknowledge the following source:

M. Morris and J.B. Williamson, "Stereotypes and Social Class: A Focus on
Poverty," in A.G. Miller (Ed.), *In the Eye of the Beholder: Contemporary Issues
in Stereotyping* (Praeger Publishers, New York, N.Y., 1982), pp. 413-416, 431
and 439. Copyright © 1982 by Praeger Publishers. Used by permission of the
publisher.

To Donna, Stephanie, and my parents

M. M.

To my mother, Nancy B. Carleton

J. B. W.

Contents

Tables

Preface

Federal poverty programs have long been the subject of controversy in the United States. Conservatives argue that many of these interventions exacerbate the very problems they are supposed to solve. This accusation is applied with particular vigor to programs which directly provide individuals with economic resources. While supporters of these programs dispute the validity of this claim, they usually agree with conservatives that a "genuine" or "permanent" solution to the poverty problem must be based in efforts that increase the economic self-sufficiency of individuals.

We believe that the evidence reviewed in this book indicates that both of these perspectives on poverty policy are seriously flawed. In reality, the strategy of direct resource provision has a substantially greater antipoverty impact than most programs which attempt to increase self-sufficiency. Moreover, it appears unlikely that sufficiency-oriented approaches can ever be strengthened to the point where they seriously challenge the resource-oriented strategy as the foundation of either a temporary or permanent solution to poverty on a national scale. The assumptions that sufficiency-oriented approaches must satisfy are simply too demanding, in terms of both quality and quantity, to allow such an achievement to occur. To the extent that this analysis is valid, a fundamental reorientation of our thinking about poverty policy's potentials and limits would seem to be called for. Such a reorientation could lead to significant progress being made in reducing poverty in the United States.

In preparing this book we received assistance from a number of individuals, and we are pleased to acknowledge them now. At the University of New Haven, Deans Ralf Carriuolo and Joseph Chepaitis, as well as Provost Alexis Sommers, provided valuable administrative support. Associate librarian Eric Johnson was a master at helping us locate hard-to-find reference materials, and graduate assistant Steve Jex was an expert at abstracting them. Linda Frisman, Dan Hungerford, and Andrew Hahn alerted us to the existence of some very useful policy analysis publications. James and Thesda Morris made countless trips to the U.S. Government Printing Office and other federal agencies on our behalf. Finally, Doreen Nuzzo and Ellen Young expertly typed numerous drafts of this work, and not once complained about nit-picky authors.

Poverty
and
Public Policy

1

Introduction

If the ultimate criterion of social welfare policy is eliminating net poverty, the War on Poverty has very nearly been won.

Charles Murray, 1982
"The Two Wars Against Poverty:
Economic Growth and The Great Society"

The faith which many may have had in the above proclamation of victory has undoubtedly been shaken in recent years. Regardless of how poverty is measured, the 1980s have witnessed significant increases in the ranks of the poor (U.S. Bureau of the Census, 1985c, 1985d). Indeed, not since the War on Poverty has the attention of policymakers and the mass media been so focused upon the plight of the homeless, the hungry, and the poor in general.

The purpose of this book is to examine the major policies and programs which combine, in an explicit and implicit fashion, to form poverty policy in the United States. Despite the vast economic resources possessed by our society, these programs have been unable to eliminate poverty or reduce it to negligible levels. Understanding why this is so, and what can be done about it, are the primary objectives of our analysis. We are certainly not the first to undertake such a task, nor are we likely to be the last. Nevertheless, we believe that our presentation makes a distinctive contribution to the poverty policy literature. This is because most discussions of poverty policy, including those with which we largely agree, fail to pursue the theoretical implications generated by their findings regarding policy efficacy.

What are these findings, and what conclusions do they justify? The evidence we review indicates that programs which provide direct economic assistance, either in the form of cash or in-kind benefits (e.g., Food Stamps, housing, medical care), have a major antipoverty impact. While social insurance programs such as Social Security clearly have the greatest impact, the substantial improvement in economic well-being experienced by those receiving a combination of welfare and in-kind benefits cannot be overlooked.

Economic growth, at least on the national level, also appears to exert a major antipoverty influence. One need not be a staunch conservative to appreciate the value to the poor of a healthy, expanding economy, and it is no coincidence that the War on Poverty was launched during such a period in the 1960s. Economic development is no panacea, however. To the extent that growth is not translated into increases in cash and in-kind assistance, its antipoverty value is greatly diminished. It is simply not possible to eliminate poverty by focusing solely on the employable poor who benefit from the increased job opportunities associated with economic expansion.

In contrast to the preceding approaches, the strategies of employment and training, education, targeted economic development, and social services have generally been found to yield very limited benefits to the poor. It is possible, of course, that the full impact of these approaches has been underestimated. For example, the impact of most cash and in-kind programs on a recipient's economic well-being is immediate and relatively easy to measure; the impacts of other types of programs are not. It is usually expected that the economic benefits of the latter programs will not be noticeable for some time. Indeed, in the case of educational interventions, it may be a decade or more before these payoffs are supposed to occur. Thus, assessing the economic outcomes of these efforts can be an exceedingly difficult and imprecise task.

Even if methodological problems in measuring impact did not exist, however, there would still be major theoretical reasons to question the antipoverty potential of the less effective strategies. The assumptions that must be satisfied in order for them to reduce poverty are usually much more demanding than those required by more successful programs. This is largely due to the fact that training, education, and social services all represent "people-changing" strategies to a great degree. That is, they rely upon changes in such personal attributes as motivation, ability, values, beliefs, and attitudes in order to be successful. Achieving such change can be a very difficult task.

Not only are the assumptions of the less effective approaches more intimidating than those of the more effective ones, they tend to be more numerous as well. This fact places the less effective strategies at a fundamental disadvantage since, all other things being equal, the greater the number of assumptions associated with a given intervention, the greater the chances are that at least one of these assumptions will not be met.

Both of these assumption-related problems can be seen in programs such as employment training. In order for training to have a substantial economic impact on participants the following conditions must be fulfilled:

1. Participants must possess or develop the motivation and ability necessary to learn the skills being taught.

2. The model of skill-training that is used in the program must be educationally sound.

3. Training must be at a sufficiently high skill level to qualify program graduates for jobs paying nonpoverty wages.

4. These jobs must actually be available in the communities where program graduates reside.

5. Graduates must have the ability and motivation to hold onto these jobs once they obtain them.

In contrast, there are only two major assumptions that must be satisfied if a direct assistance program is to significantly benefit participants. First, the dollar amount of assistance provided must be non-negligible, and second, participants must actually receive the assistance due them. Neither of these assumptions focus on the participants' motivation or ability.

On both theoretical and empirical grounds, then, we believe the following conclusions are warranted: *The greater the changes in individual characteristics required by an antipoverty strategy, the less likely that the strategy will have a major impact on a participant's economic status. More generally, the greater the number of assumptions that a strategy must satisfy, and the more demanding these assumptions are, the weaker its impact is likely to be.*

These conclusions are unsettling, for they suggest that targeted attempts to make the poor economically self-sufficient are, by their very nature, less likely to substantially reduce poverty than approaches which directly provide individuals with resources. Self-sufficiency, however, is a cherished value in American culture. It is probably safe to say that for the overwhelming majority of Americans, including most of those who strongly support direct-assistance programs, the preferred path to poverty reduction is one which involves increasing individuals' self-sufficiency and reducing their dependency on the government (Lewis and Schneider, 1985). Unfortunately, the evidence indicates that if policymakers indulge this preference at the expense of adequately funding direct-assistance programs, progress toward poverty reduction will actually be hindered. Indeed, our analysis suggests that the ultimate key to eliminating poverty, or at least to reducing it to negligible levels, is not the development of better dependency-reduction programs, but the expansion of direct-assistance ones. To the extent that such an expansion is not forthcoming, significant poverty will remain part of the American scene.

There is little reason to expect such an expansion in the near future. Huge federal deficits have combined with national political leadership which has vigorously, and with much popular support, reemphasized America's ideological heritage of individualism and aversion to federal intervention and control. This reemphasis has called into question the performance of poverty policy, especially with respect to its failure to significantly reduce the rate of prewelfare poverty (e.g., Anderson, 1984; Glazer, 1984; Murray, 1982, 1984). In this context, it is asserted that government largesse has undermined the motivation of many individuals to form strong attachments to the labor force. While the evidence indicates that this claim has overstated the modest negative impact of poverty programs on the labor supply (Burtless and Haveman, 1985; Danziger, Haveman, and Plotnick, 1981), the value symbolism involved here is potent. This potency would appear to be at least partially responsible for the fact that much of the policy agenda accompanying this claim has been legislated. The resulting budget reductions in a wide range of poverty programs (Bawden, 1984; Champagne and Harpham, 1984; Weicher, 1984b) have been justified as an effort to target resources more directly toward the truly needy who cannot be expected to work. It is maintained that those removed from the program rolls by these measures will, if they are willing to work, benefit from the national economic growth generated by a variety of macroeconomic policies. Here we see the self-sufficiency path to poverty reduction being followed in somewhat draconian fashion.

In at least the short run, these cutbacks have had a substantial negative impact on the working poor. Their standard of living has deteriorated markedly, as they have lost not only direct income assistance (in whole or in part), but in many cases eligibility for in-kind benefits such as Medicaid (Joe and Rogers, 1985; Moscovice and Craig, 1984; Sarri et al., 1984; Smeeding, 1984b; U.S. General Accounting Office, 1984b). Contributing to this deterioration has been an increased federal income tax burden imposed upon the working poor as a result of the 1981 Economic Recovery and Tax Act (Center on Budget and Policy Priorities, 1984; Congressional Budget Office, 1984a). At a more general level, these policy changes have contributed to increased income inequality in the United States (Moon and Sawhill, 1984).

Against this background it is not surprising that opinion polls show that most people believe that the poor have been treated unfairly by the executive branch in recent years (*Gallup Report*, 1983). Even more predictable has been the highly critical response of scholars and commentators who view poverty from the perspective of the political left (e.g., Beeghley, 1983; Harrington, 1984; Joe and Rogers, 1985; Levitan and Johnson, 1984; Piven and Cloward, 1982).

In many respects the policy shifts of the 1980s, and the reactions they have generated, simply represent the most recent manifestations of a fundamental ambivalence toward poverty which has characterized American society since colonial times. Accordingly, a working knowledge of the historical context within which poverty policy has developed in the United States is crucial for understanding the societal dynamics surrounding current programs.

HISTORICAL PERSPECTIVES

A review of society's treatment of the poor over the past several centuries reveals at least two key themes. One is the tendency to divide the poor into "deserving" and "undeserving" subgroups. The second is the development of the welfare state.

Dichotomizing the Poor[1]

The category of deserving poor has traditionally included those who, because of factors such as age, illness, or disability, are viewed as being poor through no fault of their own. On the other hand, the poverty of the undeserving or able-bodied subgroup has generally been attributed to a lack of motivation on their part. The available evidence suggests that this dichotomized perception of the poor has probably always existed. It was not until the fourteenth century, however, that the distinction became a focal point for public attention. Prior to that time the primary source of aid to the European poor was the local parish of the Catholic church, an institution whose "blessed are the poor" theology downplayed the importance of the deserving/undeserving categorization. While the guidelines for providing assistance accorded a lower priority to the able-bodied poor than to those in other groups (elderly, sick, widowed), the perception that an individual had unmet needs served as the ultimate criterion for rendering help (Coll, 1969).

A sharply dichotomized image of the poor having implications for relief-giving was crystallized by a number of large-scale developments in the late Middle Ages. The decline of feudalism generated an expanding class of poor, mobile laborers that was seen as posing a growing threat to societal stability. A market economy was also emerging during this period, bringing with it the phenomenon of employment cycles and regular dislocations of large segments of the new labor force. The potential for civil disorder thus increased even more, intensifying hostility toward the able-bodied poor.

The massive population reduction caused by the bubonic plague (the Black Death) of the mid-fourteenth century also played an important role. The severe scarcity of labor resulting from this reduction produced elevated wage rates, which in turn encouraged increasing numbers of the poor to become geographically mobile in the hope of improving their fortunes. The paradoxical consequence of this process was an increase in the number of individuals temporarily needing assistance because of their moving from place to place in search of higher wages and better working conditions. Inevitably accompanying this phenomenon were acts of theft and violence by a minority of this new migrant population.

While it is not surprising that antagonism toward the able-bodied poor would be generated by these developments, a cohesive ideology that could justify such hostility on a basis other than that of material self-interest awaited the emergence of the Protestant Reformation and Calvinism in the sixteenth and seventeenth centuries. Traditional Catholic views of the poor were challenged by the Protestant ethic, which presented an individualistic explanation of poverty and placed it within the context of religious dogma. The poverty of the able-bodied thus came to be interpreted as a sign of defective character. The problematical nature of poverty now extended beyond the threat of mere societal instability, having acquired supernatural significance (Feagin, 1975).

Along with the rest of their European cultural heritage, the settlers of the American colonies brought with them a dichotomized image of the poor. As time passed, however, this image took on characteristics which reflected the distinctive aspects of the American experience. One such characteristic was the development in the second half of the nineteenth century of the "poor as apprentices" view of the able-bodied poor (Bird, 1973). Poverty is portrayed in this schema as a temporary condition which strengthens the character of the poor. Through education, training, and self-discipline the poor are expected to take advantage of the myriad opportunities for upward mobility provided by American society. At the core of this image, then, is the perception of an open rather than a closed stratification system.

A second, and related, major development of the late nineteenth century was the enthusiastic endorsement which Social Darwinism received from many quarters of American society (Bannister, 1979; Hofstadter, 1955). A basic premise of Social Darwinism was that the social and economic life of society was a "survival of the fittest" struggle among individual competitors. Economic stratification was considered one of the inevitable consequences of such competition. Thus, over time there would accumulate in the lower classes a group of individuals whose psychological characteristics indicated weakness and a lack of ambition, while in the upper classes the opposite characteristics would predominate.

The historical significance of Social Darwinism lies less in its stereotyped images of the poor, which are very similar to those implied by the Protestant ethic, than in the fact that it was presented as a *scientific* justification for strongly held negative views of the poor. It could now be argued that these views were ultimately grounded neither in material self-interest nor in religious faith, but in the conclusions generated by a systematic, value-free analysis of societal dynamics.

Non-individualistic theories of poverty also emerged during this period, most notably those of Marx in Europe and social reformers in the United States (Bremner, 1956; Marx and Engels, 1848/1932). These perspectives emphasized the extent to which *all* poverty was rooted in the fundamental economic and social structure of society. From this vantage point the abilities and motivations of individuals, even those in the so-called undeserving category, do not represent key variables for explaining poverty's existence.

Against this historical background, the recent emphasis on

restricting assistance to the truly needy (i.e., deserving poor) can hardly be seen as unprecedented. Indeed, the roots of many current poverty policy issues can be traced, directly or indirectly, to ramifications of the deserving/undeserving distinction. Whether or not assistance should be given, how much assistance should be given, and what form assistance should take are all questions whose answers are greatly influenced by beliefs concerning the current deservingness of potential recipients and the fear that, over time, assistance may induce the deserving poor or their offspring to become the undeserving poor (e.g., Murray, 1984).

As a result, the impact of assistance programs on the behavior of recipients has received a substantial amount of research attention. And a veritable academic research industry has devoted itself to questions surrounding the relative efficacy of individualistic vs. structural explanations of poverty and economic stratification. Finally, the "poor as apprentices" perspective represents one of the foundations of programs that attempt to directly influence the skills and motivation of the poor, an approach that was especially popular during the War on Poverty (Patterson, 1981).

The Emergence of the Welfare State

The crystallization of a dichotomized view of the poor was not the only major consequence of the events of the late Middle Ages. Traditional church-based mechanisms for dealing with the poor became increasingly inadequate as the decline of feudalism, the industrial revolution, the development of a market economy, and the labor mobility generated by the plague expanded tremendously the number of needy individuals (Trattner, 1984). It was within this context that the state gradually began to supplant the church as the primary source of both policymaking and assistance with respect to poverty. A landmark in this regard was the Statutes of Laborers, a series of English laws passed between 1349 and 1388. These were fairly repressive measures whose primary purpose was to control the labor market activities of the undeserving poor (the able-bodied, mobile unemployed) rather than to assist the deserving poor. The laws set maximum wages, restricted travel by the poor, and prohibited begging by the able-bodied, among other things.

The next two centuries saw the enactment of a variety of English laws, culminating in the Elizabethan Poor Law of 1601, which established the foundations of the welfare state. These measures further translated into public policy the distinctions between different subgroups of the poor. The 1601 law, for example, divided the poor into the three categories of children, able-bodied, and impotent (disabled, blind, ill, etc.) for the purposes of assistance. Children were given apprenticeships, the able-bodied received work relief, and the impotent were assisted either at home or in an almshouse. The Poor Law prohibited begging, and any able-bodied individual who refused to work could be imprisoned, publicly whipped, or even put to death (Trattner, 1984).

The principle of financing poor relief through taxation was also strongly reinforced by the 1601 legislation. It is important to note, however, that responsibility for both collecting these funds and administering assistance was fixed at the local community level. The development of the welfare state as a truly national institution was yet to come.

The Poor Law served as the model for relief policies in colonial America. From this starting point, however, America's path to the status of welfare state has been longer than that traveled by her European counterparts. An initial reason for this difference was the difficulty of establishing standardized approaches to poor relief in colonies which lacked well-developed transportation and communication networks (Segalman and Basu, 1981). A much more important cause was the federal system of government that was established after the American Revolution (Trattner, 1984). The high degree of state control permitted under this system contributed to the development of a relatively uncoordinated set of poverty policies. Within this context the role of the national government in assisting the poor was deemphasized. The legacy of this orientation can still be seen today in programs such as Aid to Families with Dependent Children (AFDC) and General Assistance.

Another important influence has been the strong tradition

of voluntarism and private charitable organizations that has characterized American society (Trattner, 1984). The belief that helping the poor through private means is more effective and efficient than public aid has undoubtedly slowed the growth of the welfare state. This appears to have been particularly true during the early years (c. 1870–1890) of the scientific charity movement in the United States, when a strong individualistic interpretation of poverty was championed by its leaders.

By the early twentieth century, however, it was becoming increasingly clear that the private sector did not possess the resources to cope with the poverty-related problems caused by the rapid industrialization, urbanization, and immigration of this period (Trattner, 1984). Activists in the Progressive Movement lobbied vigorously for federal and state governments to assume greater responsibility in meeting the needs of the poor. Success came primarily at the state level, where a variety of laws dealing with workmen's compensation, mothers' aid, and old-age assistance were passed (Coll, 1969). These achievements helped pave the way for much of the New Deal legislation that passed in response to the Great Depression of the 1930s.

It is with the arrival of the New Deal that the United States began to resemble a true welfare state, in the sense of the federal government playing a major role in promoting individuals' economic security. It is important to recognize, however, the highly constrained fashion in which this development took place (Heclo, 1984). New Deal legislation focused on the poverty caused by the high unemployment rates of the Depression. Thus, the emphasis was on providing temporary assistance, preferably through work relief, to the recently impoverished. As stipulated by the 1935 Social Security Act, the federal mechanisms used to increase aid to the more chronically poor enabled states to retain considerable discretion with respect to program design and implementation. Consequently, in many states there was little movement in the direction of providing these individuals with the types of support consistent with welfare state objectives.

The most heralded provision of the Social Security Act, of course, was its old age component. As was the case with most of the other assistance legislation of this period, however, the focus here was on those with stable, productive work histories, not the chronically poor. Thus, as noteworthy an achievement as this program was, it did not signal a qualitative change in policymakers' treatment of the lower class.

To be sure, many of the policies and proposals generated during the New Deal era have evolved over the years into an impressive network of welfare state programs for the very poor: AFDC, Social Security, Food Stamps, Supplemental Security Income (SSI), and housing assistance. Nevertheless, as we shall see in the following chapters, the ability of most of these programs to provide significant benefits to the poor is a function of their being, in Heclo's (1984) terms, "covert poverty policies." The distinguishing characteristic of such policies is that they "tuck away the poor as such in some larger more encompassing set of program commitments" (Heclo, 1984, p. 26).

In all likelihood there is a ceiling on the amount of poverty reduction one can achieve through covert policymaking. To the extent that poverty reduction for its own sake does not at some point become an explicit, primary policy objective, welfare state programs will simply serve to institutionalize poverty at a certain level. Unfortunately, focusing specifically on poverty does not guarantee that poverty will be eliminated either, as historians of the War on Poverty can attest (e.g., Friedman, 1977; Heclo, 1984; Patterson, 1981). It is with these considerations in mind that we examine the phenomenon of poverty in the next chapter.

2

The Nature of Poverty

Because the definition of a problem is a crucial determinant of the interventions deemed appropriate for solving it, there are three major issues regarding poverty we must address before evaluating poverty programs per se. The first concerns how poverty is measured. Far from being a purely technical matter, the task of measuring poverty is one that is fraught with political overtones (Beeghley, 1983, 1984; Danziger and Gottschalk, 1983; Girschick and Williamson, 1984; Rodgers, 1984). Different approaches not only can yield varying estimates of how much poverty actually exists, they can also represent fundamentally different views about how poverty should be conceptualized as a phenomenon within an overall distribution of income.

Second, we will examine the characteristics of the poor from both a cross-sectional and longitudinal perspective. While this is a relatively noncontroversial area of inquiry when viewed in isolation, the findings of such an examination become politically volatile when placed within the context of analyzing the causes of poverty, the third major focus of this chapter. It is here where deeply rooted political, cultural, religious, and scientific ideologies regarding the deserving and undeserving poor are mobilized, frequently in conflicting fashion.

MEASURING POVERTY

People without the economic resources to maintain an adequate standard of living are poor, but adequacy is a matter of
degree and social values. Thus, there is no clear dividing line
between the poor and the rest of society. The interests of policymakers, social researchers, and other constituencies have
nevertheless motivated numerous attempts to establish such
a dividing line. Policymakers must have some sense of the size
and characteristics of the low-income population if they are to
design social programs. Researchers need similar information
if they are to accurately analyze the causes and consequences
of low-income status. And constituencies of all sorts (including
those just mentioned) frequently need poverty-line data to bols-
ter their claims concerning the degree of justice or injustice
inherent in the political system.

By far the most commonly used measure of the extent of
poverty in the United States is the Social Security Administration's (SSA's) poverty line index, which was developed in
1964 and revised in 1969 and 1981 (Orshansky, 1965; U.S.
Bureau of the Census, 1985b). This index is based on the "economy food plan," the least expensive of four food plans prepared
by the Department of Agriculture in 1964. Each of these plans
was designed to provide an adequate diet, but the lower cost
plans allowed less variety and called for more skill in food
preparation. The SSA set the poverty line equal to three times
the cost of the economy food plan, because a 1955 Department
of Agriculture survey had indicated that families of three or
more persons spent approximately one-third of their income on
food. Prior to 1969, the SSA index was adjusted annually for
increases in the cost of the economy food plan; since then the
Consumer Price Index (CPI) has been used.

For any given year there is not just one SSA poverty line
but many. Prior to 1981 there were 124 poverty lines calculated
each year; the number now stands at forty-eight. The reason
for multiple poverty lines is that the dollar amount of the line
is adjusted to take into account family size and the number of
children under eighteen years old. Unrelated individuals (i.e.,
those not living with relatives) and two-person families are

further differentiated by the age of the individual or family head. The most frequently cited poverty-line figure is the average threshold for a family of four persons. In 1984 this figure was $10,609. Thus, a family of four whose total income in 1984 was less than this amount would have been classified as poor by the federal government.

The merits of the SSA's approach to measuring poverty notwithstanding, it is the official nature of this index which is most directly responsible for its wide use. Since 1969 the description of the poverty population generated by this instrument has been employed by all federal agencies (U.S. Bureau of the Census, 1985b, p.2). With the SSA index enjoying such powerful sponsorship, all other approaches to measuring poverty occupy the role of challenger. Thus, the SSA index receives additional attention each time a researcher contrasts the results of an alternative method with those produced by the SSA approach.

Despite, or perhaps because of, its widespread use, the SSA poverty line index has been the subject of extensive criticism in recent years. Many of these criticisms, however, are not so much directed at the SSA methodology per se as they are at the estimates of annual income to which this methodology is typically applied. These estimates come from the Current Population Survey (CPS) conducted each March by the Census Bureau. In the CPS a representative sample of the noninstitutionalized civilian population and the Armed Forces is interviewed; approximately 57,000 households provided data in the 1985 CPS (U.S. Bureau of the Census, 1985d).

The CPS defines annual income as the sum of the following (U.S. Bureau of the Census, 1985b, pp. 176–177):

1. Earnings from wages/salaries and self-employment (including losses);

2. Social Security, Supplemental Security Income, and public assistance payments;

3. Dividends, interest on savings and other investments, income from estates and trusts, net rental income, and royalties;

4. Unemployment compensation, workers' compensation, and veterans' payments;

5. Private and government employee pensions;

6. Annuities, alimony, child support, and other periodic income.

Capital gains (or losses) and lump sum one-time payments such as life insurance settlements are not counted.

This approach to calculating annual income is problematical in a number of respects, the most important of which are discussed below.

In-Kind Transfers

The CPS income measure does not include assistance received in the form of basic goods and services such as Food Stamps, medical care, and housing. This omission has probably received more attention in recent years than all of the other problems with the CPS measure combined. Numerous researchers claim that this failure to count in-kind transfers as income causes official poverty estimates in the United States to be spuriously high (e.g., Danziger and Gottschalk, 1983; Hoagland, 1982; Paglin, 1982; Smeeding, 1982; see however, Beeghley, 1984).

In response to this concern the Census Bureau has started reporting unofficial poverty rates which reflect the inclusion of in-kind transfers in the determination of annual income (U.S. Bureau of the Census, 1985c). In the event that one of these new measures is ultimately chosen as the official indicator of income, it almost certainly will become the dominant measure in the field of poverty research.

Net Worth

The CPS does not include assets of a family or individual in calculating total income. Thus, resources such as equity in a house, land, savings, insurance, and stock holdings are not counted. While households with low money income also tend to have few assets, research indicates that the poverty count would be reduced somewhat if they were taken into consideration. The reduction would be greatest among the aged, whites, and the self-employed (U.S. Department of Health, Education, and Welfare, 1976).

Taxes and Other Payments

The original poverty thresholds were based on the average proportion of aftertax income spent on food (Committee on Ways and Means, 1983, p. 122). The CPS, however, defines annual income as the money income received *before* payment of personal income taxes and deductions for Social Security, union dues, Medicare premiums, etc. Thus, a household can be officially classified as nonpoor even though its disposable, aftertax income places it below the SSA poverty line. It has been estimated that the poverty rate would be at least 10% higher if state and federal income and payroll taxes were taken into account when measuring income (Smeeding, 1983).

Annual Accounting Period

The CPS focuses on the total money income received during the preceding calendar year. As Moon and Smolensky (1977) point out, however, "year-to-year fluctuations in total income cast serious doubt on the use of money income in any one year as the appropriate measure of economic welfare. Permanent income or life-cycle measures smooth out these fluctuations, yielding a more reasonable estimate of what a family could consume in a single year" (p. 5). Use of an accounting period which is longer than one year would reduce the poverty rate, but by how much is unclear (Committee on Ways and Means, 1983).

Low-income families are especially likely to have unstable incomes from year to year, since they are more vulnerable than higher-income families to occurrences (unemployment, illness, etc.) which affect the labor income of the head of the household (Grosse and Morgan, 1981). A long-term income estimate would not differentiate, however, between families with steady incomes and those with highly fluctuating incomes. This is unfortunate, since income instability itself can affect a family's sense of economic well-being. A family with a highly variable income is likely to feel less financially secure than one with a more stable income.

Underreporting

In household surveys such as the CPS there is a tendency for respondents to underreport their income. Income that is not derived from earnings is especially likely to be underreported. Given the important role that non-labor-market income (e.g., public assistance) plays in the life of many of the poor, the failure of the CPS to correct for underreporting results in inflated estimates of the extent of poverty. Studies indicate that the official poverty rate would be 14% to 26% lower if underreporting did not occur (e.g., Hoagland, 1982; Paglin, 1980).

We now turn to criticisms of the SSA index itself. While the first four points we address are largely technical in nature, the last two raise fundamental ideological issues.

The Economy Food Plan

The economy food plan, upon which the SSA index is based, is now regarded as outdated (Fendler and Orshansky, 1979). This plan was designed for short-term, emergency use by a family when its resources were very low (Orshansky, 1965). Thus, a family could not expect to maintain a nutritionally adequate diet by following this diet on a long-term basis.

In 1975 the Department of Agriculture replaced the economy plan with a "thrifty" food plan designed to reflect new nutrition standards, more current food preferences, and changes in food manufacturing. Though several poverty commentators assert otherwise (e.g., Beeghley, 1983, 1984; Rodgers, 1982), the thrifty plan has *not* replaced the economy plan for the purpose of computing poverty thresholds (U.S. Bureau of the Census, 1985b, pp. 177–178; C. Fendler, personal communication, May 9, 1984). Given that the long-term nutritional adequacy of the thrifty plan has also been questioned (Beeghley, 1984; Center for Community Change, 1979), its use for poverty-line purposes would probably not represent a significant improvement over the status quo. The cost of a food plan whose long-term adequacy was well-established would undoubtedly be higher than that of the economy plan. Consequently, the poverty line itself would be raised, with the number of individuals being classified as poor also increasing.

Multiplication Rate

The factor by which the economy food plan is multiplied to obtain a poverty-line figure has been criticized as being either too large or too small. Those who believe it is too large point out that low-income families spend up to 50% of their cash income on food, a significantly higher percentage than the rest of the population (U.S. Department of Health, Education, and Welfare, 1976). This implies that the multiplier should be closer to two than to three, the latter figure being the one currently in use for families of three or more. Such a change would lower the poverty line and thus decrease the number of people classified as poor.

The argument in favor of a higher multiplier is based on findings which suggest that the average American family currently spends a smaller portion of its income on food than it did when the nonfood/food ratio of 3–1 was established in 1955 (U.S. Department of Health, Education, and Welfare, 1976). Surveys conducted since that time have obtained ratios ranging from 3.4–1 to 5–1 (Committee on Ways and Means, 1983; U.S. Department of Health, Education, and Welfare, 1976). Using these larger figures in poverty-line calculations would significantly increase the ranks of the officially poor.

Regional Variations

There is evidence to suggest that the cost of living varies significantly from city to city and region to region in the United States. Consequently, the failure of the SSA index to adjust for these differences results in a distorted official picture of the poor. Some families are classified as poor who should not be, while others are erroneously placed above the poverty line. Without knowing which error is more frequent, the net impact of this problem on the official poverty rate cannot be determined.

Annual Adjustment for Inflation

The use of the CPI to update poverty thresholds on a yearly basis has been criticized. If the goods and services which consume a substantial portion of the poor's income, such as food, increase in price at a faster rate than the other components of the CPI, the CPI annual adjustments will generate poverty thresholds that are too low. This certainly seems to have been the case during much of the 1970s, when food prices increased much faster than the overall CPI (Center for Community Change, 1979). In the long run, however, the price of food appears to increase at about the same rate as the other items in the CPI (U.S. Department of Health, Education, and Welfare, 1976). Since it is also possible for poverty-relevant goods and services to increase at a *slower* rate than the overall CPI, this index would not appear to have an inherent tendency to understate or overstate changes in poverty thresholds.

Absolute vs. Relative Poverty

The SSA index is generally seen as representing an absolute approach to measuring poverty. At the core of the absolute approach is the notion of a fixed minimum standard of living, one that does not extend much beyond mere subsistence. Those who fall below this standard are considered poor. In a society where everyone enjoyed at least this minimum standard of living, poverty would not exist. Even if the average standard of living in such a society were many times higher than the minimum standard, individuals living at the minimum level would not be considered poor from the absolute perspective.

Consistent with such an orientation, the only annual adjustment applied to the SSA poverty line by the Census Bureau is for inflation. Thus, in 1959 the ratio of the poverty line to the median income for four-person families was 49%, while in 1984 it was only 34% (Committee on Ways and Means, 1985b; U.S. Bureau of the Census, 1985d).

Not surprisingly, this view of poverty has been strongly contested by those who believe that

> In a country like the United States, where average income greatly
> exceeds bare subsistence levels, poverty is more appropriately
> viewed as a problem of inequality in the distribution of income
> than as one of low absolute levels of income. . . . In a materialistic
> society, households with incomes substantially below the av-
> erage are effectively excluded from participating in the main-
> stream social and political life of their country. As a result, such
> households are viewed by society and themselves as poor. (Plot-
> nick and Skidmore, 1975, pp. 37–38).

This perspective regards poverty as a relative phenomenon:
A poor person is one whose income is significantly less than
the average or median income of the population as a whole.
Thus, as the average income rises so will the relative poverty
line. Fuchs (1967), for example, has proposed a relative poverty
line equal to one-half of the national median income, though
this fraction is not inherently superior to many others that
might be used to indicate relative poverty (one-third, one-fourth,
two-fifths, etc.).

Eliminating relative poverty requires that the societal distribution of income become more equal. Thus, it would be possible for absolute poverty to be eliminated in a society while
the number of those experiencing relative poverty remained
unchanged. In the case of the United States, use of any of the
more frequently mentioned relative poverty lines significantly
increases the percentage of the population classified as poor
(e.g., Danziger, Haveman, and Plotnick, 1985).

Girschick and Williamson (1984) claim that supporters of
income redistribution favor relative measures of poverty, while
others prefer absolute ones. To the extent that this is true it
should not be surprising. Inherent in the relative approach is
the claim that economic inequality per se can represent a social
problem. The social problem suggested by the absolute approach is much narrower in focus: lack of the material resources
necessary to insure a minimum level of physical well-being.
Accordingly, it implies much less income redistribution than
the relative perspective (see Plattner, 1979).

Insofar as the SSA index is an absolute measure, it contributes to the *social problem* of poverty being defined in a way that
focuses attention on individuals at the bottom of the income

distribution rather than on the income distribution as a whole. Against this background the absolute/relative debate represents much more than just a difference of opinion regarding measurement techniques. The more fundamental issue is: Which conception of the social problem will be legitimated by society's policymaking institutions? Thus far it has been the more restrictive one.

It is possible, of course, to use both approaches when studying poverty, as long as the differences between them are kept in mind. A family can experience an absolute improvement in its standard of living even though its relative position in the income distribution does not change. Both pieces of information are important. Economic well-being is almost certainly a function of both absolute levels of consumption and individuals' positions relative to one another.

In this context it should be noted that absolute and relative measures of poverty do not represent dichotomous categories; they are more properly regarded as existing on a continuum. Advocates of the relative approach are unlikely to recommend poverty thresholds which totally ignore the absolute levels of consumption implied. Similarly, supporters of the absolute approach are not likely to choose poverty lines that completely disregard the overall standard of living in the society (Schiller, 1984). Indeed, the SSA index itself is regarded as a "relatively absolute" measure of poverty by its developer (Orshansky, 1965). It is absolute because the economy food plan focuses on *minimum* nutritional standards, and relative because the multiplier is based on the average proportion of income spent on food by *all* families (Smeeding, 1982, p. 13).

Public Opinion

The SSA index does not take into account individuals' beliefs concerning the minimum level of income that is needed in order to be nonpoor. Studies which have taken a subjective approach to defining the poverty line have generated thresholds that are in some cases higher, and in others lower, than the official poverty line (Colasanto, Kapteyn, and van der Gaag, 1984; Danziger, van der Gaag, Taussig, and Smolensky, 1984; Dubnoff, 1985; *Gallup Report* 1985). Methodological differences between the studies preclude the drawing of definitive conclusions regarding the impact of failing to include a subjective component in the official definition of poverty. Even so, it is interesting to note that Americans believe that the percentage of the population below the official poverty threshold is much higher than it actually is (*Gallup Report*, 1985, p. 22; "Poverty in America," 1985). Among other things this finding probably reflects a perception of poverty on the part of respondents which incorporates both absolute and relative components.

Table 1 lists the major criticisms of the CPS income measure and the SSA index and indicates the probable impact of each factor on official poverty estimates.

It should be clear from the preceding discussion that assessing the validity of the official poverty line is as much an ideological exercise as it is a technical one. Depending on the mix of criticisms selected, one can claim that the federal government's poverty estimates range from far too low to far too high. Indeed, the adoption of the SSA index itself was due more to the political acceptability of the line's low level than it was to the line's ability to guarantee a long-term adequate diet, an ability it did not have. Nevertheless, once the poverty line was selected, it was usually justified in terms of the latter type of concern rather than the former. As a result, public attention and discussion have been directed toward issues which are seen as primarily technical rather than ideological.

A PROFILE OF THE POOR

Use of the SSA poverty-line index results in 14.4% of the U.S. population being classified as poor in 1984 (U.S. Bureau of the Census, 1985d). This figure represents approximately 33.7 million individuals. Table 2 reveals that the poverty rates of the 1980s have significantly exceeded those of the 1970s, a trend that has been the subject of considerable political debate (e.g., Murray, 1984). Even so, rates of the 1980s are well below those recorded in the late 1950s and early 1960s.

CPS Procedure	Impact
In-kind transfers excluded	+
Net worth excluded	+
Taxes and other payments excluded	-
Annual accounting period (vs. longer period)	+
Underreporting not corrected	+
SSA Procedure	
Economy food plan	-
Multiplication rate of 3	?
Regional variations excluded	?
Use of CPI for inflation adjustment	?
Poverty defined in absolute, not relative, terms	-
Public opinion excluded	?

Note: A (+) indicates that the procedure results in upwardly biased estimates of the poverty rate. A (-) indicates that the procedure results in downwardly biased estimates. A (?) indicates that the net effect of the procedure on poverty-rate estimates is uncertain or subject to disagreement.

TABLE 1.
Impact of CPS and SSA Methodology on Estimates of the Poverty Rate

Year	Percent of total population	Number (in millions)
1984	14.4	33.7
1983	15.3	35.5
1982	15.0	34.4
1981	14.0	31.8
1980	13.0	29.2
1979	11.7	26.0
1978	11.4	24.4
1977	11.6	24.7
1976	11.8	24.9
1975	12.3	25.8
1974	11.2	23.3
1973	11.1	22.9
1972	11.9	24.4
1971	12.5	25.5
1970	12.6	25.4
1969	12.1	24.1
1968	12.8	25.3
1966	14.7	28.5
1965	17.3	33.1
1960	22.2	39.8
1959	22.4	39.4

Source. U.S. Bureau of the Census, 1985d, p. 21.

Note. The Census Bureau has revised its 1983 estimate, lowering it from 15.3% to 15.2%.

TABLE 2.
Persons Below the Poverty Level: 1959–1984

Demographic Characteristics

An adequate examination of the characteristics of the poverty population requires that at least three questions be addressed:

1. What percentage of the poor population exhibits a given characteristic?

2. What percentage of the entire population exhibits that characteristic?

3. Of all the people who exhibit that characteristic, what percentage are poor?

The answers to these questions for a number of characteristics can be found in Table 3. Of particular interest are the following elements of a profile of the poor.

Most of the poor are white (68%), but an even larger percentage of the entire population is white (85%). In contrast, blacks constitute 28% of the poor but only 12% of the overall population. The percentage of blacks who are poor is almost three times that of whites (34% vs. 12%). The pattern for Hispanics is similar to that of blacks. The higher poverty rates for blacks and Hispanics help to clarify why so many people view programs to help the poor as programs to help minorities.

Children also account for a disproportionate percentage of the poor. While only 27% of the total population is under eighteen years old, 40% of the poor are in this category. The chances of a family being poor increase as the number of children increases, to a point where 53% of all families with five or more children are poor.

Over half (52%) of all related poor children reside in female-headed households, and thus represent an important component of the much discussed "feminization of poverty" (Garfinkel and McLanahan, 1985). Although families headed by women with no husband present represent only 16% of all families, they account for 48% of all poor families. From an historical perspective it is important to note that female-headed families have always had high poverty rates. The more striking trend is that the number of these families has grown substantially over the past quarter century. In 1959 only one out of every eleven families with children was headed by a woman with no husband present; by 1984 the proportion was one out of five.

Employment and education are, not surprisingly, also strongly associated with poverty status. The less education a family head has, and the weaker his or her attachment to the labor force, the greater the likelihood that the family will be poor.

When several demographic factors are considered simultaneously, it is possible to classify many people into categories which show a higher (or lower) risk of poverty than is indicated when the same factors are considered separately. For this reason any description of the poor which considers only one factor at a time tends to understate (or overstate) the risk of poverty

Persons	Percent of total population	Percent of poor population	Poverty rate for characteristic
White	85	68	12
Black	12	28	34
Spanish origin[a]	7	14	28
Under 18 years old	27	40	22
65 years and older	11	10	12

Families

	Percent of total population	Percent of poor population	Poverty rate for characteristic
Female head, no husband present	16	48	35
Married-couple families	81	48	7
Head worked 50-52 weeks	61	22	4
Head worked 1-49 weeks	16	28	20
Head did not work	23	51	26
Education of head less than 8 years elementary school	7	18	26
8 years elementary school	6	10	16
1 to 3 years high school	13	23	20
4 years high school	36	32	10
1 or more years college	37	17	5
Number of related children under 18			
None	47	22	5
1	22	24	13
2	19	26	15
3	8	16	24
4	2	7	35
5 or more	1	5	53

[a]Persons of Spanish origin may be of any race.

Source. U.S. Bureau of the Census, 1985d.

TABLE 3.
Characteristics of the Poor, 1984

faced by many groups in the population. For example, in 1983 the poverty rate for black children living in households headed by nonworking mothers (no husband present) was a startling 96%. In contrast, the poverty rate for white children living with both parents, where the mother worked full time for the entire year, was only 3% (U.S. Bureau of the Census, 1985b).

Findings such as these are clearly of more than academic interest. When population subgroups are found to exhibit high poverty rates, perceptions of deservingness become particularly important in influencing policy decisions concerning assistance. Groups that would probably be judged unequivocally deserving on the basis of one characteristic (e.g., age) can become vulnerable to less positive assessments when their status on other dimensions (race, family structure, employment status of householder) are taken into consideration.

Duration of Poverty

Longitudinal studies reveal that most individuals who become poor do not stay poor for a long time (Bane and Ellwood, 1983b; Duncan, 1984; Hill, 1981; Levy, 1977; Rainwater, 1980). For example, the Panel Study of Income Dynamics (PSID) found that nearly one-fourth (24.4% of its national sample experienced poverty at some point during the 1969–1978 decade (Hill, 1981). Over two-thirds (67.6%) of this subgroup were poor for three years or less during this period, however. In contrast, 10.7% of those who experienced poverty were "persistently poor," i.e., poor for eight or more years during the decade. Analysis of the PSID data by Bane and Ellwood (1983b) indicates that the persistently poor account for a substantial portion, perhaps even a majority, of the poverty population at any given point in time.

The persistently poor differ on a number of dimensions from those who are poor in any given year. The most significant one is race. Over 60% of the persistently poor during the 1969–1978 decade lived in families headed by blacks, while only 42% of those who were poor in 1978 lived in such families. The persistently poor are also more likely to be residents of rural areas and the South, and live in families headed by elderly or disabled individuals (Duncan, 1984).

Revised Poverty Estimates

In view of the abundant criticism which the SSA index has received, it should not be surprising that alternative estimates of poverty are readily available. The single most important change most of these revisions make is to translate in-kind benefits (e.g., food, medical care, housing) into money income for the purpose of calculating a household's economic status. This translation can be made in a number of ways, however, and currently there is no consensus regarding the best approach to use. This lack of agreement is important, since different approaches lead to different revised poverty rates (e.g., Hoagland, 1982; Paglin, 1982; Smeeding, 1982; U.S. Bureau of the Census, 1985c).

The Census Bureau (1985c), for example, has used Smeeding's approach to examine the impact on poverty rates of nine different methods for translating food, housing, and medical care benefits into income. For 1984, these revised poverty rates (for all persons) range from 9.7% to 13.2% compared with the official rate of 14.4%. This represents a reduction of anywhere from 8% to 33% in the official rate, depending on which revised rate is used.

When a *relative* concept of poverty guides poverty rate revisions, the resulting estimates are usually higher than any of the rates we have examined thus far. For example, when Danziger, Haveman, and Plotnick (1985) set poverty lines at 44% of the median income, they found 18.6% of the population to be poor in 1983 (vs. an official rate of 15.2%).

CAUSES OF POVERTY

As we previously implied, a comprehensive evaluation of strategies *against* poverty requires that the question of what *causes* poverty be addressed first. This question needs to be considered not because a definitive answer is available (there is none), but because poverty policies are based on notions of

what these causes are. Thus, understanding these causal theories contributes to an understanding of the strategies themselves, especially as these strategies embody historically based
notions of deservingness.

"What causes poverty?" is a question that must be examined
at two levels. First, there is the issue of why poverty exists at
all in a particular society—a *macro* question. At the second
level of inquiry, poverty's existence is taken as a given. The
pertinent question thus becomes: Why are some groups in a
society more likely to be poor than others?—a *micro* question.

We will examine these questions from two different perspectives. One emphasizes individualistic factors in explaining
poverty; the other stresses structural ones. In reality, both individualistic and structural factors contribute to poverty. Considerable disagreement exists concerning their relative
importance,however. The interdependence of these two factors
makes it unlikely that this disagreement can be resolved solely
on empirical grounds. Consequently, ideological predispositions play a major role in determining which perspective one
favors. Historically, those on the political left have emphasized
structural causes of poverty, while those on the right have
emphasized individualistic causes.

Individualistic theories of poverty tend to answer both levels
of the poverty question in the same way. The macro-level causes
of poverty are seen as residing in the characteristics of the poor
themselves. And the reason that some groups are more vulnerable to poverty than others is that some groups have more
of these characteristics—in number and/or degree—than others.

What are these characteristics? Virtually all of them involve,
at some level, either the motivation or the ability of the poor.
These two factors, it should be noted, tend to exist in a recip-
rocal relationship. Consequently, in individualistic theories they
are frequently portrayed as operating jointly to cause poverty.
We shall separate them here, however, for the purposes of
discussion.

Motivational Factors[1]

The individualistic perspective claims that the poor have
values, attitudes, beliefs, and, in some cases, an overall culture

that are not conducive to upward economic mobility (see, for example, Banfield, 1974; Gilder, 1981; Lewis, 1969; Miller, 1958; Segalman and Basu, 1981). Among the most frequently mentioned characteristics of the poor in this regard are the following:

- low need for achievement;
- low educational aspirations;
- low occupational aspirations;
- weak commitment to the work ethic;
- little ability to defer gratification and plan for the future;
- strong present-time orientation;
- low self-esteem;
- feelings of marginality, helplessness, and alienation;
- feelings of powerlessness and high external control;
- sense of resignation and fatalism.

People who have these interrelated characteristics are likely to engage in behaviors that render them highly vulnerable to poverty. These behaviors include:

- doing poorly in, and/or dropping out of, school;
- having erratic work histories characterized by employment in low-wage, dead-end jobs, which frequently have a high risk of disease or disability. Regardless of the jobs they hold, their performance rarely exceeds a minimum level of competence or productivity;
- becoming parents at an early age, with offspring often being supported primarily or solely by the mother due to disruption of the parents' relationship;
- other activities (e.g., crime, alcohol and drug abuse) which decrease their attractiveness to potential employers.

The emphasis here is clearly on characteristics that have traditionally been associated with undeservingness in the minds of the public. This is especially true with respect to the specific *behaviors* focused upon.

The individualistic theory of poverty that has received the most attention from social scientists over the past twenty-five years is the Culture-of-Poverty thesis. It is probably the most fully developed and systematized of all the individualistic approaches, and is closely associated with the work of anthropologist Oscar Lewis (1966, 1969). On the basis of his studies of families and communities in Latin America, Lewis concluded that in class-stratified, highly individuated capitalistic societies a segment of the poor population (roughly 20% in the United States) is likely to develop a culture of poverty. This culture represents an obstacle to upward economic mobility and is characterized by an interrelated network of approximately seventy economic, social, and psychological traits. His list includes most of the psychological characteristics we have previously named.

A major reason for Lewis's application of the term "culture" to this trait network was his belief that this way of life is transmitted from one generation of poor people to another through the socialization process. In this regard he states:

> Once it [the culture of poverty] comes into existence, it tends to perpetuate itself from generation to generation because of its effect on the children. By the time slum children are aged six or seven, they have usually absorbed the basic values and attitudes of their subculture and are not psychologically geared to take full advantage of the changing conditions or increased opportunities that may occur in their lifetime. (Lewis, 1969, p. 188).

It is clear that Lewis's analysis includes structural components as well as individualistic ones, since it is the economic and social structure which determines whether or not a culture of poverty will initially emerge. In addition, the culture of poverty itself constitutes a normative structure into which individuals are socialized. We have nevertheless classified the Culture-of-Poverty thesis as an individualistic approach because, in the final analysis, it claims that the Culture-of-Poverty population remains poor because of their own values and attitudes.

Evaluation of Motivational Factors

The poor do differ from the nonpoor on many motivational dimensions (e.g., Allen, 1970; Blum and Rossi, 1969; Hill et al., 1985; Inkeles, 1960; Kerckhoff, 1972; Lundberg, 1974). These differences are frequently modest in size, however, and thus are of questionable practical significance for explaining poverty in any large-scale sense. For example, it is true that the educational, occupational, and economic aspirations of lower-class respondents tend to be lower than those expressed by middle- and upper-class persons (e.g., Della Fave, 1974, 1977; Della Fave and Klobus, 1976; Dillingham, 1980; Rodman and Voydanoff, 1978; Rodman, Voydanoff and Lovejoy, 1974). Nevertheless, these same studies clearly demonstrate that the overwhelming majority of lower-class individuals seek an education, occupation, and income that would move them out of the lower class and poverty. Indeed, if measures of aspiration level took into account the respondent's current social-class standing, the already modest motivational differences that are found between the poor and the nonpoor on these dimensions would be even smaller.

It also needs to be emphasized that on some motivational dimensions there is no convincing evidence of significant differences between the poor and nonpoor. The work ethic, for example, is endorsed just as strongly by the poor as by the nonpoor (Davidson and Gaitz, 1974; Kaplan and Tausky, 1972, 1974). This has been found to be the case even when the sample of poor respondents is composed of welfare recipients (Goodwin, 1972).

In view of the above discussion it should not be surprising that relatively little empirical support has been obtained for the Culture-of-Poverty thesis (Beeghley, 1983; Hill et al., 1985; Morris and Williamson, 1982; Waxman, 1983). To be sure, persistent poverty does characterize a sizable segment of the poor population (Bane and Ellwood, 1983b), and children from poor families are more likely to be poor as adults than children from nonpoor families (though most poor children do not become poor adults; Hill et al., 1985; Levy, 1980). Suggestive as these findings may be, they are no substitute for research documenting the existence of a subcultural framework transmitted intergenerationally by the poor. This documentation has yet to be provided. Indeed, in their longitudinal analysis of a fourteen-year national sample from the Panel Study of Income Dynam-

ics, Hill et al. (1985) found that the influence of parental attitudes on children's economic mobility was neither strong nor
consistent enough to warrant the conclusion that these attitudes are the major obstacle to economic mobility across
generations.

Finally, intragenerational studies have found that motivational and other noncognitive traits are, at best, only moderately useful predictors of future economic status (e.g., Andrisani,
1977, 1978, 1981; Buchele, 1983; Duncan, 1984; Duncan and
Liker, 1983; Duncan and Morgan, 1981a, 1981b; Featherman,
1972; Hill et al., 1985; Jencks et al., 1979; Kiker and Condon,
1981; Otto and Haller, 1979; Sewell and Hauser, 1975). These
results provide us with yet another reason to be wary of claims
that the poor's distinctiveness on motivational dimensions represents a major explanation of their poverty.

Ability-Related Factors

There is a strong belief in our society that prestigious, well-
paid occupations require significantly more ability than low-
prestige, poorly paid jobs (Villemez, 1974). Consequently, lack
of ability is regarded by many as an important cause of poverty.
Factors related to ability can be arranged in a sequence that
roughly approximates the order in which they appear in the
life of the individual. Generally speaking, the factors appearing
early in life are regarded as more important than those occurring later.

Genetic and Prenatal Factors

Included here are all genetic/prenatal influences on one's
capacity to behave in ways that society rewards economically.
For example, any role that these factors play in the development of motor skills or mental disorder would be deemed relevant. Moreover, to the extent that any of the previously
discussed motivational traits are genetically/prenatally determined, they can be subsumed under this category as well.

It is the role of heredity in intelligence that has received the
most attention, however. There are at least two reasons for this
emphasis. First, individualistic theories regard intelligence as

an important determinant of economic success. Second, while it is not clear precisely how much influence genetic factors have in accounting for observed differences in intelligence, most social scientists would agree that these factors play a significant role. Insofar as these beliefs are accurate, genetic influences can certainly be seen as representing a major cause of poverty.

Analyses that suggest that society can never totally eliminate poverty usually emphasize genetic causes of poverty to a greater extent than do more optimistic views. This is to be expected, given that these factors are typically regarded as the ones that are most beyond society's ability to control (see, however, Jencks, 1980).

Human Capital

In order for genetic potential to be developed into demonstrated ability and proper credentials, one must have access to relevant experiences, education, and/or training. In the language of economists, this is described as developing one's "human capital," a resource which can be exchanged for attractive wages in the marketplace (Becker, 1964). According to the individualistic perspective, the poor's possession of little human capital can frequently be traced to a lack of motivation on the part of the poor themselves (e.g., Banfield, 1974; Gilder, 1981). Thus, individualists tend to be very critical of groups such as unwed welfare mothers, whose lack of marketable skills represents a major obstacle to upward economic mobility. Critics focus their attention not on the current plight of these women, but on the alleged motivational antecedents of low human capital.

Life-Cycle Factors

Four factors will be considered here: family size, family status, health, and age. All of them exacerbate the negative economic effects of low human capital, and two of them (health, age) can directly reduce this capital.

We have seen that poverty is positively associated with family size. Large families have greater economic needs than smaller ones, but wages and salaries are usually not related to need. If a family's income is already low due to the head of the household having a low-skill job, an additional child can push the family below the poverty line. Moreover, mothers are generally less available for employment outside of the home in large families because of their childrearing responsibilities. Even if a mother does take paid employment, the child-care costs that are frequently involved will diminish the net economic benefits provided by her job. Because individualistic analyses stress the role that voluntary choice plays in determining family size, the financial difficulties faced by large families are viewed as largely self-imposed.

Where family status is concerned, the high poverty rate among female-headed households is the obvious focus. The key issue is not just that these women usually have few skills. Rather, it is that the female-householder role exploits the vulnerability to poverty inherent in having low human capital. Once again, the individualistic perspective tends to hold the poor responsible for the processes leading to the formation of such households. This attribution of responsibility is tempered somewhat, however, by the recognition that single-parent status can be due to factors such as desertion or death of a spouse.

Health is a third major life-cycle factor, since injury or illness can prevent individuals from using the skills they have acquired or developing new skills. In addition, medical expenses are likely to increase significantly during these periods. These two factors combine to make the holders of low-skill jobs particularly vulnerable to poverty when health-related problems occur, since the financial resources they possess are generally less than those held by the more highly skilled. Thus, the former group has a much shorter distance to fall before reaching poverty than the latter. Motivational factors, which play so significant a role in individualistic interpretations of family size and status, receive relatively little emphasis when health-related causes of poverty are focused upon.

Finally, there is the factor of age. In 1984, persons sixty-five years of age and older represented about the same percentage of the poverty population (10%) as they did the population as a whole (11%). Nevertheless, the chances of being poor do increase with age after people reach their mid-forties. This increase in vulnerability to poverty is paralleled by a decrease in the likelihood of holding a full-time job. More to the point, retiring individuals whose previous employment mainly consisted of low-skill jobs are unlikely to have accumulated a great deal of economic protection against poverty for use during their nonworking years.

While this situation does not carry with it the strong motivational overtones associated with family size and status, there is nonetheless a certain amount of responsibility that individualistic analyses assign to the poor in this instance. This responsibility is based on the claim that retirement is a fact of life that everyone should prepare for financially, especially those in low-paying jobs. From the individualistic standpoint, the limited options available to low-skill workers in this respect make it all the more crucial that planning for the future take place on their part.

Evaluation of Ability-Related Factors

Researchers have consistently found that social class is positively associated with performance on tests of intellectual functioning and academic ability (e.g., Blum and Rossi, 1969; Kaufman and Doppelt, 1976; Yando, Seitz, and Zigler, 1979). Furthermore, longitudinal studies have shown that these test scores are useful for predicting future economic success, even when family background and educational level are controlled (e.g., Jencks et al., 1979). The effects of test performance on future earnings are not very large, however, when compared with the overall earnings gap between the rich and poor. Thus, the conclusion reached by Jencks et al. (1979) on the basis of their examination of these data seems appropriate: "Our findings . . . do not characterize the United States as a 'meritocracy,' at least when merit is measured by cognitive skills" (p. 121). Overall, however, the evidence does suggest that cognitive factors contribute to poverty, though its *direct* effect is probably minor.

Educational level is much more powerful than either cognitive abilities or motivational traits at predicting future earnings (e.g., Jencks et al., 1979; see, however, Krauze and Slomczynski, 1985). Thus, low levels of schooling do seem to play a significant causal role with respect to poverty. The data also suggest, however, that the positive relationship between education and income is only partly explained by the skills one acquires in school. To a certain extent employers appear to reward credentials per se (i.e., high school or college degree) in making hiring decisions (Jencks et al., 1979). This latter occurrence would appear to be at odds with at least the spirit of the individualistic perspective (see also Collins, 1979).

Of the four life-cycle factors we have discussed, family status probably has the most significant impact on poverty. For example, of all the poor female household heads in the PSID study, nearly half (49.2%) became poor *as a result* of becoming a household head (Bane and Ellwood, 1983b). This transition is a more powerful cause of poverty among whites than blacks, since blacks are much more likely than whites to be poor prior to becoming members of female-headed households (Bane, 1985). Overall, 14.6% of the non-elderly who became poor during the PSID study did so because they were part of a female-headed household.

Where aging and poor health are concerned, Schiller (1984) estimates that 10–15% of the poor are impoverished by these two factors. Luft (1978) estimates that between 9% and 18% of all poverty among the nonaged is caused by disability (see also Chirikos and Nestel, 1985). Finally, increases in family size do not appear to be a very important cause of poverty (Bane and Ellwood, 1983b; Schiller, 1984). Most large families that are poor were also poor when they were smaller.

In summary, then, ability-related factors appear to be much more useful for explaining poverty status than motivational ones. In the next section, we shall see that the structural perspective on poverty acknowledges this conclusion, but interprets it within a context that is very different from the individualistic view.

Structural Perspectives

In contrast to the individualistic orientation, structural approaches tend to explain the *existence* of poverty in a different way than they explain the *distribution* of poverty. In accounting for poverty's existence emphasis is placed on general economy-wide problems rather than individual characteristics. This emphasis draws much of its analytical power from the Marxist perspective on the class system (e.g., Marx and Engels, 1848/1932; Piven and Cloward, 1971). In essence, the structural view claims that the labor markets of capitalist economies cannot provide sufficient employment at above-poverty-line wages to keep poverty at a negligible level (Tussing, 1975). Moreover, in order to maximize the likelihood that below-poverty-line jobs are filled, welfare systems for the able-bodied are either non-existent or designed according to the principle of "less eligibility," an approach formally introduced in England in 1834 (Trattner, 1984). This principle stipulates that welfare benefits should not exceed the wages of those at the bottom of the laboring class. Thus, it is primarily the interaction of two major structural forces—the labor market and the welfare system—which serves to produce poverty. A third societal process which is included in most structural analyses of poverty is discrimination (e.g., Beeghley, 1983; Rodgers, 1982; Schiller, 1984; Tussing, 1975). A more detailed discussion of these factors follows.

The Labor Market

During the March 1985 CPS the unemployment rate among heads of poor families was 24%; the corresponding figure for all family heads was 5% (U.S. Bureau of the Census, 1985d). Since the majority of poor family heads who work are only employed for part of the year, the 24% figure significantly underestimates the total number of poor families affected by unemployment during 1985.

The structural perspective regards unemployment as a fundamental component of the capitalist economic system. In many industries it is standard practice to lay off employees during slack periods. In some seasonal industries such as farming it is assumed that a high proportion of the workers will be unemployed for a substantial part of the year.

Published unemployment figures tend to understate the full extent of joblessness because they do not count "discouraged workers" as part of the labor force. These are individuals who want jobs but are not actively looking for them because they

believe that they will not find any. The total number of discouraged workers in 1983 averaged 1.6 million (Flaim, 1984).

In addition, there are several million individuals who work
part time because they cannot find a full-time job. Thus, even
though they are employed, it is quite possible that they are not
receiving an income from their job that would place them above
the poverty line.

Finally, it is important to note that 17% of the heads of poor
families in 1984 were employed full time for the entire year.
The jobs held by these individuals simply did not pay enough
to keep them and their families out of poverty (U.S. Bureau of
the Census, 1985d). Many of these workers had jobs in the low-
wage, low-profit industries which dual-labor-market theorists
describe as the "peripheral" sector of the industrial economy.
It is claimed that opportunities for occupational mobility are
relatively limited within this sector, with the range of task and
wage variation being restricted. To the extent that this is true,
the jobs and economic rewards here would be less sensitive to
individual differences in education and work experience than
is the case in the core sector of the economy (e.g., Tolbert,
Horan, and Beck, 1980). Peripheral-sector employment includes many service jobs such as domestic, laundry, hospital,
and restaurant work, as well as many retail and agricultural
labor jobs. It also encompasses some factory jobs, especially
those in nonunionized industries. Many of these jobs are not
covered by minimum-wage legislation.

Discrimination

Discrimination on the basis of such factors as race, sex, age,
physical handicap, and economic status is regarded as a significant cause of poverty within the structural perspective. Of
particular relevance to poverty is discrimination in education
and the labor market (e.g., Beeghley, 1983; Rodgers, 1982;
Schiller, 1984). Unfairness in the former area can include segregated schools, substandard facilities, curriculum tracking,
discriminatory treatment by teachers, and tuition costs for
quality education which exceed family resources. These factors
can prevent individuals from acquiring the skills and credentials necessary for employment above the poverty level.

Labor market discrimination can also take a variety of forms. In some cases employers and unions may deliberately exclude a certain group such as blacks or women. More frequently, perhaps, recruitment procedures are used which yield the same discriminatory outcomes, even though these outcomes were not directly intended. Employers may also be prone to doubt the abilities of individuals from certain groups, or have stereotyped images of what kinds of work are most suitable for them. The possibility that current employees, business associates, or the community-at-large might react negatively to nondiscriminatory hiring practices can also play a role in an employer's perpetuation of discrimination. Taken together, these processes contribute to blacks, women, and other victims of discrimination being employed less frequently, for fewer hours, and in less desirable jobs than they otherwise would. As a result, they run a higher risk of poverty than other groups.

The Welfare System

As we noted in Chapter 1, welfare state programs in the United States have evolved in a rather fragmented fashion. One consequence of this evolution is that welfare benefits can vary a great deal from household to household and from state to state. While many people are kept above the poverty line by the cumulative benefits of such a system, many are not. Thus, a major reason for poverty's existence in the United States is the absence of a well-integrated, national income-support system which provides benefits above the poverty level for those requiring them.

Structural theorists regard the absence of a national welfare policy as largely a consequence of American capitalism. Such a policy would result in the government taking much more responsibility for individual well-being than is deemed necessary or desirable in capitalism. Specifically, government-sponsored security is seen as dulling individual initiative, encouraging idleness, and fostering dependency, all of which are incompatible with the self-reliance emphasis of capitalism. Indeed, economic insecurity and the threat of poverty are often portrayed in a positive light by individualistic analyses, since these factors provide one source of motivation for the self-in-

terested, competitive behavior essential to economic growth
(e.g., Gilder, 1981). Indeed, from such a vantage point it has
been claimed that the U.S. welfare system contributes to poverty's existence less by its economic inadequacy than by its
destructive impact on the motivation of assistance recipients
(e.g. Gilder, 1981; Mead, 1982; Murray, 1984; Segalman, 1982).

The Distribution of Poverty

In accounting for the *distribution* of poverty the structural
perspective focuses on many of the same motivational and ability-related factors employed by the individualistic approach.
Thus, the structural position can be described as follows: The
economic system of the United States inevitably generates a
certain amount of poverty, and the individuals most likely to
be poor are those possessing certain personal characteristics.
Even at the distributional level, however, there is a difference
in emphasis between the individualistic and structural approaches. The latter tends to search for the structural antecedents of motivational and ability-related correlates of poverty
while the former places more stress on the causal role of the
correlates themselves. In addition to discrimination, the two
major antecedents that are usually focused upon are social-
class dynamics and capitalist emphasis on efficiency and profit
maximization.

With respect to the former, being born into a low-income
family, especially a female-headed one, places one in a disadvantaged position when it comes to obtaining the types of education and employment conducive to achieving nonpoverty
status as an adult (Beeghley, 1983; see also Robinson, 1984).
More affluent families and communities can offer significantly
greater resources in support of these efforts. Consequently, the
offspring of the currently poor are likely to be disproportionately represented in the next generation of poor adults (Duncan, 1984). Inherent in this conclusion is the prediction that
the future poor will embody many of the same personal characteristics as the current poor, with changes occurring at a
fairly slow rate. Within this framework the values, attitudes,
beliefs, and lifestyles of the poor are viewed as primarily a
response to poverty rather than a *cause* of it (e.g., Beeghley,

1983; Gans, 1969; Hill et al., 1985; Ryan, 1976; Valentine, 1968).

Where capitalist economic imperatives are concerned, efficient and profitable production calls for keeping labor costs to a minimum. This emphasis leads to efforts to employ the most productive persons in the available labor pool. As a result, the risk of unemployment and poverty is increased for the poorly educated, the less skilled, the aged, the partially disabled, the mentally retarded, and other low productivity workers. In this context it is important to keep in mind that certain criteria, such as education, might be used as screening devices for employment in situations where their relevance is questionable (Collins, 1979; Schiller, 1984). Individuals who do not meet these criteria are thus more vulnerable to poverty than those who do, regardless of their skills or capabilities.

The goal of efficient production and profit maximization also leads to policies that have adverse effects in localized geographical areas. In an effort to reduce labor costs companies may move from one section of the country to another, leaving behind many of the least skilled without jobs. In some industries technological advances reduce the number of workers needed; in areas that have become dependent on one industry this often means extended unemployment for many workers. Finally, companies which cannot compete successfully must leave the market; the consequences of this failure are again particularly severe in areas which have become dependent on that one industry.

While these factors contribute to poverty in specific geographical areas, the overall impact is not necessarily adverse. Some workers in one area may fall into poverty when a company fails, while those in another area may be escaping poverty due to jobs created by a competing company. However, it is not always the case that gains will exceed losses; there may be fewer nonpoverty jobs created than eliminated. In addition, these new jobs may go to those who would not have been poor in any event.

Evaluation of the Structural Perspective

Labor market forces are clearly a major cause of poverty. In their analysis of PSID data, Bane and Ellwood (1983b) found that a decline in the hours worked or wages of a household member (usually the head) accounted for 50% of the movement of non-elderly households into poverty which occurred during the study period. Moreover, at any given point in time, 45% of the poor in the study could trace their entrance into poverty back to such an event.

Focusing specifically on unemployment, Blank and Blinder (1985) estimate that a sustained one point rise in the prime-age male unemployment rate increases the overall poverty rate by 1.1 points. This is consistent with other analyses which conclude that the major increases in unemployment which characterized the early 1980s (Urquhart and Hewson, 1983) played a significant role in raising the poverty rate during that period (e.g., Danziger, Gottschalk, and Smolensky, 1984). Traditional husband-wife families constituted a substantial portion of the increase in the poverty population (Smeeding, 1983), even though families of high-wage earners were usually able to avoid poverty when unemployment struck (Terry, 1983).

In non-recessionary periods, unemployment per se appears to be less important than other labor-market factors, such as low wage rates, in explaining poverty (Taggart, 1982). There are two related reasons for this. First, a substantial proportion of poor families (48% in 1984) are headed by individuals who are not even in the labor force (Corcoran and Hill, 1980; U.S. Bureau of the Census, 1985d). Second, since many poor household heads lack marketable skills, it is difficult for them to obtain full-time employment doing anything other than low-wage work. Such employment does not represent a major escape route from poverty.

Overall, the state of the labor market would appear to place severe constraints—at least in the short run—on the ability of individualistic factors to do anything more than explain the distribution of poverty. If there are only a limited number of jobs available which pay nonpoverty wages, the primary result of a significant increase in the motivation, abilities, and/or educational credentials displayed by the poor would be to increase the amount of competition for those jobs. In some cases there would be nonpoverty jobs filled that otherwise would have gone vacant, but any reduction in the overall level of poverty would probably be slight. In contrast, the characteristics of the poor population would have changed dramatically, rendering them virtually indistinguishable from the rest of the population on these dimensions.

It can be argued, of course, that an increase in the motivation and ability of a significant portion of the population would, in the long run, generate an overall increase in nonpoverty employment. Documenting such a claim is understandably difficult. It is difficult to be optimistic on this score, however, when employment projections indicate that, at least in the short term, labor market growth is going to be greatest in areas (e.g., service and clerical work) that are relatively unattractive in terms of wages (National Commission for Employment Policy, 1982).

Where discrimination is concerned, the role that this factor currently plays in poverty is controversial and difficult to quantify in a definitive manner. Hence, it is likely that ideological preferences exert a particularly strong influence on the conclusions one draws in this area. At this point in history it would appear that discrimination affects the distribution more than the extent of poverty. This is because labor market forces shape the economic impact of discrimination in much the same way that they interact with motivation and ability. To be sure, eliminating discrimination would make competition for existing jobs more equitable. It would only increase the number of nonpoverty jobs, however, by bringing about an elevation in the wage rates of low-income jobs currently dominated by the victims of discrimination (e.g., custodial and secretarial work). To the extent that one considers these low wage rates as a sign of discrimination, discrimination may be regarded as a major cause of poverty at the macro level. Indeed, those who argue in favor of the "comparable worth" approach to job compensation appear to be making precisely this case (see Treiman and Hartmann, 1981), at least where female jobholders are concerned.

With respect to the distribution of poverty, analyses of black/ white and male/female earning differentials yield findings that are clearly consistent with explanations emphasizing the role of discrimination (e.g., Jencks et al., 1979; Kaufman, 1983; Mallan, 1982; Sandefur and Scott, 1984; Treiman and Roos,

1983). Other, more individualistic interpretations of this evidence are also possible, however (e.g., Cain, 1985; Daymont and Andrisani, 1984; Duncan, 1984; Gilder, 1981, ch. 5; Filer, 1985; Kamalich and Polachek, 1982). Even so, there is little doubt that at least some portion of these income gaps is due to the cumulative effects of educational and labor market discrimination. In addition, discrimination has an indirect effect on the distribution of poverty. This is because the low-income status fostered by discrimination is itself a contributor to future poverty.

Turning to welfare policy, the experiences of countries such as Sweden and Denmark clearly indicate that a welfare system can be designed to insure greater economic security than currently exists in the United States. Accomplishing such a task, however, would undoubtedly require modifying our economic system in ways that many, if not most, citizens and political leaders would strongly oppose. Consequently, the primary motive behind most discussions of the welfare system appears to be the value question: "What role *should* the welfare system play in poverty?" rather than the factual question: "What role *does* the welfare system play in poverty?" It should nevertheless be pointed out that cutbacks in welfare programs (especially AFDC) were partially responsible for the substantial poverty rate increases of the early 1980s (Committee on Ways and Means, 1983; Danziger, Gottschalk, and Smolensky, 1984).

The role which social class and the opportunity structure play in the distribution of poverty is nearly as controversial as that of discrimination. There is widespread agreement that family background exerts a significant influence on educational, occupational, and economic success (e.g., Corcoran and Datcher, 1981; Hetherington, Camara, and Featherman, 1983; Hill et al., 1985; Jencks et al., 1979; Levy, 1980; McLanahan, 1985). Jencks et al. (1979), for example, found that in the early 1970s nearly half of the variance in occupational status and up to 35% of the variance in earnings among men aged twenty-five to sixty-four could be accounted for by family background.

What is disputed are the reasons for this social class effect. Individualistic theorists emphasize the motivational and ability deficiencies of the lower class. This interpretation is consistent with Jencks's finding that the impact of family background on education and cognitive skills accounted for over half of family background's effect on occupation and earnings. It is also consistent with research on adoptive and biologically related families by Scarr and Weinberg (1978) which suggests that, at least for the working class to upper-middle-class range, genetic differences account for the major part of the long-term effects of family background on IQ scores.

On the other hand, research employing a more representative social-class sample has found that family structure and childhood experience play a significant mediating role in the relationship between class origin and test performance (Mercy and Steelman, 1982). Such a result is consistent with the structuralist view that cognitive development and educational credentials can reflect the tangible opportunities or "life chances" associated with class position (Beeghley, 1983). Additional support for the structural perspective comes from McLanahan's (1985) study of children from female-headed families. She found that high school graduation rates were more strongly related to the economic deprivation associated with living in these families than to father absence per se.

In this context it should be noted that analysis of the PSID data indicates that children born into poverty during the study period were likely to be poor for an average of nine consecutive years (Bane and Ellwood, 1983b). This figure actually underestimates the predicament of most children in the poverty population *at any given point in time*, since a significant percentage of this latter group is made up of the persistently poor. Thus Bane and Ellwood estimate that, at any given point during the study, a poor child who was also born poor was experiencing a spell of poverty that would last an average of seventeen years. It is hard to imagine such an extended period of economic deprivation not having a lasting impact on an individual's development, regardless of the genetic potential involved.

In sum, both individualistic and structural factors appear to contribute to the observed relationship between social-class origins and adult inequality and poverty. Concluding that one

ECONOMIC

1. Poverty insures the availability of a low-wage labor pool to do society's "dirty work": Jobs which are physically dirty, temporary, dead-end, underpaid, undignified, or menial.

2. Poverty creates jobs for a number of occupations and professions that serve the poor, or shield the rest of the population from the poor (e.g., social work, penology, legal services, fundamentalist ministries).

SOCIAL

3. The poor can be identified and punished as alleged or real deviants in order to uphold the legitimacy of dominant norms.

4. Poverty helps to guarantee the status of those who are not poor. In a society which places a high value on economic success, satisfaction can be derived from comparing one's own financial lot with those of the less fortunate. The poor thus serve as an important reference group for the working class.

POLITICAL

5. The poor serve as symbolic constituencies and opponents for several political groups (e.g., the radical left, the far right).

6. The poor, being relatively powerless, can be made to absorb the economic and political costs of change and growth in American society (e.g., industrialization of agriculture, urban renewal).

CULTURAL

7. The "low" culture created by and for the poor is often adopted by the more affluent (e.g., jazz, slang).

Source. Gans (1973), pp. 106-114.

TABLE 4.
Some Functions of Poverty

factor is significantly more important than the other, however, is probably more of an ideological exercise than an empirical one, given the limited data currently available.

Finally, the role that capitalist efficiency and profit maximization play in the distribution of poverty is significant and not denied by the individualistic perspective. Indeed, these economic imperatives are regarded as societal givens by the individualistic perspective, establishing the framework within which personal traits operate. The practice of rewarding educational credentials irrespective of the traits they are supposed to represent is a process less consistent with the individualistic model, however.

CONCLUSION

The policies and programs we examine in the following chapters reflect the influence of both individualistic and structural perspectives on poverty. When evaluating the relative success of these efforts, it will be helpful to keep in mind Gans's (1973) structurally based claim that poverty's existence is functional for the nonpoor in a variety of ways. Indeed, for many of these functions Gans doubts whether alternatives could be developed that would benefit the nonpoor as much as current processes do. A representative sample of these "positive functions of poverty" is provided in Table 4.

To the extent that an antipoverty program threatens to disrupt these functions, Gans's analysis suggests that strong resistance to the program is likely to occur. The evidence we review in the following chapters concerning a wide range of interventions provides, in our view, a great deal of support for this hypothesized relationship.

3

Direct Income Strategies: Public Assistance and Social Insurance

Giving people money is undoubtedly the most straightforward way of dealing with the problem of poverty, but considerable disagreement exists over whether it is the most effective way (e.g., Ellwood and Summers, 1985; Murray, 1984). Those who favor individualistic explanations of poverty tend to be skeptical of the value of direct income approaches. This skepticism is largely based in the belief that many of these programs decrease the motivation of recipients to earn and save money on their own. Program supporters, on the other hand, generally claim that this decrease is small in both magnitude and importance. While they acknowledge the need to revise many direct income programs, they stress even more strongly both the demonstrated and potential antipoverty effectiveness of this strategy.

Direct income strategies clearly play a major role in reducing poverty in the United States. Danziger, Haveman, and Plotnick (1985) estimate that if it had not been for these income transfers, the official 1983 poverty rate would have been 24.2% rather than 15.2%.[1] Moreover, these programs were instrumental in generating the poverty reductions which occurred during and after the War on Poverty years (Danziger, Haveman, and Plotnick, 1985; Gottschalk and Danziger, 1985; Plotnick and Skidmore, 1975).

The overall performance of direct income strategies should not obscure the fact that some of these programs reduce poverty much more than others. Social Security, for example, is without question the nation's most effective antipoverty program. AFDC, on the other hand, has never realized the antipoverty potential inherent in the direct income approach. Issues of perceived deservingness and political influence are at the core of these differences. Accordingly, a major goal of this chapter is to develop an understanding of why some direct income programs outperform others.

Public assistance and social insurance are the two most important direct income strategies currently used in the United States.[2] The major public assistance programs are Aid to Families with Dependent Children (AFDC), Supplemental Security Income (SSI), Veterans' Pensions, and General Assistance. The major social insurance programs are Social Security, Unemployment Insurance, Workers' Compensation, and Veterans' Compensation.

Even though all of these programs share the characteristic of being direct income approaches, it must be emphasized that they do not combine to form a well-integrated or unified system of economic support for the entire population; they were not designed with that purpose in mind. Rather, programs were developed individually to deal with specific causes of low-income status (e.g., old age, unemployment, absence of household head). Thus, each program has its own set of objectives associated with serving a well-defined population (Lurie, 1975).

PUBLIC ASSISTANCE

The goal of this strategy is to provide money to certain categories of people who are in need and, in theory at least, are regarded as deserving of public support. For the most part, these individuals are not viewed as having earned the right to assistance in an active sense. Rather, it is their state of need that is seen as requiring public intervention on their behalf.

Some commentators view this categorical approach to assistance as an appropriate one, recognizing as it does the multiple causes of poverty (e.g., Ellwood and Summers, 1985). Others regard this approach as a major obstacle to providing economic security to all segments of the population (e.g., Lurie, 1975; Garfinkel, 1982). Whatever one's opinion on this issue, it is clear that some groups of recipients tend to be viewed as much more deserving than others, resulting in their needs for economic security being taken more seriously. Also significant in this regard is the fact that the former recipient groups tend to exert greater political pressure than the latter through the vehicle of well-organized interest groups.

AFDC is the largest public assistance program, both in terms of total expenditures and number of recipients. It is the program most people think of when they hear the word "welfare." AFDC is also the most controversial public assistance program, and thus will be examined closely in this chapter. SSI will be discussed in detail as well. It is a substantial program in terms of expenditures, though its caseload is much smaller than AFDC's. SSI's recipients are generally seen as being more deserving than AFDC's, with predictable and important results in terms of the levels of support provided. Both Veterans' Pensions and General Assistance illustrate key issues with respect to poverty policy and thus merit our consideration. Because they are relatively small programs in terms of expenditures, however, our consideration of them will be brief.

Aid to Families with Dependent Children

No other poverty program generates the heated debate concerning recipient deservingness that AFDC does. Indeed, in many ways AFDC epitomizes the dilemmas faced by policymakers with respect to prioritizing their goals for the welfare state. AFDC *could* be structured in a way that would all but eliminate poverty among female-headed families. That it has not been designed in such a fashion is a non-event of great policy significance.

Viewing AFDC from an historical perspective helps to place the current controversial status of the program in its proper context. In 1935 the Social Security Act established Aid to

Dependent Children (ADC), a cash assistance program in which payments were made to needy families on behalf of children deprived of support due to parental absence, disability, or death. During the program's early years its caseload was mainly composed of widows and their children. While this group is generally seen as more deserving of assistance than families headed by unwed mothers (who currently represent nearly half of all AFDC families), it is important to recognize that even widowed families were subject to pejorative perceptions at the time of ADC's passage.

The ADC program was modeled after Mothers' Aid laws which had been enacted in most states in the early 1900s. Most of these laws only provided aid to families headed by widows, and even then they emphasized the need to investigate whether the widowed applicant was morally deserving of assistance. Given these circumstances, it is not surprising that rejection rates were high and assistance payments low (Dunn, 1984), patterns that persisted under ADC. It is a mistake then, to regard the current disenchantment with AFDC as a recent phenomenon caused by the particular racial and marital status characteristics of its recipients. While these factors have intensified discontent with the program, they did not create it.

Over the years the scope of AFDC has been expanded. Beginning in 1950, ADC payments took into account the economic needs of the adult relatives (usually the mother) who cared for the children. An Unemployed Parents component was added in 1961, which allowed (but did not require) states to assist children in two-parent families where one of the parents was unemployed. In 1962 these unemployed parents also became eligible for assistance, and the overall program became known as Aid to Families with Dependent Children.

In 1967 an optional Emergency Assistance program was established under the general provisions of AFDC (see Handler and Sosin, 1983). Emergency Assistance provides aid for up to thirty days in a twelve-month period to families with children under twenty-one. As its title implies, the program focuses on families requiring immediate financial assistance due to a crisis situation. Many families on Emergency Assistance receive regular AFDC payments as well.

While every state currently offers AFDC, only about half participate in the Unemployed Parent (AFDC-UP) and Emergency Assistance programs. The failure of many states to participate in the optional programs is no doubt partly due to the economic burden involved, since AFDC is jointly financed by federal, state, and, in some cases, local governments.

Policymaking for AFDC also takes place at both the federal and state levels, while program administration is a state and/or local responsibility. The interaction of these multiple funding, policymaking, and administrative processes generates not one AFDC program but fifty, with each state having its own, somewhat distinctive, version of AFDC. Each state, for example, possesses considerable freedom with respect to defining need and establishing need standards, setting income and poverty limits above which families are not eligible for assistance, and determining the amount of assistance it wishes to provide families (Chief, 1979). Thus, the same family might receive relatively generous AFDC benefits in one state, relatively meager benefits in a second state, and no benefits at all in a third state.

Virtually all of the major debates in the United States concerning the welfare state and the undeserving poor come to a head in the case of AFDC. In the following sections we review those aspects of the debate for which empirical data are available. The picture of AFDC that emerges is, we believe, different from the one presented in most popular discussions of the program.

Welfare Dependency

The fear that individuals will prefer living off the public dole rather than earning their own way in society is a concern that is nearly as old as public assistance itself. A related criticism asserts that AFDC contributes to intergenerational dependency, with the children of welfare families growing up to become welfare recipients themselves as adults.

As a general characterization of AFDC caseload dynamics this scenario is clearly false, in view of the longitudinal studies reported by Bane and Ellwood (1983a) and others (e.g., Boskin and Nold, 1975; Coe, 1981; Rein and Rainwater, 1978; Rydell,

Palmerio, Blais, and Brown, 1974). Of all those who ever receive AFDC benefits, only a minority become long-term clients. Indeed, 50% of all AFDC episodes last less than two years. Because long-term clients accumulate on the rolls over the years, however, they constitute a majority of the recipients at any single point in time and consume most of the program's resources. Consequently, for those families on AFDC at a single point in time, the average length of stay will be over ten years.

Long-term AFDC mothers are more likely than short-term ones to be nonwhite, high school dropouts, and without previous earnings. They are also more likely to have become a household head by having a child, and to have more children than the average (Bane and Ellwood, 1983a).

The fact that a subgroup of AFDC recipients becomes long-term clients does not, in and of itself, justify the conclusion that the program fosters welfare dependency. It is nonetheless true that the likelihood of leaving AFDC through earnings decreases sharply after one has been in the program for two years. Moreover, women who have received AFDC for more than two years tend to become long-term recipients (Bane and Ellwood, 1983a). These findings are more suggestive than those on duration of stay per se regarding the role of AFDC in fostering dependency. Even so, it must be kept in mind that there is no strong evidence indicating that long-term recipients remain on AFDC because they prefer welfare to working (Goodwin, 1983).

Where intergenerational dependency is concerned, relevant research is confounded. The major studies have not focused upon AFDC per se, but upon receipt of assistance in any number of forms, such as AFDC, Food Stamps, General Assistance, and SSI (Coe, Duncan, and Hill, 1982; Dickinson, 1975; Hill et al., 1985; Levy, 1980; Rein and Rainwater, 1978). While these investigations can shed considerable light on the issue of intergenerational dependency on welfare programs in general, they are less helpful in clarifying the nature of AFDC dependency in particular. Nevertheless, the more recent studies (Coe et al., 1982; Hill et al., 1985; Levy, 1980) have found that growing up in a welfare household does increase the likelihood of receiving welfare as an adult by a factor of 1.4 to 2. In absolute terms, however, the data also indicate that most children from welfare families do not grow up to receive welfare themselves, and that most adults in welfare families did not receive welfare as children (Coe et al., 1982).

Thus, while there is evidence that some intergenerational welfare dependency occurs, the role of an intergenerational factor in accounting for adult welfare status appears modest. Moreover, Hill et al., (1985) found little evidence to indicate that this modest amount of intergenerational transmission is caused by the attitudes of welfare parents. The extent to which these findings characterize AFDC recipients is unclear, given their methodological constraints. Insofar as they are applicable, however, major questions must be raised concerning those analyses which suggest, either explicitly or implicitly, that a sizable "underclass" has developed in the United States which is intergenerationally dependent on, and highly accepting of, AFDC (e.g., Auletta, 1982; Banfield, 1974; Mead, 1982; Murray, 1984; Segalman, 1982).

Work Effort

Closely tied to the issue of welfare dependency is concern over the impact which AFDC has on work effort. Interestingly, when ADC was established in 1935, the goal of the program was to provide assistance to the children of widows so that the latter would not have to enter the labor market. At that time it was felt that a mother's proper place was in the home caring for her children, not in the arena of paid employment. Furthermore, it was expected that the ADC caseload would decrease significantly over the years, as more and more widows became eligible for the Survivor's Insurance component of the Social Security program.

This expectation has not been confirmed. The number of divorced, separated, and never-married mothers receiving assistance has grown substantially, resulting in an expansion rather than a contraction of the program. In addition, there has been a dramatic, nationwide increase in recent years in the labor force participation of mothers with young children (Hayghe, 1984). The interaction of these two factors has generated a social norm that questions the appropriateness of some mothers staying at home with their children at public expense while others with similar responsibilities engage in paid employment which contributes to the economic support of both groups. The growth of public interest in the work incentive aspects of AFDC has paralleled these developments.

AFDC does appear to have a significant, though modest, negative impact on recipients' work behavior. On the basis of their review of the relevant research literature, Danziger, Haveman, and Plotnick (1981) estimate that AFDC reduces the work effort of the average recipient by about 600 hours per year. In addition, preliminary research by Bassi (1984a) strongly suggests that during the 1970s workers increasingly displayed a tendency to reduce their incomes in order to become eligible for AFDC.

Whether modest or large, any reduction in labor supply associated with AFDC is going to be evaluated very negatively by policymakers and the public, in view of the social trends we have previously discussed. From a policy perspective, however, it can be argued that these evaluations are perhaps a bit misplaced. Given their low level of human capital, it is by no means clear that AFDC mothers could generate above-poverty-line incomes even if they avoided AFDC and focused instead on increasing their labor market participation. Indeed, there is strong evidence to suggest that in many cases such a strategy would not even enable them to command wages that matched their AFDC benefits (e.g., Sarri et al., 1984). Thus, to the extent that one regards poverty reduction as a primary goal for poverty policy, the labor supply impact of AFDC does not necessarily represent an inherently undesirable outcome. On the other hand, for those who view dependency reduction and self-sufficiency as poverty policy's main goals, the findings on work reduction are clearly troubling. It is an indication of the priorities of American policymakers and the public that the latter reaction to the labor supply issue is much more common than the former.

Family Composition

It is frequently claimed that AFDC affects family composition in numerous ways that society evaluates negatively. For example, in states without an AFDC-UP program a family with an able-bodied male is not eligible for assistance. Thus, if the earnings of the male head of a household in these states fall substantially below the benefits provided by AFDC, there is an economic incentive for him to leave his family. Moreover, the federal eligibility requirements associated with the AFDC-UP program are sufficiently stringent that a significant incentive for poor husbands to leave their families remains even in those states which have the program. In some cases, of course, the leaving may be more apparent than real: The man may remain in the community, continuing to fulfill the role of husband and father to a limited degree, often to the point of providing some financial support to the family.

The availability of AFDC also decreases the need for a couple to stay together for financial reasons when one or both parties regard the relationship as unsatisfactory. Not everyone would view these breakups as undesirable, but those who place a high value on marital stability question whether the government, in the form of AFDC, should be subsidizing them.

A review of the relevant research indicates that AFDC's strongest impact is on the decision of young single mothers to establish their own households (i.e., to move out of their parents' home). Ellwood and Bane (1984) found that in states offering relatively generous AFDC benefits, young single mothers were much more likely to be living independently (and receiving AFDC) than young mothers in low-benefit states. AFDC benefit levels also appear to exert a moderate influence on the divorce and separation rates of young mothers (Ellwood and Bane, 1984). Not all studies have found that AFDC contributes to marital dissolution, however (for reviews see Bishop, 1980; MacDonald and Sawhill, 1978; Mayo, 1976; Phillips, 1981; Sanger, 1979). Most of AFDC's influence in this context seems to operate through the "independence effect," whereby the availability of AFDC benefits makes it easier for a woman to leave an unsatisfactory relationship. In contrast, there does not seem to be much support for the hypothesis that AFDC encourages a husband to leave his family for the purpose of maximizing its income.

There is also evidence that AFDC's availability reduces the

likelihood that a woman will decide to marry or remarry (e.g., Danziger, Jakubson, Schwartz, and Smolensky, 1982). The role of AFDC in these decisions seems to be minor relative to other considerations, however.

The claim that many low income, unmarried females bear illegitimate children in order to become eligible for AFDC has received no convincing empirical support (e.g., Ellwood and Bane, 1984; Keefe, 1983). Sanger (1979) provides an apt summary of this research with her observation that "illegitimacy has been found to be the result of unplanned and unanticipated pregnancies, and welfare receipt is more often the result than the cause" (p. 84). A related concern—that women on AFDC are encouraged by its benefit structure to have additional children—also doesn't seem to be warranted at this point in time, if it ever was (Ellwood and Bane, 1984; Placek and Hendershot, 1974; Presser and Salsberg, 1975).

Thus, while AFDC does exert a significant impact on family composition in certain respects, it does not appear to account for the decision of unmarried females to have children. Moreover, most analysts believe that major policy changes would be needed to alter the effects that AFDC does have on family composition. These changes could exacerbate problems of program performance in other areas, such as equity and antipoverty effectiveness (see MacDonald and Sawhill, 1978; Phillips, 1981).

Vertical Equity

As applied to public assistance programs, the concept of vertical equity encompasses at least three related principles (Allen, 1981):

1. Those in greater need should receive larger benefits than those in lesser need;

2. The receipt of welfare benefits should not have the effect of reversing the positions of households in the income distribution; and

3. Not only should the positions of households not be reversed, the distance between them in the income distribution should not be "unduly compressed."

With respect to AFDC, concern over vertical equity has traditionally focused upon the claim that some AFDC families have incomes as high or higher than those of many working families not on AFDC. This situation also represents a violation of the principle of less eligibility discussed in Chapter 1, which holds that assistance should be kept below the income of the poorest category of employed workers. Indeed, this is precisely the line of argument used in justifying many of the recent changes in the AFDC program which have greatly reduced the financial incentives for working while on AFDC (Rubin, 1983).

Even with these changes, it is still possible for an AFDC family to end up with an income that exceeds that of a non-AFDC family with an employed member. How frequently this occurs has never been determined with any precision. As a conservative estimate, it can be noted that in 1983 there were approximately 9,000 families above the poverty line whose sole source of income was AFDC or General Assistance. An additional 221,000 families above the poverty line had a combination of earnings, AFDC, and/or General Assistance. In contrast, there were 1.4 million families below the poverty line whose only source of income was earnings (U.S. Bureau of the Census, 1985b).

It must be recognized, however, that there will always be some people who choose to work at very low wages rather than seek public support. Consequently, efforts to keep AFDC assistance levels below that of the lowest paid workers not on AFDC would result in benefits that are extremely low. In this context it would probably be more appropriate to criticize the labor market for offering such poorly paid jobs than to find fault with AFDC for providing assistance that exceeds the income of some of the working poor.

At a more general level, this issue underscores a key dilemma which the principle of vertical equity raises. It is not possible to simultaneously honor vertical equity *and* employ a direct income approach to eliminate poverty or reduce it to negligible levels. Achieving such an antipoverty goal would require that the bottom of the income distribution be compressed upward to an extent that would be deemed unacceptably unfair to those who were only slightly above the poverty line. Furthermore, it is unlikely that enough direct income assistance could be given to those just above the line to substantially alter this perception of injustice. If the antipoverty impact of other poverty strategies were substantial, this particular conflict between vertical equity and the direct income approach would be of mere academic interest. As we shall see in the following chapters, however, the performance of other approaches is not strong enough to compensate for the decision of policymakers to resolve this conflict in favor of the principle of vertical equity.

Horizontal Equity

A deceptively simple concept, the principle of horizontal equity stipulates that those in similar circumstances or with similar needs should be treated the same (Lindeman, 1981). The simplicity is deceptive because the principle does not specify the factors to be taken into consideration when determining similar circumstances or needs. Nevertheless, at a practical level the AFDC program is generally seen as violating horizontal equity in at least two major areas, both of which are a result of interstate variation. First, the limited availability of AFDC-UP means that two-parent families can receive assistance in some states but not others. Second, benefit levels can vary dramatically from state to state. While regional differences in the cost of living undoubtedly account for some of the differences in assistance levels across states, there is little doubt that recipients in high-benefit states are more adequately supported than recipients in low-benefit ones. Indeed, the manner in which the federal government subsidizes state AFDC expenditures actually contributes to this benefit variation (Moffitt, 1984a). The availability of Food Stamps on a nationwide basis to all needy families who meet eligibility requirements reduces, but does not eliminate, these disparities.

A lack of horizontal equity is inevitable in a program that is as decentralized as AFDC. This problem has persisted in spite of two major attempts on the part of the executive branch in the past twenty years to replace AFDC with a national income support system: President Nixon's Family Assistance Plan and President Carter's Program for Better Jobs and Income. To be sure, the failures of both of these efforts can be described in terms of their idiosyncratic causes (e.g., Leman, 1980; Moynihan, 1973). The more fundamental message contained in these episodes, however, is that any proposal for a national program which standardizes direct cash assistance will encounter formidable obstacles when it includes those whose deservingness is regarded as questionable.

Stigma

It is frequently claimed that welfare programs in general, and AFDC in particular, stigmatize their recipients. Stigmatized individuals "have attributes, either alleged or real, that detract from their character and reputation making it difficult for others to relate to them in a normal way" (Williamson, 1974, p. 213). According to Rainwater (1982), supporters of the stigmatizing argument usually maintain that:

1. Nonrecipients have negative attitudes toward AFDC recipients;

2. As a result of these negative attitudes, recipients are treated differently than nonrecipients;

3. Recipients develop negative attitudes toward themselves because they appreciate the social significance of "being on the public dole;" and

4. The preceding three processes cause AFDC recipients to be perceived as behaving in ways that reflect the derogated status they occupy.

A measure of empirical support can be found for all four of these claims. Numerous studies have shown that a significant segment of the American public views welfare recipients, and especially AFDC mothers, in pejorative terms (e.g., Alston and Dean, 1972; Coleman, Rainwater and McClelland, 1978; Feagin, 1975; Goodwin, 1972, 1973; Williamson, 1974). The disproportionate number of AFDC families headed by women who are black or Hispanic, unmarried, and not in the labor force undoubtedly plays a major role in this perception (Glazer, 1969).

Documenting negative behavior toward AFDC recipients is more difficult than documenting negative attitudes. Perhaps the clearest evidence is the low level of support that is provided in most states. It is no coincidence, for example, that SSI is a more generous program than AFDC. A major reason is that the former's beneficiaries—the aged, blind, and disabled—are generally regarded as more deserving of assistance than the latter's. In this context Wohlenberg (1976) found that the least generous and most restrictive welfare programs are in those regions of the country where attitudes toward the poor on the part of the general public are most hostile. In a similar vein, Piliavin, Masters, and Corbett (1979) found that welfare case aides with negative attitudes toward the poor committed greater underpayment errors in their decisions regarding AFDC recipients than did aides with more positive attitudes.

At a more general level, it is frequently charged that AFDC is administered in a fashion that is demeaning to potential and actual recipients, especially when compared with the administration of programs such as SSI and Veterans' Pensions. To be sure, a "presumption of dishonesty" does appear to characterize the regulations and procedures of AFDC to a greater extent than the other two programs (Handler, 1972). Even so, it must be acknowledged that, in an administrative sense, AFDC-eligible persons receive much fairer treatment now than they did twenty years ago. This is due to a major shift in AFDC policy during this period from a high level of administrative discretion to a more standardized and bureaucratized approach, one which encompasses the protection of certain constitutional rights (Sosin, 1985). While the interests of AFDC participants have not been served by all of these changes, especially those occurring in the 1980s, the overall impact has clearly been positive.

Where the issue of internalization of stigma by AFDC recipients is concerned, the most that can be said is that people *believe* that AFDC recipients feel highly stigmatized as a result of receiving assistance (Williamson, 1974). Studies of AFDC recipients themselves generate a somewhat different picture (e.g., Goodban, 1985; Goodwin, 1972; Handler and Hollingsworth, 1968; Horan and Austin, 1974; Kerbo, 1976; Lowenberg, 1981). Most recipients appear to experience relatively little stigma, with a minority feeling highly stigmatized. To be sure, ego-defensiveness on the part of some recipients may partially account for this finding (Rainwater, 1982). Nevertheless, on the basis of the available evidence it appears that characterizations of the AFDC population that emphasize the feelings of shame and self-criticism associated with recipient status are somewhat overdrawn. This conclusion is consistent with those analyses that suggest that during the 1960s welfare recipiency came to be viewed by many potential and actual program participants as an economic right, rather than as something to be ashamed of (e.g., Patterson, 1981; Sosin, 1985).

Fear of stigmatization can, of course, prevent eligible individuals from applying for assistance (Moffitt, 1983). Indeed, welfare conservatives (e.g., Gilder, 1981) cite this as a desirable consequence of stigma, because it encourages individuals to be self-sufficient. It nevertheless appears that the great majority of those eligible for AFDC do in fact participate in it. It is hard to imagine this occurring if the program were as subjectively distasteful in a general sense as some have claimed (see, however, Rainwater, 1982). Perhaps the most accurate observation in this regard has been made by Lowenberg (1981), who concludes on the basis of his literature review that "welfare stigma has not been eliminated, but those who need help and those who depend on public programs seem to be less and less deterred by stigma" (p. 450).

The fourth component of stigma—the belief that recipients engage in behaviors responsive to their derogated status—is difficult to evaluate. To be sure, a number of commentators assert that the welfare system fosters the development of a dependent underclass characterized by a variety of behavioral pathologies (e.g., Gilder, 1981; Mead, 1982; Murray, 1984; Segalman, 1982). In the eyes of the general public, however, is recipient status seen as causing deviance, or are deviants regarded as simply being more likely than others to end up as recipients? The answer is not clear.

A similar question applies to the actual behavior of recipients. While their lifestyles are distinctive in a number of respects, establishing recipient status as the cause of this distinctiveness is extremely difficult. There is evidence, however, that recipients who are long-term and/or feel highly stigmatized tend to express negative, passive attitudes in a variety of contexts (e.g., Goodban, 1977, 1985; Kerbo, 1976; Rainwater, 1970).

Antipoverty Impact

It is clear that AFDC has a significant economic impact on participating households. In 1983, for example, AFDC benefits reduced the poverty rate among recipients by 15% (Committee on Ways and Means, 1985b). Even so, 76% of all families on AFDC or General Assistance in 1983 were below the official poverty line after receiving their benefits (U.S. Bureau of the Census, 1985b). In this context it is instructive to compare the number of families who are below the poverty line when welfare (primarily AFDC) payments are *not* included in income calculations (the prewelfare poor) with the number below the line when these payments are included (the postwelfare poor). The results indicate that less than 4% of the prewelfare poor were raised above the poverty line by AFDC in 1983 (Committee on Ways and Means, 1985b).

The major role of AFDC benefits, then, is to lessen the extent of a family's poverty rather than to lift them above the poverty line. In recent years, however, AFDC's ability to accomplish either of these objectives has declined markedly. As long as states have the freedom to establish need standards and benefit levels, this trend is almost certain to continue. The real value of AFDC benefits has been seriously eroded by the failure of states to increase payments to keep pace with inflation, and Food Stamp allotments to participating families have not been large enough to fully compensate for this decline. Given that AFDC is just one of many programs competing for the state's financial resources, and that AFDC recipients are relatively weak as a political pressure group, these results are not surprising.

Caseload

Given the negative perceptions to which AFDC recipients are vulnerable, any significant increases in the program's caseload can be counted on to generate high levels of concern among policymakers and the public. That such increases have occurred is undeniable. Between 1960 and 1984 the average monthly number of recipient families increased by 470%, from 787,000 to 3.7 million. While this increase is substantial, it is important to note that the bulk of this growth had taken place by the mid–1970s.

What were the causes of this dramatic increase in AFDC enrollment? The interaction of three factors appears to be mainly responsible: changes in welfare policies and regulations which increased the number of those eligible for assistance; an increase in the percentage of eligible families who actually applied for assistance; and an increase in the percentage of eligible applicants who actually received assistance (Patterson, 1981). These changes reflected the growing influence in the 1960s of interest groups claiming that citizens possessed fundamental social and economic rights, not just political and civil rights (Gronbjerg, 1977; Patterson, 1981; Ritti and Hyman, 1977).[3] With the declining influence of these groups in the 1970s, the liberalization of welfare policy and administration largely came to an end. Thus, as the number of those applying for and receiving benefits approached the total number who had been made eligible by the earlier changes, the AFDC caseload began to stabilize (Rence and Wiseman, 1978).

The modest increase in the number of AFDC families since the mid–1970s appears to be primarily due to continued growth in the number of poor female-headed families, a fundamental demographic trend. It should be noted, however, that during this period the number of female-headed AFDC families has grown much more slowly than the number of poor female-headed families overall (Committee on Ways and Means, 1985b). Thus, there has been an actual decline in the percentage of poor female-headed families served by AFDC. This decline reflects, at least in part, the failure of state eligibility standards to keep pace with inflation. This increases the likelihood that a family can be below the poverty line and still not qualify for assistance. A second reason for the decline in coverage is recent changes in AFDC regulations which render many poor families with a working female head ineligible for benefits. These changes were proposed by the executive branch, which maintained that social and economic rights were in fact overextended during the 1960s, resulting in assistance being granted to those not truly needing or deserving assistance.

It is a telling comment on the public's view of deservingness and the poor's lack of political influence that the declining relevance of AFDC to poor female-headed families has received scant public attention in comparison to the controversy generated by the caseload explosion of the 1960s and early 1970s. The significance of this situation will become clear when we examine the results of attempts to restrict the access of more favored groups to poverty program benefits.

Implications

Viewed in its entirety, the evidence we have reviewed in the preceding sections would seem to justify several conclusions. First, AFDC does have an impact on work behavior and family composition, an impact that may contribute directly and/or indirectly to caseload increases and the welfare dependency of a subgroup of recipients. Second, these impacts appear to be quite modest in magnitude, and certainly do not justify portrayals of AFDC as a Venus's-flytrap of social policy, a program that entices and then ensnares most of those who are unfortunate enough to come near it. Third, AFDC's role as an antipoverty program has diminished markedly in recent years. It assists a smaller fraction of its target population than it used to, and those that it does assist receive benefits that have shrunk considerably in real terms over the years.

There is a certain irony to this third development. As we noted previously, the original ADC program was expected to wither away over the years as widows became increasingly eligible for Social Security benefits. In the 1980s, it is not the AFDC program that is withering away so much as it is the antipoverty potency of the program, as states use in-kind programs such as Food Stamps to partially offset this decline. A crucial question thus emerges: With a group as low in perceived deservingness as AFDC recipients, how far can erosion of benefits proceed before policymakers take significant remedial action? We shall address this question in Chapter 6.

Supplemental Security Income

If AFDC epitomizes the problems inherent in providing cash assistance to a population whose deservingness is suspect, SSI illustrates the wider range of policy options available when more favored groups are assisted: the aged, blind, and disabled. This program also illustrates, however, the constraints under which any direct income strategy operates when it focuses on a group whose political influence is relatively weak and whose right to assistance is passively rather than actively earned.

The 1972 Social Security amendments established the SSI program to replace three separate direct income programs that had been administered by state and local governments and jointly financed by the state and federal governments under the 1935 Social Security Act: Old Age Assistance, Aid to the Permanently and Totally Disabled, and Aid to the Blind. Implemented in 1974, the basic SSI program is financed and administered entirely by the federal government. In sharp contrast to AFDC, program guidelines, eligibility requirements, methods of income measurement, and assistance payments made in the basic federal SSI program are uniform nationwide (Farrell, Parent, and Tenney, 1984). States are permitted, and in some cases required, to supplement the basic federal benefits (Hawkins, 1983).

For the aged, blind, and disabled who qualify, SSI represents a guaranteed annual income, and as such is the only national guaranteed income program in the United States. Its cash benefits, while modest, are nonetheless more generous than either AFDC or most of the state/federal assistance programs it replaced. Of particular significance is the fact that automatic cost-of-living increases have been applied to federal SSI payments since 1975. Consequently, SSI benefits have not declined in real terms over the years, as has been the case with AFDC.

SSI has a much smaller caseload than AFDC, with 3.9 million recipients in 1984 versus AFDC's 10.8 million. Over half (60%) of SSI recipients were eligible for assistance due to disability, and 38% qualified because of old age (i.e., sixty-five years of age and over). Only 2% were recipients due to blindness. The number of individuals receiving assistance because of old age has declined fairly steadily since the program began, while the number of disabled and blind recipients has increased (Committee on Ways and Means, 1985a).

Having the SSI program primarily administered by the Social Security Administration rather than state and local welfare departments reflects, and reinforces, the distinctions between the SSI and AFDC populations in the public's mind. The Social Security Administration has traditionally been associated with programs in which the benefits are viewed as earned rather than charity. This difference in orientation toward clients is perhaps most vividly illustrated by the millions of dollars that have been spent on national outreach programs in an attempt to locate and enroll potential SSI recipients (Menefee, Edwards, and Schieber, 1981). No such efforts characterized the years when the AFDC participation rate was very low. Indeed, in many locations the emphasis was exactly the opposite: to keep the AFDC rolls as low as possible through a variety of regulatory and discretionary mechanisms (Sosin, 1985).

In view of the above discussion, it is clear that SSI represents a significant improvement over the three programs it replaced. It assists many low-income aged, blind, and disabled individuals who did not receive, or would not have received, benefits from the latter programs. For many of those who were being aided under the old system, the benefits provided by SSI are more generous than they were getting. From an antipoverty perspective, however, the program could be improved in two major respects: participation rate and antipoverty impact.

Participation Rate

A large number of individuals who are eligible for SSI benefits do not participate in the program. This appears to be particularly true of the aged, whose participation rate ranges from 50% to 60% (Coe, 1985b; Menefee et al., 1981; Warlick, 1982). In their study focusing on the elderly and the disabled, Menefee et al. (1981) concluded that nonparticipation in SSI had four major causes:

1. *Nonparticipants' evaluation of their level of need and attitudes toward the welfare system.* With regard to the former, it

was found that nonparticipants viewed their quality of life and quantity of income in relatively positive terms. In addition, many of these individuals, especially the elderly, expressed negative attitudes toward welfare. Indeed, nonparticipants were less likely than recipients to have had contact with any public assistance program, a finding replicated by Drazga, Upp, and Reno (1982).

These results are helpful in understanding why only 3% of the eligible nonparticipants contacted by the Social Security Administration after the latter study subsequently applied for SSI benefits. They also suggest that there is stigma associated with the SSI program for at least some nonparticipants, even though relatively little stigma appears to be felt by the recipients themselves (Tissue, 1978).

2. *Lack of knowledge about SSI*. In the Drazga et al. (1982) study, 45% of the nonparticipants claimed that they had never heard of the program. And of those who were aware of it, many thought they would not qualify for benefits. In a similar study, Coe (1985b) found that 75% of nonparticipating households cited informational problems.

It is also likely that some nonparticipants underestimate the amount of cash assistance that SSI would provide them. Warlick (1984) estimates that nonparticipants could, on the average, increase their cash income by 160% by enrolling in the program. This figure actually underestimates the economic benefits available, since SSI participants can in many cases automatically qualify for in-kind benefits such as Medicaid and Food Stamps.

3. *Financial status*. Nonparticipants tend to have higher incomes than participants. Consequently, the former have less to gain from SSI than the latter. Many nonparticipants may regard the benefits as not large enough to justify the effort involved in becoming and remaining an SSI recipient. In this context Drazga et al. (1982), Warlick (1984), and Coe (1985b) report that participation of eligibles in SSI is positively associated with higher benefit levels.

4. *Family support*. Menefee et al. (1981) found that many nonparticipants appear to rely on their relatives for the financial support they might otherwise receive from SSI and other public programs. The percentage of this group of nonparticipants who hold negative attitudes toward welfare is not reported, but we predict it would be large. Family support networks should appear particularly attractive to those who perceive public assistance as stigmatizing.

Antipoverty Impact

Unfortunately, the most recent data on SSI's antipoverty performance is for 1978, when SSI was estimated to have reduced the number of elderly below the poverty line by 12% (Warlick, 1984). This figure would have risen to 27% if there had been 100% participation in the program. To the extent that the former percentage is currently applicable, SSI's antipoverty impact significantly exceeds AFDC's. That should not be surprising, given that in 1985 the federal SSI benefit for a single individual was 75% of the poverty line, and the corresponding benefit for a couple was 89% of the line. In contrast, the median maximum AFDC benefit for a family of three in that year was only 47% of the poverty line (Committee on Ways and Means, 1985a).

The fact remains, however, that 76% of all single individuals receiving SSI were poor in 1983, as were 36% of all SSI couples (U.S. Bureau of the Census, 1985b). To be sure, a large number of these individuals and families did receive in-kind benefits. For example, of those households receiving SSI that were below the poverty line in 1983, 64% received Food Stamps (U.S. Bureau of the Census, 1985a). No estimates are available of what the poverty rate for these recipients would be if these benefits were counted as income. In all likelihood a sizable number would still be poor.

Implications

The case of SSI highlights an obvious but fundamental assumption of direct income programs: Eligible persons must participate in order to benefit. It is not enough to have a program that provides relatively generous benefits. The overall structure of the program must be such that barriers to enrollment are minimized. This is particularly important when lack of information and perceived stigmatization are involved. Given the evidence that suggests that SSI's antipoverty impact could be more than doubled by achieving 100% participation, focusing on increased enrollment would appear to be a very inexpensive way of improving program performance. In an era of high federal deficits this is an important consideration.

Increased participation does not represent the entire solution, since many of those who currently receive SSI remain poor. It is easier to recommend increased benefits than it is to achieve them, of course. Though SSI's population is generally viewed as a very deserving one, as a political constituency it is relatively weak. Part of this weakness derives from the fact that the three groups served by SSI have little in common other than low-income status, a status that is associated with low levels of political mobilization, at least in American society. Consequently the fortunes of SSI recipients have depended greatly on the influence wielded by those who advocate on their behalf. To be sure, this advocacy has resulted in significant achievements, especially when compared with the accomplishments of those advocating for the AFDC population. Even so, the record of SSI is clear testimony that a group's deservingness, in and of itself, is no guarantee that its economic needs will be fully met by policymakers.

Veterans' Pensions

Of all the groups served by public assistance programs, wartime veterans are probably seen as the most deserving. Preferential treatment of veterans has a long history in America, predating even the Revolutionary War (Levitan, 1985). The current Veterans' Pension program, enacted in 1933, assists low-income wartime veterans who are sixty-five or older, or are permanently and totally disabled due to causes that are not service-connected. Benefits are also available to survivors of wartime veterans whose deaths were not service related.

Most people probably do not think of Veterans' Pensions as public assistance or welfare. The fact that these pensions are income-tested, i.e., eligibility and payments are tied to current financial need rather than to past earnings, clearly places them in the category of public assistance, however. The reason for the confusion is that wartime military service is generally viewed as a very active, commendable behavior which entitles veterans to the assistance they receive. In a normative sense, then, these benefits are earned rather than being the result of charity. It is the latter characteristic that most people associate with public assistance, and the circumstances of the AFDC and SSI populations.

Veterans are also much better organized as a political constituency than either of these groups. This combination of deservingness and political power results in benefits that exceed those of other public assistance programs, and are subject to automatic cost-of-living adjustments.

Because the pension program is planned, financed, and administered entirely at the federal level, it is not vulnerable to the fiscal and political pressures at the state level that can negatively affect other public assistance programs (see Grubb, 1984). In this context, the administration of the program by the Veterans' Administration has proven to be particularly beneficial to recipients. Procedures to establish and maintain eligibility are relatively simple, with disclosure of one's private affairs kept to a minimum. This presumption of honesty is consistent with the high level of deservingness attributed to recipients. The overall impact of this approach is perhaps best summarized by Levitan (1985), who observes that "veterans' benefits are administered with maximum consideration to the recipients' dignity and self-respect" (p. 45).

General Assistance

General Assistance is a public assistance program, but it is not a federal program. It is designed, financed, and administered entirely at the state and/or local level. Nevertheless, there are two reasons for including it in the present discussion. First, General Assistance is a program of great historical importance. As a direct descendant of the 1601 English Poor law, General Assistance represents the oldest form of public assistance in the United States. Prior to 1900 it was the only assistance program offered in most states, and during the Great Depression of the 1930s served approximately six million families (Brinker, Klos, and Kesselring, 1982). Its caseload is smaller now; in 1983, for example, there were fewer than 1.3 million recipients of General Assistance (Levitan, 1985).

A second reason for discussing General Assistance is that its continued presence is an indication of the extent to which the

United States has yet to fully mature as a comprehensive welfare state. General Assistance functions as a residual program for those who fall between the cracks of the current income support system. Included here are individuals who are ineligible for federally based public assistance programs and those who require temporary assistance until the benefits from these programs begin. The former group can include, but is not limited to, childless couples and single persons; the partially handicapped or blind; families in which the head has exhausted his/her unemployment benefits; and transients (Segalman and Basu, 1981).

Because General Assistance is totally controlled by states and localities, policies and administrative procedures concerning such matters as eligibility and the level of assistance provided are more varied than in any other public assistance program. A major consequence is that General Assistance is rife with horizontal inequities. A common thread that runs through nearly all General Assistance programs, however, is that (1) only those desperately in need are aided, and (2) the amount of aid rendered is the least of all public assistance programs (Segalman and Basu, 1981). Though systematic estimates are not available, it is likely that the percentage of the prewelfare poor removed from poverty by General Assistance is close to zero.

SOCIAL INSURANCE

The lessons which social insurance programs have to offer to students of poverty policy begin with one crucial fact. These programs play a much greater role than public assistance in reducing poverty in the United States. Approximately 34% of the "pretransfer poor"[4] were removed from poverty by social insurance in 1983. Less than 4% of the pretransfer poor escaped poverty via public assistance (Danziger, Haveman, and Plotnick, 1985). This substantial difference reflects two factors. A greater percentage of the pretransfer poor receive social insurance than public assistance, and the average social insurance benefit is larger than the average public assistance benefit.

That social insurance and public assistance should differ in these ways is one of the great ironies of public policy. Social insurance programs were not designed as antipoverty programs per se, if that label is taken to mean a program that directs the bulk of its resources to the low-income population. Rather, the primary goal of social insurance is to replace a portion of the earnings that are lost when employment, retirement, disability, or death occurs. This objective focuses on the employed population, a group in which the poor are underrepresented.

Within this context social insurance has a second major goal, social adequacy, whose relevance to antipoverty objectives is more direct. The purpose here is to ensure that the incomes of social insurance recipients do not fall below some minimum standard of acceptability. To this end social insurance generally replaces a higher proportion of the earnings of low-income workers than high-income ones.

We shall examine three major social insurance programs in this section: Social Security, Unemployment Insurance, and Workers' Compensation. Their overall performance illustrates both the opportunities and dilemmas that the social insurance approach presents to policymakers committed to poverty reduction.

Social Security

Since its enactment in 1935, Social Security has evolved into the most effective poverty program in the United States, if effectiveness is measured by the number of recipients it keeps above the poverty line. Not all of these individuals were covered by Social Security at its inception, however. The program's old age benefits were originally provided only to aged workers who had retired. In 1939 the program was expanded to cover retirees' dependents, as well as the survivors of deceased workers. In 1956 the program was further expanded to provide coverage to disabled workers and their dependents, and in 1966 an in-kind health insurance component was added. Today, the Social Security system is made up of old age and survivor's insurance, disability insurance, and health insurance.

Social Security is a very complex program, even as federal programs go. The basic principles upon which the program operates are fairly straightforward, however. That these principles have not always been candidly communicated to the public by policymakers is one of the more fascinating chapters in the history of public policy, for it can be argued that this process has actually contributed to the antipoverty effectiveness, and certainly the popularity, of the program. In recent years, however, serious questions have been raised concerning Social Security's ability to sustain its performance in either of these areas. It is with this issue in mind that we review the key features of the program.

As is the case with virtually all social insurance programs, eligibility for Social Security benefits is a function of one's employment history. In order to be a "fully insured" participant one must have worked for at least ten years in jobs whose earnings are subject to the Social Security payroll tax. In 1982 approximately 89% of the civilian workforce were employed in such jobs (Committee on Ways and Means, 1985a; see also Nelson, 1985). While this is an impressive figure, it should be noted that the remaining 11% tend to be drawn disproportionately from the ranks of the poor. The job-linked nature of Social Security, in conjunction with the fact that the payroll taxes of future beneficiaries help to finance the program, contribute greatly to Social Security recipients being viewed as a very deserving population.

While the payroll tax used to finance Social Security is slightly regressive, the formula used to compute benefits is quite progressive. It replaces a higher percentage of the earnings of low-income workers than high-income ones. In absolute terms, however, the former ends up with smaller benefits than the latter. In this fashion the program attempts to simultaneously achieve individual equity and social adequacy. Equity is served by providing greater absolute benefits to those who paid more in payroll taxes when they were working. Adequacy is served by replacing a greater proportion of low-income workers' wages.

The fact that Social Security benefits are available to the nonpoor as well as the poor has at least two interrelated consequences of considerable importance. First, Social Security is by far the largest direct income program, both in terms of beneficiaries and expenditures. In 1984 over $180 billion was provided to thirty-six million recipients (Committee on Ways and Means, 1985a).

The second consequence is that a large and powerful segment of the population has a vested interest in maintaining and expanding the program. This is a major reason why increases in Social Security payments have, since 1975, been automatically adjusted to reflect increases in the cost of living. This change has contributed significantly to increases in the program's cost, with current expenditures being approximately three times greater than they were in 1975.

This growth in cost takes on added significance when one realizes that Social Security is very different from a conventional private pension plan. In a private plan, workers' contributions are invested and paid back with interest when they retire. Thus, each generation of workers pays for its own benefits. In Social Security, on the other hand, workers' contributions are used to pay current beneficiaries of the program. When these workers retire, they will be supported by the contributions of the individuals then employed, and so on. What is taking place is a redistribution of income from the young to the old and disabled. Nevertheless, Social Security has at least two features that foster the impression that it is just a public version of a private pension plan. First, it is funded by workers' (and employers') contributions rather than by general revenues. Second, in absolute terms high-wage earners pay more into, and get more out of, the program than low-wage earners.

Further complicating matters is the peculiar way in which the unearned component of Social Security benefits are distributed. This component consists of the portion of the Social Security benefit that exceeds the payment one would have received from participating in an actuarially fair private pension plan. Thus far in the history of Social Security, all cohorts have benefited from this unearned component, and most individuals have gotten back more in benefits than they have paid out in payroll taxes (Burkhauser and Warlick, 1981; Moffitt, 1984b). Furthermore, Ozawa (1982) has shown that retired workers with a record of high earnings receive subsidies of this type that are larger in absolute terms than those received by retired low-income workers. The purely redistributive aspect of Social

Security thus serves to allocate benefits in a fashion which is inversely related to economic need.

Social Security's idiosyncratic mechanisms for financing and benefit distribution have received increasing attention in recent years, as concern over the financial stability of the program has grown. In this regard there are at least three major issues that need to be addressed in order to put these concerns, and Social Security's role as a poverty program, in their proper context: antipoverty impact, incentives to work and save, and program cost.

Antipoverty Impact

The antipoverty effectiveness of social insurance programs is mainly attributable to Social Security. Overall, social insurance programs removed 34% of the pretransfer poor from poverty in 1983; Social Security alone accounted for almost 90% of this total (Committee on Ways and Means, 1985a; Danziger, Haveman, and Plotnick, 1985). As one might expect, Social Security's impact is concentrated on the elderly (i.e., those sixty-five and over). Approximately 59% of the pretransfer aged poor were raised above the poverty line by Social Security (Committee on Ways and Means, 1985a). Indeed, this is the primary reason why the elderly poverty rate has declined substantially in recent years, from 25% in 1970 to only 12% in 1984 (U.S. Bureau of the Census, 1985d). This is a major social policy accomplishment. At a more general level, studies indicate that the economic status of the elderly population as a whole has reached a point where it closely approximates, and may even exceed, that of the nonaged (e.g., Danziger, van der Gaag, Smolensky, and Taussig, 1984). Social Security has played a major role in this development.

These figures mask considerable variation in economic well-being among various subgroups of the aged. Individuals with weak links to the labor market frequently do not receive enough support from Social Security to stay out of poverty, a situation that can only be partially compensated for by participation in the SSI program. In particular, blacks and females do not fare as well as whites and males. Elderly black females thus represent a very disadvantaged group, having a 1984 poverty rate of 36% (Ozawa and Alpert, 1984; Ross, 1984; U.S. Bureau of the Census, 1985d; Warlick, 1983).

More generally, 8% of all families with Social Security income in 1983 were below the poverty line, as were 26% of all unrelated individuals (U.S. Bureau of the Census, 1985b). To be sure, many of these households would not be classified as poor if their in-kind benefits such as medical care and Food Stamps were counted as income. Indeed, the elderly represent the demographic group whose poverty rate is most dramatically reduced when adjusted for in-kind benefits, with the resulting poverty rate ranging from 2.6% to 7.6% for 1984, depending on the estimating procedure used (U.S.Bureau of the Census, 1985c).

All of the qualifications and adjustments we have discussed should not obscure a basic message: Social Security is the most powerful of all direct income programs. If all poverty programs were as effective with their target populations as Social Security is with the elderly, the goal of reducing poverty to negligible levels in our society would be a realistic one.

Work Effort and Savings

The estimates of antipoverty impact we have presented have not gone unchallenged (e.g., Plotnick, 1984). To the extent that Social Security reduces work effort and the tendency to save money through private channels, recipients' pre-Social Security incomes are lower than they would be in the absence of the program. Estimates which fail to take these effects into account thereby exaggerate Social Security's antipoverty influence.

These are legitimate concerns. Where work effort is involved, Social Security enables many individuals to retire earlier than they otherwise could afford. In addition, once individuals begin receiving Social Security benefits, payments are reduced if recipients continue to work and earnings exceed a certain amount. The Disability Insurance (DI) component of Social Security has received special attention in recent years, due to the fact that a substantial decline in the labor force participation of older males has paralleled major increases in both DI benefits and the DI caseload (e.g., Parsons, 1980, 1984).

On the basis of their review of the relevant research, Danziger, Haveman and Plotnick (1981) estimate that Social Security has reduced the labor force participation of men sixty-five and over by 12% since 1950. Where DI is concerned, the evidence also indicates that, at least through 1978, the increasing generosity and/or leniency of the program had a significant but small negative effect on the work effort of older workers (Haveman and Wolfe, 1984). These factors have also contributed to caseload growth in the program. DI's impact on labor supply, however, appears to be mainly confined to older disabled men with low expected earnings. Consequently, it is unlikely that the incidence of pretransfer poverty among these individuals has been greatly altered by DI's availability.

The impact of Social Security on private savings has been the subject of considerable controversy, with widely varying estimates of its influence being offered. It is thus noteworthy that two of the most recent reviews of this literature find the overall evidence to be inconclusive (Aaron, 1982; Lesnoy and Leimer, 1985). Even if Social Security has reduced savings in the past, however, it may not do so in the future. Currently, many workers are concerned that during their retirement years they might not receive the same high rate of return on their Social Security contributions that previous beneficiaries have. Consequently, these individuals might not reduce their private savings as much as they would if they viewed Social Security's future more optimistically (Watson, 1982).

In sum, the evidence on work effort and savings suggests that only minor adjustments in estimates of Social Security's antipoverty impact need to be made. These changes would certainly not be of a magnitude that would call into question the major conclusions drawn in the preceding section.

Cost

Can Social Security sustain its antipoverty effectiveness in the decades to come? Social Security is an enormously expensive social program, and the problem of financing it in both the long and the short run became the focal point of policymaking debate concerning direct income strategies during the early 1980s (e.g., Birdsall and Hankins, 1985; Harpham, 1984; National Commission on Social Security Reform, 1983; Thompson, 1983). The major concern was that the pay-as-you-go nature of the system had become untenable due to (1) the growing ratio of elderly beneficiaries to tax paying workers, and (2) the relatively generous, inflation-indexed benefits provided by the program. In the bleakest scenario Social Security was portrayed as being on the verge of bankruptcy, with the long-term future of the system in doubt. The most sanguine view presented by critics was that young workers would receive a much poorer return on their Social Security contributions at retirement than that enjoyed by current beneficiaries.

In reality, the first scenario was clearly false in any politically meaningful sense. In 1983, a series of amendments to the Social Security Act was passed. These amendments resolved the short-term financing problem of Social Security and eased its long-term problems, while keeping the basic structure of the program intact (National Commission on Social Security Reform, 1983; Svahn and Ross, 1983).

Several of these changes (e.g., taxing benefits) had been recommended on their own merits for years by reformers, quite apart from any financial crisis (e.g., Pechman, Aaron, and Taussig, 1968). Indeed, for students of poverty policy the individual amendments were less significant than their collective thrust. The principles of individual equity and social adequacy were retained, and the economic interests of virtually all current beneficiaries were protected.

The extent to which this protection can be maintained for future beneficiaries is the subject of disagreement. As long as Social Security is financed on a pay-as-you-go basis, it is a certainty that the overall rate of return on payroll contributions will begin to decline at some point as the system approaches maturity. Some projections indicate a more drastic decline than others, however (e.g., Burkhauser and Warlick, 1981; Feldstein, 1977; Leimer and Petri, 1981; McKay, 1982; Russell, 1982).

For our purposes, the key issue is that as the system matures, the goals of individual equity and social adequacy come increasingly into conflict (Birdsall and Hankins, 1985). If the full antipoverty impact of the program is to be preserved, the rate of return to high-wage earners might eventually have to be lowered to a point that is actuarially unfair. Such an action, to the extent that its significance was understood by the public, could undermine support for what has traditionally been a very popular social program (Coughlin, 1980; Goodwin and Tu, 1975).

On the other hand, resolving this conflict at the expense of the social adequacy objective could also generate substantial negative reaction, given the sympathetic response that low-income beneficiaries usually elicit from the public. Finally, proposals that would ease the equity vs. adequacy conflict by using general federal revenues, in addition to payroll taxes, to finance the program are not without problems of their own. Such a move would increase Social Security's resemblance to public assistance, which is bound to generate hostility among those who have disdain for such programs. It is possible, of course, that the perceived deservingness of Social Security recipients would outweigh the negative connotations accompanying this structural change, resulting in the program being viewed in a positive manner similar to that associated with Veterans' Pensions.

Given the complex matrix of vested interests involved, all of the preceding approaches are likely to play a role in the attempts of policymakers to ensure Social Security's long-term viability. In view of the program's great antipoverty impact, the mix of strategies that is eventually chosen is certain to have profound implications for the future success of poverty policy in the United States.

Unemployment Insurance

The objectives of Unemployment Insurance (UI) are to provide economic assistance to temporarily unemployed workers and to help stabilize the economy during recessions (Congressional Budget Office, 1985). Since the program focuses on earnings replacement, it is invariably grouped with social insurance programs in discussions of poverty policy. Even so, in several key respects UI closely resembles public assistance programs such as AFDC. This resemblance is partially responsible for

UI's antipoverty impact being much more limited than Social Security's.

The major similarity between UI and AFDC lies in the area of state control. States can exercise considerable discretion in UI matters such as eligibility determination, benefit levels, and duration of benefits. This discretion has resulted in serious violations of horizontal and vertical equity, especially with respect to eligibility and benefit amounts. For example, it is frequently the case that low-income workers have to work longer than higher-income ones in order to qualify for benefits (National Commission on Unemployment Compensation, 1980).

In addition, low-wage jobs such as agricultural work, domestic work, and casual labor are covered much more extensively in some states than others. Overall, however, the percentage of the labor force in jobs covered by UI is very high, approximately 90%.

In view of this high level of coverage, it is striking that in 1984 only about 34% of the unemployed received UI benefits. In contrast, during the 1975 recession an average of 76% received UI assistance (Committee on Ways and Means, 1985a). The recent low percentage appears to be largely due to a variety of legislative and administrative changes enacted in the program at the federal and state levels beginning in the late 1970s (Burtless, 1983a, 1983b; Burtless and Saks, 1984; Vroman, 1984). These changes have rendered some potential recipients ineligible, reduced the net benefits available to certain eligible recipients, raised the costs of applying for benefits, and deterred some eligible individuals from applying for assistance.

For the unemployed who do receive UI benefits, the benefit amounts depend on their state of residence and the type of job held. The state-determined weekly benefit is usually between 50% to 70% of the recipient's weekly earnings prior to unemployment, up to a specified maximum benefit limit. This procedure results in high-income workers receiving greater absolute benefits than low-income ones, giving the program its insurance-like quality. As is the case with Social Security, however, low-wage earners tend to have a greater percentage of their wage replaced than high-wage earners. This latter fact, along with the maximum benefit limit, helps explain why the national average weekly benefit in 1984 was only 35% of the average weekly wage (Committee on Ways and Means, 1985a). The maximum benefits vary substantially from one state to another, and represent fixed amounts or fixed proportions of the state's average weekly wage. Interestingly, however, the benefits actually awarded to UI recipients exhibit more interstate variation than can be accounted for by differences in the prevailing wage rates of the states (Baron and Mellow, 1981). Thus we have another example of horizontal inequity.

Interstate variation, at least that portion attributable to state discretion, is less evident in the case of benefit duration. In most states the maximum benefit period is twenty-six weeks. Through the Extended-Benefits program states with high unemployment rates can lengthen this period by up to thirteen weeks. Finally, in response to the recession of the early 1980s, temporary legislation (Federal Supplemental Compensation) was passed to provide up to fourteen weeks of additional benefits in high-unemployment states. This program ended in early 1985. In this context it is important to keep in mind that those who exhaust their benefits while still unemployed represent a minority of Unemployment Insurance beneficiaries. In 1982 this percentage was approximately 39% (Congressional Budget Office, 1985).

In view of the issues we have discussed, how effective is UI at preventing households from falling below the poverty line? The population of interest here is households whose incomes in the absence of UI are below the poverty line. Of households in this category having a head or spouse who had been unemployed for thirteen or more weeks in 1982, 16% were kept out of poverty by UI benefits. In this regard, husband-wife families fared better than single-parent families or unrelated individuals. UI prevented the poverty of 22% of the husband-wife group, but only 12% of the other two groups (Burtless, 1983a).

While these figures indicate that UI has a significant anti-poverty impact, its effectiveness has declined in recent years. For example, in 1975 UI was responsible for an overall reduction of 27% in the poverty rate of households with thirteen or more weeks unemployment, compared with 16% in 1982 (Burtless, 1983a). This decline reflects both a drop in the percentage of the unemployed who are receiving UI due to the policy changes previously discussed, as well as an apparent decrease relative to the poverty line in the amount of UI assistance provided to low-income recipients. This latter trend is consistent with Hamermesh's (1982) research, which indicates that upper-income households tend to receive greater UI benefits than are necessary to maintain their level of consumption, while low-income families frequently receive less than is necessary.

The recent history of UI suggests that the label "social insurance" should not blind one to the important differences between programs included in this category. Indeed, the decline in UI's antipoverty effectiveness over the past decade calls to mind AFDC rather than Social Security. Both UI and AFDC have undergone their own distinctive patterns of retrenchment during this period. While UI recipients are generally seen as more deserving than AFDC recipients, both programs are closer to one another in their levels of perceived stigma than either is to Social Security (Williamson, 1974).

These differences and similarities are undoubtedly caused in large part by attributions about the work statuses of the three programs' populations. Social Security beneficiaries are viewed as having fully earned their benefits through a lifetime of productive work and payroll tax contributions. The desire of AFDC recipients to work, on the other hand, has traditionally been regarded as highly suspect. UI recipients are subject to mixed evaluations. They typically have a more stable work history than AFDC mothers but a shorter one than Social Security beneficiaries. Moreover, because in nearly all states UI is financed by a tax on employers but not employees, UI recipients resemble AFDC recipients insofar as neither group directly contributes to funds designated for the program which benefits them.

Finally, there is the long-standing belief that UI payments induce a significant number of able-bodied individuals to prolong their unemployment, a belief which has empirical support (Congressional Budget Office, 1985). Danziger, Haveman, and Plotnick (1981), for example, estimate that UI lengthens the mean duration of unemployment by five weeks per recipient (see also Corson and Nicholson, 1982; Moffitt and Nicholson, 1983; Solon, 1979). While the work-disincentive criticism is widespread and intense with respect to AFDC, it carries less force in Social Security, since there is less of an expectation that the affected groups (older and disabled workers) should display high work effort.

In an overall sense, then, our analysis of UI leads to a troubling conclusion. Both the administrative structure of the program and the work-related perceptions relevant to its functioning make UI vulnerable to policy changes that are typically associated with programs serving the minimally deserving, rather than the highly deserving, poor. To the extent that UI's antipoverty impact either continues to decline or plateaus at its current level, the role of complementary assistance programs (e.g., Food Stamps) becomes increasingly important. As we have seen in the case of AFDC, however, these other programs do not appear to have filled the gap produced by retrenchment. Insofar as UI follows a similar pattern, the economic well-being of the unemployed will be seriously compromised.

Workers' Compensation

Workers' Compensation is the third major income replacement program, serving the victims of work-related injuries and their families. Approximately 87% of all wage and salaried workers are covered by the program, with farm workers, household workers, and casual laborers being the most frequently excluded.

It is primarily a state-run program, which is almost entirely funded by employers. As a result, many of the horizontal inequities which characterize UI apply to Workers' Compensation as well, such as differential coverage and widely varying benefits. These benefits typically include (1) cash payments for disability and death, replacing a portion of lost earnings; (2) cash payments for partial disability, frequently as a scheduled payment for loss of specific body parts and functions; (3) medical care; and, to varying degrees, (4) rehabilitation services. Benefits are usually paid on a weekly basis, though lump-sum payments also frequently occur.

The majority of compensation cases involve temporary total disability, which results in the worker being incapacitated for several weeks. The benefits in these cases are generally based on a percentage (e.g., 66⅔%) of the worker's average wage during a particular period. But due to other provisions such as upper limits on allowable payments, in some states the worker will end up receiving benefits that are significantly less than the specified percentage.

Expenditures have increased significantly in recent years due to three major factors: (1) the initiation in 1970 of the federal black lung program to provide assistance to coal miners disabled by black lung disease; (2) extensive liberalization of state benefit formulas, maxima, and coverage provisions; and (3) the effect of inflation on wages and medical care costs, which in turn are tied to benefit levels (Price, 1980). Benefit growth has slowed down considerably in the 1980s, however (Price, 1984).

Systematic estimates of Workers' Compensation's antipoverty effectiveness are not currently available. To the extent that its overall benefit structure resembles that of UI, Workers' Compensation probably has a similar impact on its recipients. Indeed, when one considers that the recent history of the program has been characterized by liberalization rather than retrenchment, it is likely that Workers' Compensation reaches a greater proportion of its target population than does UI.

CONCLUSION

At least three themes have emerged in our analysis of the direct income approach to poverty policy. First, the impact of these programs on poverty is relatively straightforward, at least in the short run. Depending on the amount of assistance provided, the recipient's standard of living is affected to a greater or lesser degree. Within this context the only major assumption that has to be met in order for a direct income program to have an economic impact is that those eligible for the program actually participate in it. To be sure, this can be a difficult assumption to satisfy in some cases (e.g., SSI). This should not obscure the fact, however, that the number of assumptions associated with direct income programs is relatively few.

A second theme is that some direct income programs display much more antipoverty effectiveness than others. Programs that serve constituencies which are relatively powerful and/or perceived as highly deserving tend to perform better than those that do not. Hence the disparate fortunes of Social Security beneficiaries and AFDC mothers. From this perspective, the reason that some direct income programs are more effective than others is only secondarily a function of their design. This is because the designs themselves primarily reflect the direct and indirect influence wielded by various recipient constituencies. In this context we have seen that traditional distinctions between public assistance and social insurance programs do not fully capture all the aspects of their differential influence.

Finally, the evidence indicates that direct income programs do have modest behavioral impacts on participants, which could contribute to a small subgroup's low-income status in the long run. We believe that the links between these impacts and low-income status are sufficiently tenuous that it would be unwise to substantially alter direct income programs solely on the basis of these presumed relationships.

Not everyone would agree with this judgment, of course (e.g., Gilder, 1981; Murray, 1984). Some commentators interpret the behavioral impacts as substantial rather than modest, and perceive the causal linkages to poverty as solid rather than tenuous. Ultimately, such disagreements would appear to reflect more fundamental ideological differences in perceptions of the causes of poverty, which we discussed in Chapter 2. These disagreements and differences have major implications for views of how direct income programs should be improved, implications we shall address in Chapter 6.

4

In-Kind Benefits

The programs we examine in this chapter do not focus on income provision per se. Rather, their primary objective is to provide the poor with some of the basic goods and services upon which individuals typically spend a portion of their income. Differences in the standards of living of the poor and nonpoor are thus narrowed, even though the gap between their cash incomes remains stable. A subgroup of in-kind programs also has a second objective: to eliminate some of the major *causes* of poverty, such as teenage pregnancy.

In recent years in-kind assistance to the low-income population has increased (in real terms) at a much faster rate than benefits from cash public assistance programs. Between 1965 and 1984, for example, the market value of means-tested noncash benefits grew by nearly 800%, while public assistance increased by just 56%. While these noncash benefits only accounted for 24% of the total amount of direct assistance (cash plus in-kind) to the poor in 1965, in 1984 they represented 64% of the total (U.S. Bureau of the Census, 1985c). Nearly 59% of all poor households received some form of means-tested in-kind benefit in 1983 (U.S. Bureau of the Census, 1985a). Clearly, then, an examination of in-kind programs is essential if the overall nature and impact of poverty policy is to be understood.

There are both individualistic and structural reasons for supporting at least some types of in-kind benefits. The individualistic perspective is skeptical that the poor, left to their own devices, will spend money in ways which maximize the well-being of themselves and their families. One solution to this problem is to aid the poor in ways which restrict their choices to socially approved alternatives. Food Stamps, for example, can be used as cash, but only for the purpose of purchasing certain broad categories of food. At a structural level, the dynamics of the marketplace can frequently make it difficult for the poor to translate cash assistance into adequate medical care or housing. In-kind benefits can be very helpful in these cases.

Supporters of the in-kind approach also claim that the total amount of assistance that the poor receive through a number of separate noncash programs significantly exceeds what they would be likely to get if all assistance took the form of unrestricted cash grants. There are at least three major reasons for this belief. First, policymakers and the public have traditionally been reluctant to provide the poor with sizable amounts of no-strings-attached cash assistance. Second, suppliers of housing, food, social services, and the like are more inclined to see their vested interests being served by in-kind than direct income programs. Consequently, strong lobbying efforts by these groups are much more likely to occur on behalf of the former programs. Third, the highly differentiated Congressional committee structure fosters an environment within which problems are addressed on a piecemeal basis through separate legislative acts. Such a system is much more supportive of the categorical approach represented by in-kind programs than it is of the more generic cash assistance strategy.

While critics of the in-kind approach acknowledge the validity of the preceding observations, they maintain that in some instances it can be more efficient to aid the poor via direct cash assistance than with in-kind benefits. It is claimed that the value that recipients attribute to in-kind benefits, frequently referred to as the "recipient value" or "cash equivalent" value, is usually less than their market (i.e., dollar) value (Smeeding, 1984a). To the extent that this is true, it implies that the degree of recipient satisfaction generated by in-kind benefits of a certain market value could be achieved with an unrestricted cash grant whose market value was lower. Alternatively, an unrestricted cash grant which equalled the market value of an in-kind benefit could be counted on to generate more recipient satisfaction than the in-kind benefit. Either way, the unrestricted grant emerges as the preferred policy option, if recipient satisfaction is regarded as the most important program objective.

Whether recipients actually value in-kind benefits less than direct income transfers is, of course, an empirical question which we shall address at various points throughout this chapter. In order to appreciate the relevant research, however, it is important that the basis for this prediction be understood. First, it is assumed that in-kind benefits can distort the consumption patterns of recipients. Benefits will cause some recipients to consume more of a specific good or service than would have been the case if they had received the market value of those benefits in cash. For example, the Food Stamp program may cause some families to spend more money on food, and less on things such as housing and clothes, than they would like.

Second, there may be a stigma associated with receiving in-kind benefits for some individuals. Recipients can be more readily identified in everyday interaction as public dependents than can recipients of cash grants. Being a resident of a low-income housing project is a twenty-four-hour-a-day advertisement for one's dependency; having to cash a welfare check at the bank once a month is not.

Both of these processes, to the extent they occur, reduce the value of in-kind benefits to recipients relative to that of unrestricted cash assistance. Moreover, some potential recipients might refrain from participating in the programs altogether because of these factors. Constituencies such as policymakers and taxpayers, however, may derive social, political, and psychological benefits from the provision of in-kind benefits which exceed the economic inefficiency involved (Smeeding, 1984a). Stigma, for example, may be viewed favorably as a deterrent to public dependency rather than as a dimension to be minimized or eliminated. In a more humanitarian vein, prompting individuals to consume more food or medical care than they otherwise would can represent a source of altruistic satisfaction. There can also be a patronizing assumption operating here, of course, which holds that many in the recipient population do not have the motivation and/or the ability to care for these needs when allowed freedom of choice in spending their income.

Whatever one's views concerning the merits of the in-kind strategy, it is hard to deny the sizable impact which these programs have on the economic well-being of the poor. Even the most conservative estimates of this impact indicate that the overall poverty rate would have been 8% lower in 1984 (13.2% vs. 14.4%) if food, housing, and medical care benefits had been counted as income. More liberal estimates place the reduction as high as 33% (U.S. Bureau of the Census, 1985c). Using the more conservative approach, Danziger, Haveman, and Plotnick (1985) estimate that the number of pretransfer poor persons removed from poverty in 1983 by in-kind programs was over 2½ times the number removed by public assistance (9.2% vs. 3.4%). This difference reflects the growing dominance of the in-kind strategy in federal policymaking for the poor.

In the following sections we shall examine four major categories of in-kind benefits: food, medical care, housing, and social services.[1] It is the assistance given in the first three areas which commentators focus upon when claiming that official poverty rates are spuriously high. The fourth area is important because it includes programs that attempt to modify some of the poor's attitudes, beliefs, and behaviors that are believed to play a causal role in poverty.

FOOD

At the core of the absolute approach to defining poverty is the notion of subsistence, and at the core of subsistence is the ability to obtain enough food to survive. In this context it would certainly seem plausible to assume that the poor are more likely to be underfed and malnourished than the nonpoor. The extent to which this is the case in the United States has been the subject of considerable disagreement in recent years, however (Bovard, 1983b; Citizens' Commission, 1984; Food Research and Action Center, 1984; Graham, 1985; U.S. General Accounting Office, 1983c). Controversy over this issue peaked in 1984, when a Presidential task force issued a notorious report suggesting that it was not possible to document hunger's extent in America (President's Task Force on Food Assistance, 1984). In spite of this report, most analysts agree that the evidence overwhelmingly indicates that hunger increased significantly during the recession of the early 1980s (e.g., Citizens' Commission, 1984; Food Research and Action Center, 1984), a conclusion consistent with opinion poll results and the marked increase in the number and utilization of community soup kitchens during that period ("Harris Survey Reports," 1984). Whether malnutrition has increased in a corresponding fashion is much less clear.

Against this background it is instructive to consider how the nature and scope of federal food assistance policy have changed over the years, especially with respect to the Food Stamp program. In 1935 the Federal Surplus Commodities Corporation was established and assigned responsibility for distributing surplus farm products to the poor. The primary objective of this program, however, was not the satisfaction of the poor's nutritional needs. Rather, it was the support that such a program could provide for farm prices (MacDonald, 1977).

Criticism of this approach to food assistance by both recipients and food retailers helped to bring about the first Food Stamp program in 1939. In this program participants purchased stamps which could then be used to buy food from authorized retailers. Because the market value of the stamps exceeded the amount paid for them, participants' purchasing power with respect to food was increased. In 1943 the Food Stamp program was terminated due to the decline in unemployment and the elimination of the food surplus brought about by World War II.

The shift from a food assistance policy dominated by commodity distribution to one emphasizing Food Stamps began in 1961, when eight pilot Food Stamp projects were authorized by

President Kennedy. In 1964 the Food Stamp Act permitted states to switch from the Commodity Distribution program to a Food Stamp program, and twenty-two states immediately did so. Congress enacted major increases in Food Stamp benefits for participants in 1971 and required national participation in the Food Stamp Program in 1974.

With the elimination of the purchase requirement in 1977, recipients no longer had to buy their Food Stamps. Instead, the bonus value of the stamps (i.e., market value minus purchase price) was given directly to participants in the form of stamps. This change was especially helpful to those who had frequently found themselves with insufficient cash to purchase the stamps.

In 1983, 41% of all poor households received Food Stamps. This group represented 72% of all households participating in the program (U.S. Bureau of the Census, 1985a). As one would expect, most Food Stamp households also receive benefits from at least one direct income program, such as AFDC, SSI, or Social Security (Committee on Ways and Means, 1985a). The mean annual market value of the stamps received by the 7.1 million participating households in 1983 was $1,042, amounting to $11.1 billion in benefits.

The available evidence indicates that Food Stamps are more effective as a public assistance program than as a food and nutrition program. It is clear that the overall purchasing power of the poor is enhanced by Food Stamps. Indeed, the value of the stamps to the average recipient has been estimated to be 97% of their market value (Smeeding, 1982). Thus, the overwhelming majority of recipients view the stamps as being nearly equivalent to direct cash transfers. Only the poorest of the poor, for whom the average recipient value is 85%, appear to be constrained in any significant way by the program, and even this constraint is not large in absolute terms.

Estimates of the antipoverty effectiveness of Food Stamps typically do not partial out its influence from that of the National School Lunch Program (NSLP) and housing assistance (e.g., U.S. Bureau of the Census, 1985c). In 1984 the combined impact of these three in-kind programs would have lowered the poverty rate from 14.4% to somewhere between 12.9% and

13.2%. Given that the number of Food Stamp and NSLP house-holds greatly exceeds the number of households receiving hous-ing assistance, it seems safe to assume that food assistance accounts for significantly more poverty reduction than housing assistance. This assumption is most justified when recipient values, rather than market values, are the basis for calculations.

Food Stamps also help to compensate for interstate differ-ences in the levels of support provided by direct income pro-grams, such as AFDC and General Assistance. Thus, families whose cash income is low due to the fact that they live in states where welfare benefits are skimpy are usually eligible for larger Food Stamp allotments than those living in more generous states. In this fashion disparities across states in the size of the total welfare package (cash transfers plus Food Stamps) are smaller than they would otherwise be.

Moreover, unlike many poverty programs, the Food Stamp program does not penalize the working poor for being employed. Because it emphasizes the income level of the potential recip-ient in determining eligibility, the working poor are just as entitled to Food Stamps as the poor who cannot work. Indeed, there are few categorical restrictions of any sort on eligibility, such as age, disability, or the presence of children in the house-hold. This characteristic of the program makes it particularly useful for providing temporary assistance to individuals and families during periods of economic decline. For many house-holds this may be the only poverty program to which they can readily turn to soften the financial impact of a recessionary period.

Critics of the Food Stamp program frequently emphasize the fact that most participants end up spending little more for food than they would have if they had simply received the cash equivalent of the stamps. Moreover, because the stamps can be used to purchase just about any type of food, the program provides recipients with little incentive to upgrade the basic nutritional quality of their diets. As a result, the impact of the program on the nutritional adequacy of participants' diets has been found to be minimal (Akin, Guilkey, Popkin, and Smith, 1985; Butler, Ohls, and Posner, 1985; MacDonald, 1977; President's Task Force on Food Assistance, 1984). The improvement that has occurred appears to be mainly due to the fact that the stamps enable the poor to buy more, rather than better, food.

Given these findings, many critics maintain that the efficiency and coverage of the program would be improved if it were "cashed out," that is, turned into a direct cash assistance program resembling a guaranteed income (e.g., Barmack, 1977; Isserman, 1975). Administering such a program would be simpler than administering the current Food Stamp program. In addition, many believe that the nonwelfare poor would participate in a direct cash program in significantly greater numbers than they do in the Food Stamp program, where their participation rate is low relative to that of AFDC and SSI recipients. Overall, it has been estimated that only 50–65% of all those eligible for Food Stamps actually receive them (Coe, 1983, 1985a; President's Task Force on Food Assistance, 1984).

Whether cashing out the program would significantly increase participation depends on the extent to which nonparticipants view receipt of the stamps as stigmatizing, administratively inconvenient, and/or unduly constraining in terms of purchasing power. In contrast, to the degree that nonparticipation results from lack of information about the program, there is little reason to expect that a direct cash program, in and of itself, would generate greater participation. While all of these factors contribute to the nonparticipation currently observed, lack of information appears to be a particularly important reason (Coe, 1983, 1985a). It is especially useful for explaining why Food Stamp participation is positively associated with being a public assistance recipient and negatively associated with being a member of the working poor. Informational problems are also one of the reasons why nonparticipation is positively associated with age, though it appears that fear of stigma and perceived administrative problems are more potent factors in this instance.

It should also be noted that nonparticipating eligible households tend to have higher incomes than participating ones, and that nonparticipating elderly and working poor households in particular tend to claim that they do not need Food Stamps (Coe, 1985a; President's Task Force on Food Assistance, 1984).

The greater the Food Stamp benefits available to a household, however, the greater the probability that the household will participate in the program (Coe, 1985a).

Whatever the implications of the research on nonparticipation, it must be kept in mind that a successful attempt to cash out Food Stamps could, in the long run, result in less aid being given to the poor than would have been the case under the in-kind program. Fear of this outcome is one reason that critics are unlikely to press very hard for such a reform in the fore-seeable future (Giertz and Sullivan, 1982), especially in view of the high recipient value that the stamps possess.

Where the nutritional shortcomings of the Food Stamp program are concerned, significantly increasing the stamp allotment to participants would represent an indirect, and expensive, response to the problem. Enabling participants to buy more food would increase the chances, but by no means guarantee, that their nutritional needs would be met. Allotments are currently a function of household size, monthly income, and the cost of food included in the Department of Agriculture's Thrifty Food Plan (Committee on Ways and Means, 1985a). It is the use of the Thrifty Food Plan that has been most severely criticized, since the plan was not designed to be nutritionally adequate for long-term use. Furthermore, even for effective short-term use the plan assumes sophisticated nutritional knowledge on the part of participants and access to low-cost supermarkets, storage space, and equipment (Food Research and Action Center, 1981).

Another avenue to nutritional adequacy is to use the Food Stamp program to exercise more direct control over the diets of the poor, by restricting purchases to certain types of foods. Such a step would probably lower the participation rate significantly, and does not appear to be a realistic political option. In the area of child nutrition, however, there are a number of government programs that attempt to exert this type of influence.

Child Nutrition Programs

The oldest and largest child nutrition program is the National School Lunch Program (NSLP), which was permanently authorized in 1946. In this program the federal government provides cash and/or commodities to participating public and private schools (pre-primary, primary, and secondary) for the purpose of preparing and serving lunches to enrolled children. These lunches must adhere to federally specified meal patterns and standards of nutritional quality, such as providing one-third of the child's recommended daily allowance of vitamins and minerals (Congressional Budget Office, 1980).

The price a child pays for the lunch is determined by his/her family income, with some children paying nothing, others paying a reduced price and still others (those least in need) paying the full price. The cost of even the full price lunches is less than what it would be in the marketplace, given that the overall lunch program is federally subsidized. In 1983, nearly two-thirds (65%) of all poor households with school children from five to eighteen received free or reduced-price lunches through this program (U.S. Bureau of the Census, 1985a). Overall, about half (52%) of the school children in the United States were enrolled in the program in 1983, and 91% of all children attended schools which participated in it (U.S. General Accounting Office, 1984c).

The School Breakfast Program is similar to the lunch program, except that it focuses on low-income areas, rural areas, and areas where there are a large proportion of working mothers (Congressional Budget Office, 1980). Consequently, the program is only offered in about one-third of the nation's school districts (President's Task Force on Food Assistance, 1984). Fewer than 8% of all U.S. students participate in the program, with the great majority of enrollees coming from low-income families.

Studies of the impact of these two programs have produced mixed but generally positive results (for reviews, see Bovard, 1983b; Congressional Budget Office, 1980; President's Task Force on Food Assistance, 1984; Vachon, 1983). The most recent investigations indicate that the lunch program is stronger in nutritional terms than the breakfast program. Not surprisingly, research also suggests that low-income participants in these programs are more likely to benefit nutritionally than middle-income ones, especially when they participate in multiple programs (Congressional Budget Office, 1980).

The second largest and fastest growing child nutrition program is the Special Supplemental Food Program for Women, Infants, and Children, known as the WIC program. Established in 1972, the program served about three million participants in 1984. WIC provides food supplements to pregnant, breast-feeding, and postpartum women and their children (up to five years old). In order to participate in the program a mother and her child must be low-income and nutritionally at risk.

In contrast to Food Stamp enrollees, WIC participants obtain items from a fairly restricted list of foods high in protein, iron, calcium, Vitamin A, and Vitamin C, such as fortified cereal, eggs, juice, milk, formula, and cheese. The great majority of participants receive vouchers that can be used at local supermarkets to obtain only these items. Numerous studies have found the WIC program to have positive effects on participants (for a review see U.S. General Accounting Office, 1984d). Most convincing is the evidence indicating an increase in the mean birthweights of children born to WIC mothers, and a decrease in the percentage of low-birthweight infants.

Dollar for dollar, child nutrition programs are probably better than Food Stamps at achieving nutritional goals. Nevertheless, the effectiveness of these programs is not so striking that they have been immune to blistering criticism. Some commentators (e.g., Bovard, 1983b), for example, claim that the modest nutritional impact of these programs does not justify the significant public expenditures involved. It is furthermore observed that families whose incomes place them well above the poverty line are frequently able to participate in nutrition programs (e.g., the lunch program), thus reducing their target efficiency.

Supporters of nutritional programs, on the other hand, emphasize the significant long-term benefits that may result from even minor nutritional gains achieved during infancy and childhood (e.g., Beeghley, 1983; Food Research and Action Center, 1984). They also stress the fact that many poor children do not have the opportunity to benefit from nutrition interventions because they are not entitlement programs. Consequently, these programs lack horizontal equity. Schools that do not participate in the lunch program, for example, are frequently in low-income areas that lack the resources to meet federal matching requirements (Levitan, 1985). And of those schools with the lunch program, only a minority have the breakfast program. The WIC program is also not available in all locations.

It should be noted that recent changes in the National School Lunch Program have increased the cost of full-price lunches to participants and the strictness of eligibility standards associated with qualifying for reduced-price and free lunches (Hoagland, 1984). As a result, the benefits of this program are now more focused on low-income children. In addition, federal reimbursement rates for all NSLP lunches have been lowered. The overall effect of these changes has been to decrease the number of schools participating in the program (U.S. General Accounting Office, 1984c). The low-income children in these schools thus lose the opportunity to obtain free or reduced-price lunches, even though poor children in general are supposed to be the main beneficiaries of the program. This is probably one of the reasons there has been a greater increase during the 1980s in the overall number of low-income children than in the number of low-income children participating in the lunch program (Committee on Ways and Means, 1985b). Consequences such as these focus attention on the side effects of attempts to reduce program expenditures by greater targeting of benefits toward the poor.

MEDICAL CARE

Medical care can be causally related to poverty in at least two major ways. First, inadequate care can result in the perpetuation of poor health or deterioration of good health, both of which can make it difficult for an individual to acquire or maintain employment. Second, the expense of medical care can thrust a previously nonpoor family below the poverty line (Luft, 1978). Within this context federal health care policy has traditionally had two explicit goals: providing the poor with greater access to medical care of acceptable quality and reducing the cost to the poor of obtaining such care.

While these two objectives provide the framework within which policymaking takes place, the enormous growth of federal expenditures for health care in recent decades has brought to the fore a set of alternative and, to a great extent, competing priorities (Freeland and Schendler, 1983). Among these are pressures to reduce federal spending for, and regulation of, medical care, and to simultaneously increase the role of the states and the private sector in these areas (Feder, Holahan, Bovbjerg, and Hadley, 1982). Against this background we shall examine three major health programs relevant to the poor: Medicaid, Medicare, and Community Health Centers.

Medicaid

Medicaid is the most important government program focused on the poor's medical care. When enacted in 1965 as Title XIX of the Social Security Act, it received relatively little attention, primarily because the highly controversial Medicare program was established at the same time. Medicaid thus represents a prime example of the covert approach to poverty policymaking described by Heclo (1984).

Through a system of federal matching grants the Medicaid program enables individual states to provide a wide range of free (or nearly free) medical services to public assistance recipients (primarily AFDC and SSI) and certain other subgroups of the population whose low level of income falls within public assistance guidelines. States can also provide Medicaid to the medically needy if they wish. The medically needy have incomes that exceed the eligibility limits for public assistance, but that are not high enough to cover their medical expenses. At the end of 1984, thirty-one states had medically needy programs (Committee on Ways and Means, 1985a).

In Medicaid, payments are made by the states to vendors who provide services to program participants. Certain services must be provided in a state Medicaid program (e.g., inpatient and outpatient hospital care), while others can be included at the state's option (e.g., prescription drugs, inpatient psychiatric care).

In 1983, 40% of all poor households were covered by Medicaid, and 61% of all Medicaid households were poor (U.S. Bureau of the Census, 1985a). AFDC recipients represented 66% of the 21.4 million Medicaid recipients in that year. Only 26% of Medicaid expenditures were for these individuals, however, the majority of expenditures (72%) were for those who were disabled or elderly (Committee on Ways and Means, 1985a).

Medicare

The objective of Medicare is to cover the hospital, physician, and certain other medical expenses of the aged. As such, the program is not explicitly focused on the poor. For many individuals, however, Medicare serves as a protection against the poverty that could result from paying large medical bills. In addition, 17% of the 20.8 million Medicare households in 1983 were already below the poverty line (U.S. Bureau of the Census, 1985a). The eligible population for Medicare includes individuals sixty-five and older, certain disabled persons entitled to Social Security benefits, and most individuals with end-stage renal (kidney) disease.

There are two basic program components to Medicare. The Hospital Insurance program covers short-term hospitalization, skilled nursing care, home health care services, and hospice care. The Supplementary Medical Insurance program is oriented toward ambulatory care, and pays for 80% of the reasonable charges for physicians' services and a variety of other medical and health services. While individuals must pay a monthly premium to participate in this program, the overwhelming majority of the elderly and disabled who are enrolled in the Hospital Insurance program do so (Congressional Budget Office, 1982a).

In general, Medicare focuses on acute needs rather than the chronic, long-term medical needs of the elderly and disabled. Nursing home costs, for example, are for the most part not covered by Medicare. Moreover, deductibles and copayments are associated with many of the covered services in Medicare.

Consequently, while the financial burden that these services impose on individuals is significantly reduced by Medicare, it is by no means eliminated (Congressional Budget Office, 1983a).

Community Health Centers

Developed as part of the Economic Opportunity Act of 1964, Community Health Centers represent an ambitious attempt to restructure health care delivery to low-income areas. The wide-ranging goals of the centers include (Geiger, 1984):

• actually *providing* care to the poor, rather than just removing financial barriers to care;

• creating a new type of health care institution which serves a defined population and provides comprehensive curative and preventive services;

• shifting the service base from the hospital to the local community and the emphasis from tertiary to primary care;

• emphasizing multidisciplinary health care teams which include local paraprofessionals;

• broadening the scope of service to include health-related environmental and social issues;

• providing for local community participation in center decision-making; and

• using health services as a vehicle for wider social change.

Thus, at least in theory, Community Health Centers embody orientations of both service and social activism, with the latter focus being a direct reflection of the community action emphasis which characterized a major component of the War on Poverty. As one might expect, an activist, community participation orientation is much more pronounced in some centers than in others. The goal of comprehensive care is more routinely met, with the typical center offering medical and dental services, laboratory, X-ray, and pharmacy centers, as well as a variety of support services. There are over 800 centers nationwide, serving approximately 4.2 million individuals (Geiger, 1984).

Evaluation of Medical Care Programs

Virtually all analysts agree that Medicaid, Medicare, and Community Health Centers have had a dramatic impact on the ability of the poor, elderly, and minorities to obtain health care (e.g., Aday, Anderson, and Fleming, 1980; Altman, 1983; Blumenthal and Calkins, 1984; Brown, 1984; Davis and Schoen, 1978; Geiger, 1984; Starr, 1984). For example, between 1964 and 1983 the frequency of physician visits by the poor nearly doubled. Indeed, since 1978 the poor have actually paid more visits, on the average, to physicians than the nonpoor (Altman, 1983). Gains have also been recorded in the frequency with which the poor use hospital and dental services (Davis and Schoen, 1978). In short, the evidence is clear that the poor and other traditionally underserved groups receive much more medical care now than they did prior to the establishment of these programs.

The health of the poor also appears to have improved markedly in the past two decades, though the relevant data do not always permit firm conclusions concerning differences between income groups (Altman, 1983; Beeghley, 1983; Blumenthal and Calkins, 1984; Geiger, 1984; Starr, 1984). Nevertheless, there have been significant declines in infant mortality, maternal mortality, and death rates for young children, conditions that have traditionally been high among the poor. The gap between the poor and nonpoor in the incidence of chronic illnesses has also been narrowed (Davis and Schoen, 1978). Indeed, the age-adjusted death rates for *all* Americans have declined substantially in recent decades (Altman, 1983).

These health gains do appear to be at least partially attributable to the federal programs we have discussed. For one thing, the development and growth of these programs took place during the period in which major health improvements occurred. More conclusive evidence is available, however, from econometric studies (Hadley, 1982) and research on the health impacts of geographically targeted programs such as Community Health Centers (e.g., Geiger, 1984). These positive findings are not necessarily inconsistent with research suggesting that, beyond a certain level, medical care has a weak relationship to overall health (Benham and Benham, 1975; Davis, 1981).

Counting medical care benefits as income reduces the poverty rate significantly, but the amount of this reduction varies greatly with the specific procedures used to value benefits. This is because the average recipient value of medical care is less than 30% of its average market value. The more conservative measurement approaches yield reductions in poverty that are slightly less than the combined antipoverty impact of food and housing assistance (U.S. Bureau of the Census, 1985c).

While the successes of federal health programs have been notable, major problems remain in providing adequate health care to the poor. Most conspicuous, perhaps, is the fact that less than half (40%) of all households below the poverty line were covered by Medicaid in 1983 (U.S. Bureau of the Census, 1985a). While Medicare and private insurance programs provide assistance to some of the poor not covered by Medicaid, those not covered by any health insurance program constitute a significant, and growing, percentage of the poverty population (Starr, 1984).

The lack-of-coverage problem is a reflection of the fact that Medicaid eligibility has traditionally been very closely tied to eligibility for AFDC and SSI. While this connection has become less rigid in recent years, it is still the case that many of the poor cannot qualify for Medicaid because they do not qualify for either of the other two programs. This fact takes an added importance in view of the traditional reluctance of states to raise the income ceilings associated with AFDC eligibility, and the negative impact of recent program changes on the AFDC eligibility of the working poor. States have also been reluctant to liberalize the eligibility standards for the medically needy component of the Medicaid program (Davidson, 1979).

At a more fundamental level, the state-run nature of Medicaid generates a considerable amount of horizontal inequity with respect to both coverage and services. Some states cover a large percentage of their poor residents, while others provide assistance only to the most destitute. Likewise, some states provide nearly all of the optional services allowed under the

Medicaid program, while others provide relatively few. Thus, Medicaid has many of the same faults as AFDC, the program to which it is closely linked. As with AFDC, there are really fifty state Medicaid programs, not one national program, with some of these fifty being relatively generous and many others being quite restrictive.

Furthermore, over the years Medicaid has evolved to the point where it now primarily serves three distinct populations: poor families with children; the elderly (and other functionally impaired individuals); and the mentally retarded (and other developmentally disabled individuals). The first group, which was envisioned as the major target population by Medicaid's designers, tends to receive relatively inexpensive short-term and primary care services. The other two groups generally receive long-term, residential care which is quite expensive. This mixture of recipient groups and services within a single program has caused myriad problems with respect to financing, service provision, and administration, and has even resulted in a call for the establishment of separate programs for these populations (National Study Group, 1983).

For the AFDC and SSI populations, Medicaid is basically an extension of pre–1964 welfare-oriented medical care programs, and as such does not represent a major qualitative shift in the government's approach to addressing the poor's health needs (Brown, 1984; Goggin, 1984; Starr, 1984; Stevens and Stevens, 1974). The program that was the most significant departure from that approach, Community Health Centers, has not been funded at a level that permits the majority of the poor to benefit. This is especially regrettable, given that systematic evaluations of the performance of the centers have yielded positive results in terms of such dimensions as cost-effectiveness, access to care, and quality of both preventive and treatment-oriented care (Blumenthal and Calkins, 1984; Davis, 1977; Geiger, 1984; Reynolds, 1976). In this context it is interesting to consider Sardell's assertion that "it was precisely because the neighborhood health center model challenged the basic structure of the American health care system that it could only be considered as part of a separate agenda, one limited to the poor" (1980–81, p. 210).

It must also be acknowledged that the increased access to

care brought about by Medicaid has by no means eliminated the two-track system that has traditionally characterized health care in America. The poor are still more likely than the nonpoor to see general practitioners (rather than specialists) and to go to an outpatient clinic (rather than a doctor's office). The poor also travel further and wait longer for medical care than do the nonpoor (Altman, 1983; Brown, 1984; Davis, 1977). Moreover, when health status is controlled, it is found that the poor use health services much less frequently than the nonpoor (Starr, 1984).

One factor which certainly contributes to these differences is the reluctance of many physicians to accept Medicaid patients. A major reason for this reluctance is the relatively low reimbursement rates that many states apply to physicians' Medicaid services (Sloan, Mitchell, and Cromwell, 1978). This two-track problem is likely to be exacerbated by recent legislation which allows states to restrict Medicaid recipients' freedom of choice in selecting doctors and hospitals so that program costs can be better controlled.

Where the health of the poor is concerned, the impressive gains that have been recorded in recent years should not obscure the fact that significant gaps remain between the poor and nonpoor on virtually all of the indicators (e.g., infant and maternal mortality, chronic illness) that separated them prior to the enactment of the policies we have examined (Beeghley, 1983; Blumenthal and Calkins, 1984). While the persistence of these gaps undoubtedly has multiple causes, the fact that so many low-income households are not served by Medicaid or Community Health Centers undoubtedly represents an important factor. This lack of coverage affects specific components of the Medicaid program as well. The Early and Periodic Screening, Diagnosis and Treatment program, for example, has been riddled with problems. As a preventive program directed at poor children, its health promotion potential was great. Implementation of the program by the states has been very uneven, however. Only a minority of those eligible for the program have ever been screened, and follow-up services for those identified as having problems appear to have been sporadic (Cannon, 1981; Davis and Millman, 1983; Foltz, 1982).

None of the above problems, as serious as they may be, have

generated as much policymaking discussion as the rising cost of federal health programs, especially Medicaid and Medicare (Blendon and Moloney, 1983; *Proceedings*, 1984). Indeed, just as Social Security was the center of debate during the early 1980s, Medicaid and Medicare are likely to occupy that position in the future. Among the factors that have contributed to these rising costs in recent years, the most important appear to be the following (Altman, 1983; Bovbjerg and Holahan, 1982; Congressional Budget Office, 1983a; Davis and Schoen, 1978; Freeland and Schendler, 1983; Ginsburg and Moon, 1984; National Study Group, 1983):

1. Major increases in the fees charged for medical care. While virtually every sector of the health care industry is involved, the high cost of long-term residential care for Medicaid recipients has been particularly conspicuous.

2. Expansion of the number of services covered under the programs.

3. Major increases in the number of Medicare enrollees.

4. Increases in the average number of services used per participant, due in part to overall increases in the complexity and intensity of medical care.

Attempts to control costs in Medicaid and Medicare are constrained by their entitlement nature. Federal and state governments are required to pay for all covered services received by eligible persons who participate. Within this context three basic approaches to cutting costs are available. First, eligibility standards can be tightened to decrease the number of program participants. Second, cost-sharing can be increased. This strategy makes participants responsible for a greater share of the cost of their medical services or insurance premiums. This approach would reduce government expenditures for services rendered, as well as decrease the frequency with which participants use services. Finally, limits can be imposed on the amounts paid by the government to service providers on behalf of participants (see Russell, 1983.). This can be done by paying for fewer services and/or paying less for each service (Ginsburg and Moon, 1984).

Elements of all three approaches can be seen in recent actions taken by the federal and state governments (Bovbjerg and Holahan, 1982; Feder et al., 1982; Goggin, 1984; Meyer, 1984; Russell, 1983; Starr, 1984). Eligibility restriction measures have mainly focused on Medicaid, due primarily to the low degree of political power possessed by its recipient constituency. Increased cost-sharing and budget limitations have been directed at both programs. Perhaps the most significant change to date has occurred in Medicare, where a prospective payment system for hospital insurance has been legislated.

The overall impact of these changes on the poor's access to health care has yet to be determined in a systematic fashion. Nonetheless, it appears fairly certain that the uninsured percentage of the low-income population is growing. It is also likely that the financial burden on the poor for the care that is obtained has increased. Contributing to these developments is the recent combining of many categorical health programs into block grants which states have to implement with reduced federal funding (Feder et al., 1982; Meyer, 1984). Many of these programs focus on the low-income population.

At least in the short term, then, it is very unlikely that much additional progress will be made toward increasing the poor's access to high quality health care. It can be argued, of course, that this is a necessary consequence of the financial problems that currently plague the health care system. It is also a consequence, however, of the disparities in political power which characterize the various constituencies involved. In this context the structural differences between Medicare and Medicaid take on special importance. As a social insurance program for the elderly of all social classes, Medicare enjoys a broad base of political support. In both the short and long run, its recipients are likely to be compromised less in the name of budgetary constraints than are Medicaid recipients, who are aided within a public assistance framework encompassing certain subgroups of the lower class.

The fragmentation inherent in the latter approach is well-suited to modifying eligibility standards in response to financial pressures. Moreover, the close connection between Medicaid and AFDC weakens the ability of the former program to withstand such changes, given AFDC's unpopularity with the public. Thus, while it need not be inevitable that the poor disproportionately suffer during periods of health care retrenchment, the structural arrangements for this care make such an outcome highly predictable.

HOUSING

Since 1940 the quality and quantity of housing available to Americans has increased dramatically (Congressional Budget Office 1982b; *Report of the President's Commission on Housing*, 1982; Sternlieb and Hughes, 1983). For example, 45% of all housing units lacked complete plumbing facilities in 1940, while only 4% did in 1980. Similarly, the percentage of units judged as dilapidated or in need of repair declined from 18% to 7% during that period. And the percentage of overcrowded households (i.e., with more than one person per room) decreased from 20% in 1940 to 4% in 1980. In terms of quantity, the number of housing units in the United States doubled between 1950 and 1980. This tremendous growth reflects an expansion in both single-family homes and rental units.

While the poor have benefitted from these gains, they are still disproportionately represented among those living in inadequate housing (Congressional Budget Office, 1982b). Within the low-income population, it is also the case that the long-term poor are more likely to reside in inadequate housing than the short-term poor (Newman and Struyk, 1983). Finally, poor families have to devote a larger proportion of their budget to housing costs than the rest of the population (Dolbeare, 1983).

Overall, the improvements in housing quality that have occurred since World War II have been primarily due to (1) high rates of private residential construction, which has frequently entailed the replacement of inadequate housing, and (2) the upgrading of existing inadequate housing. In contrast, federally assisted housing construction for the poor has played a very minor role in raising housing quality for the population as a whole. This fact is stressed in analyses that support the "trickle-down" theory in accounting for the housing gains of the poor in recent decades (e.g., Sternlieb and Hughes, 1983).

In this explanation, the movement of the affluent into new and better housing results in existing, but still adequate, housing being made available to lower income groups.

While this process has undoubtedly been a major factor in the improvement in the poor's housing status, it is clear that federal housing programs have played a significant role as well. In 1983, for example, 23% of all poor renting households received housing assistance. These households accounted for slightly more than half (52%) of all households receiving means-tested housing benefits (U.S. Bureau of the Census, 1985a).

Against this background, it is important to recognize that improving the quality and affordability of housing for the poor are only two of the goals of federal housing policy. Other objectives include stimulating housing production and smoothing out cyclical swings in production; increasing homeownership, especially among the middle class; increasing housing opportunities for minorities and for those with special needs; promoting neighborhood preservation and revitalization; and stimulating employment (Congressional Budget Office, 1982b, 1983b). Indeed, as Aaron (1972, p. 53) has observed, "the murky provisions of the Internal Revenue Code contain the most important housing program currently administered by the federal government." Specifically these provisions subsidize virtually all American homeowners by significantly reducing their tax bills. The treasury revenues lost due to these mortgage interest reductions greatly exceed the cost of federal housing programs directed at the low-income population. As the income group least likely to own a home, the poor benefit relatively little from these deductions. It is thus clear that the poor do not represent the primary beneficiary of federal housing policy.

The federal government has been actively involved in housing since the 1930s. However, evolution of a low-income housing strategy did not take shape until 1949, when the Housing Act initiated a basic revision of the Public Housing program and the beginnings of the controversial Urban Renewal program. Since that time, housing policy has evolved rapidly with a variety of innovations and much controversy. For many years it was guided by the assumption that the problem of housing for low-income families was primarily one of inadequate supply rather than ineffective demand. Consequently, construction of housing for the poor was stressed. More recently, however, the emphasis has shifted to the demand side, with the goal of increasing the purchasing power of the poor. The assumption here is that an adequate supply of decent housing is available, if only the poor could afford it. This shift to a demand-side emphasis has only been a partial one, however, with the result being that the current array of housing programs encompasses both supply and demand approaches. It is likely, however, that the balance will increasingly tilt in the direction of demand-oriented approaches in the coming years (Schwartz, 1984; Weicher, 1984a), despite strong criticism from some quarters (e.g., Hartman, 1982; Nenno, 1984). As we examine both types of programs in the following sections, it will become clear that this shift in emphasis is a mixed blessing for the poor.

Supply-Oriented Programs

Public housing is the oldest federal housing program for the poor. Established by the Housing Act of 1937, it was one of many federal efforts designed to generate jobs and counter the effects of the Depression. Originally, public housing was rather loosely targeted toward low-income households, with the very poor not being explicitly focused upon. With the passage of the Housing Act of 1949, however, the latter group did become the primary recipient of housing assistance. Consequently, today's 1.3 million public housing households are much poorer, relative to the rest of the population, than were the tenants of the 1940s and 1950s.

Public housing is owned and operated by local public housing authorities, with tenants paying 30% of their monthly cash income toward rent. The program is a prime example of the growth and decline of government-sponsored housing construction over the years. Although public housing represented the only form of federal housing assistance for the low-income population from 1937 to 1961, it now accounts for only 35% of all assisted units. Very little new public housing has been built in recent years.

The stereotyped image of public housing projects portrays them as problem-ridden collections of unattractive, poorly maintained, box-like buildings or high-rises located in depressed neighborhoods and inhabited by multiproblem welfare families. It is ironic that public housing, which was originally proposed as a means of eliminating slums, is now frequently viewed as a major cause of them.

This stereotype would only appear to apply to a small minority of projects. For example, in 1979 the Department of Housing and Urban Development concluded that only 7% of public housing projects could be described as "troubled" (Jones, Kaminsky, and Roanhouse, 1979). These projects tended to be large, old, and in urban areas, with female-headed families being the primary tenants. It should be noted, however, that most projects with these characteristics were not troubled.

Both Community Development Block Grants (CDBGs) and Urban Development Action Grants, (UDAGs), to be discussed in Chapter 5, permit localities to use grant monies for the purpose of housing rehabilitation. Moreover, in the UDAG program community sponsorship of new construction is permitted as well. Since so many of these rehabilitated and newly constructed dwellings house the poor, the programs increase the supply of adequate housing for this group. Indeed, housing activities represent the largest single use of metropolitan CDBG funds. Housing activity plays a smaller role in the small-cities CDBG program and the UDAG programs. It is also the case that both CDBG and UDAG have provided more assistance to low- and moderate-income homeowners than to renters, especially in recent years (U.S. Department of Housing and Urban Development, 1985; U.S. General Accounting Office, 1983d).

A number of other federal programs provide assistance for the rehabilitation and construction of housing targeted to the low-income population. These include the Rental Rehabilitation Grants program, the Section 312 Rehabilitation Loan program, rural programs, and the Section 8 New Construction and Substantial Rehabilitation program. These programs, as well as CDBG and UDAG, emphasize the private sector as the source of housing for the poor.

Demand-Oriented Programs

The most important program in this category is the Section 8 Existing Housing and Moderate Rehabilitation program. As a demand-oriented program it depends on the ability of low-income households to secure adequate housing for themselves in the existing private market. A participating household receives a subsidy that pays the difference between 30% of its total monthly income and the rent charged for the unit in which it resides. Unlike public housing and other supply-oriented programs, the subsidy can accompany the household if it moves to a new residence.

In order for a residence to be eligible for this program, two conditions have to be met. First, it has to meet the official standards of housing adequacy established for the community, and second, its rent can not exceed the fair market amount set by HUD for that locality. The "moderate rehabilitation" portion of the program allows households to participate if they occupy residences that can be brought up to standard quality with limited repairs.

In 1983 Congress authorized a demonstration program in which certain households enrolled in the Section 8 program receive a voucher whose value equals the difference between 30% of its income and the fair market rent charged in the community. The household can use the voucher in renting any unit of adequate quality, regardless of its cost. If the rent for the chosen unit is less than the fair market value, the household gets to keep the cash difference. On the other hand, if the rent exceeds the fair market value, the household ends up paying more than 30% of its income for the dwelling.

The introduction of vouchers into the Section 8 program represents a significant change in housing assistance policy, and will be discussed in the next section.

Evaluation of Housing Programs

There is little doubt that federal housing policies have a significant impact on the poverty population. As we have noted, of all renting households in 1983 that were below the poverty level, 23% lived in public or subsidized housing (U.S. Bureau of the Census, 1985a). The recipient value of this assistance appears to be fairly high, ranging from 75% to 93% of its market value, depending on the program (Mayo, 1983).

While a precise estimate of housing assistance's antipoverty impact is not currently available, the relatively high market value of these benefits suggests that these programs reduce poverty among participants to a greater extent than Food Stamps eliminate poverty among Food Stamp households. Because there are far fewer housing-assistance households than Food Stamp households, however, housing's overall antipoverty impact is probably less.

Housing programs also enable participants to decrease the proportion of their income that they devote to housing. Thus, the financial burden of housing on the poor comes to more nearly resemble that encountered by other social classes in society. This is generally regarded as a desirable result, given the assumption that the poor should not have to pay a disproportionate amount to obtain one of life's necessities.

Housing assistance has other positive features. It is generally acknowledged, by both liberals and conservatives, that government intervention on behalf of the poor in the area of housing is appropriate and necessary due to the inability of the private market to ensure the availability of quality housing at an affordable price to all Americans. Consequently, housing programs have a broad, though perhaps shallow, base of political support. In this context the growing emphasis on demand-oriented programs in recent years is promising in at least two major respects when compared with conventional public housing. First, demand-oriented programs have been found to be much more economically efficient than supply-oriented ones (Cronin, 1983; Khadduri and Struyk, 1982; *Report of the President's Commission on Housing*, 1982). Thus, an expenditure of a given level of funds can assist significantly more individuals in the former strategy than the latter.

Second, while demand-oriented programs are unlikely to greatly increase economic and racial integration within communities, they are likely to forestall the trend toward increased *segregation* that supply-oriented approaches tend to encourage (Hamilton, 1983; Rossi, 1981). This is important, because where individuals live is a significant determinant of their life chances. The location of one's home influences access to such important services as education, recreation, police protection, and transportation.

It is clear, however, that U.S. housing policy is flawed and limited in a number of fundamental ways. Perhaps most glaring is the lack of horizontal equity. Unlike AFDC, SSI, Food Stamps, or Medicaid, housing assistance is not an entitlement program. Less than 30% of those who are eligible for rental housing assistance actually receive it (Committee on Ways and Means, 1985b). Even public housing projects, with their overall negative reputation, frequently have lengthy waiting lists. Housing assistance programs would have to be expanded many times over in order to serve all of those who need and want them. There is no indication that such an expansion is forthcoming (Schwartz, 1984).

Vertical equity is also violated by housing programs. The benefits received by program participants can frequently result in them enjoying a more favorable housing situation (in terms of quality and affordability) than those whose incomes place them just above the eligibility ceiling. This is especially likely when participants reside in newly constructed housing (U.S. General Accounting Office, 1980).

Even within the eligible population it has often been the case that benefits have not gone to the neediest individuals, in large part due to eligibility requirements which encompass those above the poverty line. In other cases, such as the CDBG program, flaws in the documentation system have made it unclear to what extent housing activities have actually benefitted low-income persons (U.S. General Accounting Office, 1982a). In response to these problems Congress has enacted changes in program requirements which have resulted in sharper, and more easily identifiable, targeting of benefits to the poor (Struyk, Tuccillo, and Zais, 1982; U.S. Department of Housing and Urban Development, 1985). Unfortunately, some of these changes will make housing projects more racially and economically segregated.

While the problems associated with supply-oriented programs have contributed to the current popularity of demand-oriented approaches, a close examination of the latter reveals that they are no panacea. Our understanding of the limitations inherent in the demand-oriented approach has increased dramatically in recent years due to the research done in conjunction with the Experimental Housing Assistance Plan conducted by the federal government (Bradbury and Downs, 1981; Friedman and Weinberg, 1983a; Struyk and Bendick, 1981). This experiment, which began in 1973 and lasted up to ten years in some sites, provided low-income households with cash payments that they could use to obtain adequate housing. In most cases the size of the payment was a fraction of the difference between the cost of adequate housing in the community and household's ability to pay for it. Overall, the experiment involved more than 25,000 households in twelve locations across the country.

The results of the experiment prompted many commentators, including the President's Commission on Housing (*Report*, 1982), to call for a national policy of housing assistance that stresses housing vouchers rather than construction. This sentiment is by no means unanimous, however, with critics pointing to a number of problems with vouchers as revealed by the experiences of both the experiment itself and the Section 8 (Existing Housing) program. These problems are summarized below:

- The distinctive nature of housing markets can make it very difficult for low-income tenants to translate a housing allowance or voucher into more adequate housing. Moderately priced housing of acceptable quality is currently in short supply, and the available evidence strongly suggests that such housing will become even more scarce in the years to come (Dolbeare, 1983; Hartman, 1982; Sternlieb and Hughes, 1983; U.S. General Accounting Office, 1979). The evidence also indicates that there is little reason to believe that the demand created by vouchers will substantially increase the production of such housing. This housing scarcity is exacerbated by the fact that the groups who encounter the greatest housing discrimination (e.g., minorities, welfare families) are disproportionately represented among the low-income population which is the primary target group for vouchers.

- The participation rate of eligibles in the housing experiment was much lower than had been anticipated (Carter, Coleman, and Wendt, 1983; Cronin, 1981; Kennedy and MacMillan, 1983; Straszheim, 1981). For example, in the open enrollment condition of the experiment, in which attempts were made to enroll as many eligibles as possible, only 42% of the eligible renters and 33% of the eligible homeowners participated. Families initially living in substandard housing were less likely to participate than those in standard units. Thus, those most in need of housing assistance (at least in terms of objective housing quality) were the least likely to obtain it from the program. This is likely to occur in any allowance program that makes participation contingent on meeting standards of housing quality. Those who have to change their living situation the most (in terms of either moving or upgrading their current residence) will be the least likely to do so.

• The allowances were mainly used by participants to reduce the proportion of their income that was spent on housing, rather than to substantially improve the quality of their housing. In terms of increased housing consumption, participating households generally did the minimum amount necessary to meet the requirements for receiving the allowance (Friedman and Weinberg, 1983b; Zais, 1981). For the most part, the housing allowances were used by recipients as a straightforward direct income transfer to purchase desired services other than housing. Thus, to a great extent the allowances represented a *housing* program only in the sense that they reduced the financial burden of housing for participants (Aaron, 1981).

To be sure, these experimental results might not be totally generalizable to an ongoing, permanent program. Nevertheless, they do suggest that a demand-oriented approach to housing assistance needs to be supplemented by supply-oriented strategies if significant numbers of the poor are to receive housing of improved quality. While a voucher program could be designed to make assistance contingent on meeting high, strictly enforced standards of housing quality, at this point there is little reason to believe that a significant percentage of the poor would participate in such a program. This limitation was recognized by the President's Commission on Housing (*Report*, 1982), which recommended that a national system of housing assistance payments be supplemented by new construction authorized under the Community Development Block Grant Program. With adequate funding, this dual approach could have a major impact on the housing problems that a significant percentage of the poor face. Recent federal initiatives in the area of housing have been very limited, however (Schwartz, 1984; Struyk, Mayer, and Tuccillo, 1983; Weicher, 1984a). The funding made available for new programs such as vouchers has not been large. Thus, predictions that the housing fortunes of the poor will actually decline in the coming years are not surprising (e.g., Sternlieb and Hughes, 1983).

SOCIAL SERVICES

The range of issues and problems addressed by the programs in this category is so broad that it is difficult to formulate a precise theoretical definition of "social services." Indeed, the services provided under the federal government's Social Services Block Grant can address any one of five general objectives (*Budget*, 1985, p. I-K 43):

1. Prevention, reduction, or elimination of dependency;

2. Prevention of neglect, abuse, or exploitation of children and adults;

3. Prevention or reduction of inappropriate institutional care;

4. Admission or referral to institutions when other forms of care are not appropriate;

5. Provision of services to individuals in institutions.

Among the services provided by all or most states are child day care, home-based services (e.g., homemaker services), protective services for children and adults, information and referral, adoption, counseling, family planning, child foster care, health services, and transportation (Committee on Ways and Means, 1985a).

For the most part the poor could not afford to purchase these services in the private marketplace. Consequently, in a fashion similar to housing, food, and medical care, social services enable the poor to obtain levels of services they would not otherwise be able to obtain. Moreover, it is assumed that many of these services address problems that have a causal relationship to poverty. For example, the negative economic effects of teenage childbearing have been clearly documented (e.g., Hofferth and Moore, 1979). Family planning services are designed to provide young people with the knowledge and motivation necessary to reduce the incidence of pregnancy. And for those who have already become teenage mothers, day care facilities and other services can enable them to obtain the education, training, and employment necessary to improve their economic well-being (e.g., Polit and Kahn, 1985).

While the delivery of social services in the United States has traditionally been the responsibility of state and local governments (and private organizations), since the early 1960s the federal role in financing these activities has grown substantially. In addition, Congressional legislation in the mid–1970s gave states much greater freedom in designing federally supported social service programs and deciding who would be eligible for them.

In this regard it is instructive to examine the effect that relaxed eligibility standards have had on both the composition of the client population and the nature of the social services rendered. Nonpoor families began to consume a much greater proportion of federally financed social services in the 1970s, while the proportion of recipients who were AFDC recipients dropped dramatically (Rein, 1982). In 1980, for example, only 27% of those receiving social services under Title XX Block Grant legislation were AFDC enrollees (Committee on Ways and Means, 1985a).

The influx of a nonwelfare clientele also helped to bring about changes in the services themselves. For one thing, the emphasis shifted from relatively intangible "soft" services such as social casework to more concrete programs such as day care or day treatment centers. In addition, the poverty-reduction function of social services began to receive less attention than the potential of these activities for enhancing human development and improving the quality of life. With such a shift in orientation it became possible for states to define as a social service virtually any activity they wished (Gilbert, 1983). Given these dynamics, it is not surprising that precise definitions of the social services are so difficult to develop.

While an emphasis on block grants and flexible eligibility

standards has continued in recent years, the willingness of the federal government to expand its financial support for social services has not (Gutowski and Koshel, 1982; Hasenfeld, 1985). Indeed, federal budget allocations for block-grant activities have actually been reduced in the past few years, forcing states to explicitly address the question of where social services reside on their list of budget priorities. It is likely that the quality of services will be negatively affected by diminished funding and increased state control, given the sizable influence that non-human-service constituencies wield at the state level (Gutowski and Koshel, 1982; Lynn, 1980; Magill, 1979).

The question of priorities could be dealt with in a more coherent fashion if systematic data were available on the anti-poverty impact of social services. There is no doubt that the poor's access to legal services, professional counseling, child day care, family planning services, and the like have been greatly increased by these programs. However, in contrast to the other in-kind programs we have discussed, there are no estimates available of what the poverty rate would be if social service benefits were counted as income. This is at least partially due to the great difficulty involved in calculating appropriate market and recipient values for many of these services, a problem that also affects the valuation of medical care, but to a lesser degree.

Because many social services do not provide benefits that are essential for day-to-day subsistence, the ratio of recipient value to market value for these programs is probably much lower than for food and housing assistance. As a result, it is debatable whether the poverty rate would be reduced very much even if the recipient value of social services were included in income calculations.

For many social services, however, the market or recipient value of the service is a much less important indicator of antipoverty effectiveness than is the program's contribution to economic self-sufficiency. Counseling, social casework, family planning, substance abuse prevention and remediation, as well as employment, education, and training are examples of such services. Unfortunately, when measured against the self-sufficiency criterion the overall performance of these programs has not been impressive (e.g., U.S. General Accounting Office, 1973). It does appear, however, that the services offered by federally funded family planning clinics reduce the number of unintended births to adolescents by a substantial percentage, perhaps as much as 20% or more per year (Forrest, Hermalin, and Henshaw, 1981). While there are no published estimates of how this reduction affects the poverty rate, the impact could not be trivial. From a cost/benefit perspective, Chamie and Henshaw (1981) estimate that for every dollar spent on family planning services for teenages, nearly three dollars is saved in the first year alone in welfare and medical costs.

At least one other social service program, legal services, appears to have had a significant impact on the poor's economic status. This is ironic, since legal services do not have the explicit dependency-reduction goal that many of the other social services do. Nevertheless, a number of law reform cases won by legal services attorneys during the late 1960s brought about major changes in welfare eligibility standards that benefitted the poor economically, though they did little to increase the poor's self-sufficiency (Champagne, 1984; Champagne and Nagel, 1983; Hollingsworth, 1977). Against this background it is noteworthy that the regulations governing legal services have been tightened over the years to make it more difficult to pursue such broad-scale changes (Levitan, 1985). Currently, the program is primarily funded by the Legal Services Corporation, a private nonprofit organization which the executive branch has repeatedly attempted to dismantle in recent years (Champagne, 1984).

CONCLUSION

The evidence we have reviewed indicates that most in-kind programs have a significant positive impact on the economic well-being of the poor. In this respect social services appear to be the weakest of the four major strategies, although its family planning and legal service components have been effective.

The relatively short chains of assumptions associated with most in-kind programs hold the key to their economic impact. With the exception of social services, program success does not depend on making major changes in the skills or motivation of participants. Rather, the direct provision of resources is emphasized. In this context there would appear to be two major assumptions that need to be satisfied. First, as we noted when discussing direct income programs, those eligible for assistance must actually participate in the programs to benefit from them. As effective as in-kind programs are, they would be even more effective if the Food Stamp participation rate increased and housing assistance was made available to all who met the income guidelines for such assistance.

The second assumption is that in-kind benefits have a high recipient value, i.e., recipients view them as being functionally equivalent (or nearly so) to cash income. This assumption is most valid in the case of Food Stamps, and also is clearly warranted where housing assistance is concerned. It is much less justified in the case of medical care and social services. The market value of medical benefits is sufficiently great, however, that the antipoverty impact of this program remains substantial even when its dollar value is heavily discounted.

To the extent that self-sufficiency is a more appropriate effectiveness measure for social services, the assumptions that must be met to ensure program success are more numerous and intimidating than the ones just discussed. Because most social services that are self-sufficiency oriented require participants to significantly change some combination of their attitudes, beliefs, and behavior, the level of participant motivation needed usually exceeds that of other in-kind programs. Second, not only must participants be motivated to change, they must also have the ability to change. Third, the change model or technology used by social service providers must be theoretically and pragmatically sound, in terms of both the change process itself and the relationship of this process to increased self-sufficiency. Fourth, participants must have both the motivation and ability to sustain change once it is accomplished. And fifth, the external environment must be at least minimally supportive of the attempt to both initiate and sustain the change.

Viewed in this context, it is not surprising that the overall record of social services at promoting self-sufficiency has not been particularly impressive. How, then, are we to explain the effectiveness of family planning services? There would appear to be two major reasons. Most important, the service technology involved, that of contraception, has been developed to the point where its proper application virtually guarantees a "successful" outcome. It just so happens that this outcome, the avoidance of pregnancy, is closely related to economic self-sufficiency. No other social services technology that is directed toward self-sufficiency can claim such a high degree of effectiveness. Second, unlike many other change-oriented interventions, the successful practice of contraception requires a relatively low level of skill.

When these two factors are viewed together, it becomes clear that the major obstacle facing family planning programs is motivating eligibles to take advantage of the service technology available. Once this participation is achieved, the probability of success is high. Unfortunately, motivation is just one of the many problematical assumptions faced by most programs aimed at self-sufficiency, whether they are based in a social service approach or some other. This is one of the major conclusions suggested by the performance of the programs we shall examine in the next chapter.

5

Employment, Education, and Economic Development

In this chapter we examine programs that attempt to raise the incomes of the poor by improving their position in the labor market. Since the labor market is the major vehicle through which most households directly or indirectly receive income, it represents a natural target for poverty policy. Even so, the only strategies in this category that can *guarantee* substantial income benefits to the poor are those which actually provide them with well-paying jobs. Those who view poverty in structural terms tend to focus on this fact when criticizing job training and educational programs, maintaining that they are of little economic use to the poor if the labor market fails to provide appropriate job opportunities. Although those sharing a more individualistic perspective acknowledge this problem to varying degrees, they are less likely than structuralists to regard direct job creation by the federal government (e.g., public service employment) as a meaningful solution to it. They tend to prefer more broad-gauged policies that increase aggregate demand for labor through stimulation of economic growth and development in the private sector.

We will consider three major strategies in this chapter: employment and training, education, and economic development. The first approach emphasizes the provision of jobs and/or job-

related training to the disadvantaged. Increasing the participation and performance of the poor in the educational system
is the goal of the second strategy. This increase is expected to
make the poor more competitive when they enter the job market. Finally, economic development involves increasing the
number of jobs available to the poor as a consequence of local,
regional, or national economic growth.

EMPLOYMENT AND TRAINING

In theory, the poor have been the prime targets of federally
sponsored employment and training programs since the War
on Poverty in the 1960s. There have been major changes over
the years, however, in the administrative and management
apparatus used to pursue employment and training goals for
the poor, changes that have reflected both pragmatic and ideological concerns. The programs that evolved during the War
on Poverty were designed and controlled by a host of federal
agencies exhibiting little coordination (Clague and Kramer,
1976). The result was a policy potpourri, characterized by frequent conflict, redundancy, inefficiency, and unresponsiveness
to local needs.

In an attempt to deal with some of these problems, Congress
passed the Comprehensive Employment and Training Act
(CETA) in 1973. The act shifted management responsibility
for most employment and training programs from the federal
level to the state and local levels, and allowed communities to
choose the mix of programs that best suited their needs. Both
of these changes were consistent with, and flowed from, the
Nixon administration's overall goal of lessening the federal
government's role in nondefense programs.

From 1973 until its expiration in 1982, CETA was amended
no less than eight times and received twenty-six separate ap-
propriations. The programmatic and financial instability of
CETA, as well as of previous employment and training programs (e.g., the Manpower Development and Training Act) can
be at least partly attributed to the multiple goals and objectives
these programs have traditionally had to serve. These include
(modified from Guttman, 1983):

• retraining the experienced labor force;

• relieving the adverse effects of automation;

• reducing poverty;

• creating jobs during recessionary periods;

• serving as a backup for direct income strategies;

• encouraging high school completion;

• reducing juvenile delinquency and related antisocial behavior;

• converting welfare recipients into wage earners;

• conserving natural resources.

The relative importance assigned to these goals by policymakers and the public can, of course, shift dramatically with changes in the national economy and political climate.

CETA was replaced by the Job Training Partnership Act (JTPA) in 1983. Because JTPA has a permanent authorization from Congress that provides for advance funding of programs, it may enjoy more stability than CETA. JTPA differs from CETA in several other major ways (Guttman, 1983):

1. The role of local businesses in designing and implementing programs at the community level is greatly enhanced. This represents an attempt to establish a more cooperative relationship between the federal and private sectors than existed under CETA. To the extent that such a relationship is achieved, the ability of programs to place trainees in unsubsidized employment is increased. As we shall see, however, there is justified concern over the *types* of trainees who are assisted when the business community plays a major policymaking role.

2. Public service employment (PSE) is not permitted under JTPA. At one time under CETA, these jobs accounted for 60% of all CETA expenditures. This change is consistent with the belief, held by many, that placement in unsubsidized employment should be the major goal of employment and training programs. Within this context PSE is frequently criticized as "makework," with the implication being that it neither serves a useful public function nor results in the development of marketable skills (e.g., Bovard, 1983a).

3. Responsibilities for employment and training efforts have been realigned at the federal, state, and local levels under JTPA.

The federal government is mainly responsible for developing performance standards for evaluating programs, and for ensuring that funds are appropriately spent. States have the task of coordinating, supervising, reviewing, and monitoring programs, and are responsible for assigning performance goals and sanctioning poor performance. Primary responsibility for designing and implementing programs rests with local governments and the business community.

4. Performance and outcome standards are used instead of process and operational standards when evaluating programs for the purpose of making refunding decisions. The former standards focus on such dimensions as earnings, employment, and welfare dependency. In other words, it is not enough to simply design programs whose structures conform to general federal guidelines; the programs must produce bottom-line results as well.

Comprehensive evaluations of the bottom-line effectiveness of JTPA programs are not yet available. Even so, there has accumulated over the years a considerable body of research focusing on the basic training approaches that comprise the bulk of JTPA activities. Consequently, a review of this literature should help us predict what the impacts of JTPA are likely to be (Bassi, 1983a). We shall also examine research on a wide variety of other employment-oriented programs.

In this context it should be noted that most evaluation studies focusing on employment and training strategies have not directly addressed the issue of antipoverty impact. The most frequently used dependent measures in these investigations—employment status, earnings, and welfare dependency—are not usually analyzed in a way that permits unambiguous conclusions concerning the poverty status of program participants. Finding a job, increasing one's earnings, or leaving welfare does not necessarily mean that one has crossed the poverty line, though it probably does mean that the *degree* of one's poverty has been lessened. This observation underscores the more general point that an employment and training program might be successful in achieving some goals (e.g., reducing unemployment) but not others (e.g., reducing the poverty rate).

In reviewing these programs it is important to recognize that they can improve the economic status of the poor in at least three ways (Congressional Budget Office, 1982c):

1. by directly increasing the number of well-paying jobs available to them;

2. by upgrading their job-related skills and motivation; and

3. by assisting them in the process of job-seeking so that they can be more effectively matched with existing job openings.

Ideally, these approaches would generate an overall reduction in the poverty rate, as the number of persons making nonpoverty wages increased in absolute terms. It is possible, however, for the second and third approaches to simply result in a redistribution of poverty rather than a reduction in it. This could occur if program participants ended up displacing previously nonpoor jobholders (Bassi and Ashenfelter, 1985; Gottschalk, 1983).

Training Programs

Three major types of training were provided under CETA: classroom, on-the-job, and work experience (Congressional Budget Office and National Commission for Employment Policy, 1982). Classroom training focuses on basic education and the development of specific occupational skills, such as those involved in clerical or crafts work. In on-the-job training, on the other hand, skill development takes place in actual job settings. The expectation is that the setting will continue to employ the individual after the training period ends.

On-the-job training under CETA emphasized operative and crafts training. Given the significant commitment that employers must make in on-the-job training, it is not surprising that it accounted for less CETA training than the other two approaches. When employers have jobs to fill, they prefer to hire individuals whom they perceive as bringing more resources to the job than the typical CETA participant (see also Bresnick, 1984, ch. 4).

The distinguishing characteristic of work experience is its emphasis on socialization. Temporary subsidized employment is used to instill positive work habits and job attitudes; developing specific skills is a secondary goal. A major assumption underlying this approach is that some of the poor face significant psychological and social barriers to achieving job stability, and that these obstacles must be addressed if skill training is to be successful.

With respect to impact, CETA training did have a significant, though modest, positive effect on the post-program earnings of adult participants (for reviews see Bassi, 1983a, 1983b, 1984b; Bassi and Ashenfelter, 1985; Borus, 1980; Burtless, 1984; Congressional Budget Office and National Commission for Employment Policy, 1982; Gottschalk, 1983; Taggart, 1981). This effect was primarily due to the impact of training on the number of hours individuals worked, rather than on the wage rates they received. Those who benefitted most from CETA training in economic terms were the ones with the least amount of previous employment experience, a group which was largely female. Individuals who were chronic low earners (i.e., with more extensive previous employment but at very low wage rates) gained very little from CETA training. These latter individuals were much more likely to be male than female. In general, the poorer that participants were prior to entering CETA, the more the program helped them economically.

Given the nature of CETA training, these results are not surprising. Most training was relatively short-term and prepared trainees for entry-level jobs. It is unlikely that substantial skill development can take place under these circumstances. A trainee's ability to secure low-wage employment is likely to be enhanced by such an approach, but better paying jobs requiring moderate skill will still be out of reach for the most part. These results suggest that CETA training was much more effective at transforming the nonworking poor into the *working poor* than it was at transforming them into the *working nonpoor*. Virtually all analysts agree that job training programs in the U.S. have not substantially reduced the poverty rate among the working age population (e.g., Burtless, 1984; Bassi and Ashenfelter, 1985; Committee on Ways and Means, 1985b). Consequently, as an antipoverty strategy CETA apparently left much to be desired.

Finally, it should be noted that disagreement exists concerning the relative effectiveness of various training strategies. Some researchers have reported either unsystematic or no significant differences among classroom, on-the-job, and work experience approaches with respect to increasing earnings, and point to the nonrandom assignment of participants to different approaches as a major stumbling block to drawing definitive conclusions (e.g., Borus, 1980; Congressional Budget Office and National Commission for Employment Policy, 1982; U.S. General Accounting Office, 1983a). Others have found on-the-job training to be more effective than classroom training, which is in turn judged to be more effective than work experience (e.g., Bassi, 1983a; Johnston, 1980; Perry, Anderson, Rowan, and Northrup, 1975; Taggart, 1981).

Where work experience is concerned, however, there is evidence from a non-CETA experimental program that this approach can be designed in a way that makes it effective for at least some subgroups of the poor (Hollister, Kemper, and Maynard, 1984). The National Supported Work Demonstration (NSWD), which ran from 1975 to 1979, provided up to twelve to eighteen months of work experience to individuals with histories of severe employment problems. The day-to-day operation of NSWD was distinguished by three characteristics. First, close supervision of participants was provided by individuals with knowledge and understanding of their work histories and personal backgrounds. Second, participants worked alongside peers in crews of ten or fewer. Third, job attendance and performance standards were increased over the course of a participant's involvement in the program, until a point was reached where the standards resembled those of regular jobs. Most of the work performed by NSWD participants was relatively unskilled and involved activities such as housing rehabilitation, day care, clerical work, and buildings and grounds maintenance.

The 10,000 NSWD participants represented four hard-to-employ groups: long-term AFDC mothers, ex–drug addicts, ex–criminal offenders, and school dropouts. The program had its greatest positive impact on AFDC recipients, significantly increasing their employment rate and earnings, and reducing their dependency on welfare. Ex-addicts experienced much smaller employment and earnings gains, but their criminal activity decreased markedly. The results for ex-offenders were inconclusive, while those for dropouts indicated that the program was not effective for this group.

It would appear, then, that supported work experience clearly represents a viable approach to assisting AFDC recipients, traditionally one of the most stigmatized groups of the poor. Indeed, Danziger and Jakubson (1982) estimate that implementation of a supported work program on a national scale could reduce the poverty rate of minority female-headed families on welfare by up to 60%. The expenditures for such a program, were they to be simply used for AFDC payments, would only reduce this group's poverty rate by 36%. In addition, the work effort generated by the supported work intervention would be much greater.

Public Service Employment

The strategy of direct job creation received very little attention during the decade of the War on Poverty (1960–1970). Since that time, however, there has been a dramatic increase, and subsequent decline, in the use of this approach by the federal government. More specifically, public service employment was extensively used to deal with the cyclical unemployment caused by the economic recessions of the 1970s. The first major initiative during that decade, and indeed the first since the Great Depression, was the two-year Public Employment Program (PEP) established by the Emergency Employment Act of 1971. At its peak (summer, 1972) PEP generated 185,000 temporary jobs for the unemployed (Levitan and Taggart, 1974).

By the time of CETA's passage in 1973 the economy had improved significantly. Consequently, CETA's initial PSE provisions focused on the structurally unemployed, i.e., those who have difficulty finding jobs because they lack skills and education. The most disadvantaged of this group are frequently referred to as the "hard-core unemployed." Shortly after CETA went into effect, the recession returned and Congress passed the Emergency Jobs and Unemployment Assistance Act of

1974. The act added a substantial PSE component to CETA that focused on cyclical unemployment. In 1976 the Emergency Jobs Program Extension Act continued this emphasis. By 1978 over 750,000 persons were enrolled in CETA's structural and countercyclical PSE jobs, and PSE accounted for 60% of all CETA expenditures. Indeed, at that time nearly 5% of all state and local government employees were CETA workers (Mirengoff, Rindler, Greenspan, and Harris, 1982; Nathan, Cook, and Rawlins, 1981).

The conspicuous expansion of PSE under CETA was accompanied by a predictable increase in criticism of the program. Four aspects of the program were regarded as particularly problematical (Mirengoff et al., 1982):

1. "Creaming": The provision of PSE to the most qualified eligibles rather than to the most needy ones.

2. Inadequate training: PSE jobs frequently did not enhance the individual's ability to secure unsubsidized employment.

3. Substitution: The use of PSE funds to subsidize jobs that would have been supported in any event by local resources. In these cases PSE did not result in a net increase in the number of jobs available.

4. High wage rates: The attractive wages provided by some PSE jobs reduced the motivation of participants to look for non-CETA employment.

Concern over these and other features of CETA led to major revisions of the program in 1978. Eligibility standards were tightened, greater percentages of PSE funding were designated for training purposes, and PSE wages were reduced, among other changes. These modifications reduced the number of PSE enrollees to 328,000 by the end of the 1980 fiscal year. PSE under CETA was terminated at the end of the 1981 fiscal year. In 1983, however, Congress responded to the persistently high unemployment rate by passing job creation legislation in the form of the Emergency Jobs Appropriation Act. The act was directed at cyclical unemployment, and established jobs that provided assistance to state and local governments in repairing public roads, parks, and buildings.

PSE does have a positive impact on the post-program earnings of participants, though it does not appear to equal the modest impact achieved by on-the-job training (Bassi, 1983a; Johnston, 1980). Indeed, Bassi's research suggests that PSE is less cost-effective than either on-the-job or classroom training, but more cost-effective than work experience for adults. Neither PSE nor work experience generates economic benefits to participants that equal the cost to taxpayers of funding the programs.

As is the case with training strategies, the participants who benefit most from PSE are those with the lowest levels of earnings and employment prior to their program involvement. This finding suggests that the structurally unemployed are more likely to benefit from PSE than the cyclically unemployed. It also appears that PSE programs focused on the structurally unemployed generate smaller substitution effects than those directed at the cyclically unemployed (Bassi and Ashenfelter, 1985). Structurally oriented programs, however, tend to be much less popular with local governments (Nathan et al., 1981).

Employment Subsidies

Federally sponsored job creation in the private sector can be viewed as an alternative or supplement to job creation in the public sector (i.e., PSE). While this approach has received increasing attention from policymakers and researchers in recent years, its potential as an antipoverty strategy is far from being realized.

In private sector job creation the basic objective is to increase the demand for labor by subsidizing the employer's wage costs. Tax credit programs have served as the major vehicle through which this subsidization has taken place. In 1971 the WIN Tax Credit permitted private employers to claim a tax credit on the wages paid to AFDC applicants or recipients who were certified as employable by the Work Incentive Program. In 1975 the definition of eligibility was expanded to include any AFDC recipients who had been receiving assistance for at least ninety days prior to being hired.

While the WIN Tax Credit focused on the structural unemployment of a specific low-income group, the 1977 New Jobs Tax Credit (NJTC) represented a countercyclical strategy which did not restrict employers to hiring only certain categories of workers. Instead, this two-year program provided employers with a tax credit on the wages paid to the first fifty workers the employer hired above 102% of its previous year's employment level. Because the credit only applied to the first $6,000 of an employee's wages, however, it subsidized low-wage jobs to a greater extent than high-wage ones.

In 1979 the Targeted Jobs Tax Credit (TJTC) replaced the NJTC. As its name implies, this is a structural policy providing tax credits to employers who hire individuals from certain disadvantaged groups, most of which are characterized by low income. In 1981 involuntarily terminated CETA public service employees became eligible for the credit, and the program also became the vehicle for stimulating the employment of WIN/AFDC participants. The executive branch has recently proposed that TJTC be allowed to expire.

The WIN Tax Credit and TJTC have not been widely used by employers. Firms do not apply for these credits for the great majority of eligible individuals whom they hire (Congressional Budget Office, 1984b; Johnston, 1980; Ripley and Franklin, 1983). The NJTC, on the other hand, generated a much more positive response from the private sector, with a substantial amount of job creation resulting (Haveman and Palmer, 1982). How much of this job creation actually benefitted the poor is uncertain, given that NJTC represented a nontargeted program.

There appear to be several reasons for the low utilization of targeted programs by employers (Burtless, 1985; Congressional Budget Office, 1984b; Corbett, Masters and Moran, 1981; Ripley, 1981; Ripley and Franklin, 1983). One is that employers desire maximal freedom when making hiring decisions, and targeted programs restrict this freedom more than nontargeted programs. Moreover, targeted group members are generally viewed as having few characteristics that would make them attractive job candidates, further reducing employers' motivation to hire them. There is even evidence suggesting that TJTC vouchers actually stigmatize job applicants in the eyes of some employers, thereby reducing applicants' chances of finding work (Burtless, 1985). Given these dynamics, many target group members are understandably reluctant to advertise their credit eligibility when job hunting. Against this background it is not surprising that O'Neill (1982) argues that targeted subsidies actually end up generating fewer jobs for target group members than nontargeted subsidies do.

Inadequate knowledge of the program among employers, state government employment counselors, and potential participants is another major cause of low utilization. Additional factors that have limited use of the program include complex and confusing implementation procedures associated with underfunded administrative services, and the belief on the part of some employers that the relatively small tax savings they receive from participating in the program do not justify the effort involved. Indeed, many employers are reluctant to participate in any programs that involve government intervention.

While the importance of these obstacles to utilization should not be minimized, some commentators are optimistic that participation in targeted employment subsidy programs can be significantly increased (Bishop and Haveman, 1978; Congressional Budget Office, 1984b; Corbett et al., 1981; Haveman and Palmer, 1982). Increasing the use of employment subsidies, however, is not necessarily synonymous with substantially increasing their antipoverty effectiveness. In order to achieve the latter objective, the subsidized jobs must provide individuals with an opportunity, either in the long or short run, to work themselves out of poverty. The current structure of TJTC does not require employers to provide program participants with training to upgrade their job skills. Providing dead-end employment to participants is likely to do little more than replace one source of inadequate income (welfare) with another (low-wage jobs). While this shift may accomplish a number of worthwhile social goals, the elimination of poverty among TJTC participants is not one of them.

Youth Programs

Concern over the labor market difficulties faced by youth has increased markedly in recent years, with the high rate of youth unemployment receiving the greatest attention (e.g., American Assembly, 1980; Borus, 1984; Bresnick, 1984; Congressional Budget Office, 1982c; Freeman and Wise, 1982; Hahn and Lerman, 1985; Lefkowitz, 1982). Indeed, 40% of JTPA's local training funds have been targeted for disadvantaged youth. It should be noted, however, that the overwhelming majority of young people who look for jobs find them. Only a small percentage, perhaps less than 10%, experience persistent unemployment. Membership in this latter group is associated with being black, a high school dropout, and a resident of a poverty area (Freeman and Wise, 1982).

It should also be pointed out that youth unemployment and adult unemployment are virtually unrelated. That is, being unemployed when one is young does not significantly increase the likelihood of being unemployed when one reaches adulthood. What it does increase is the likelihood of being employed in a low-wage, dead-end job as an adult (Freeman and Wise, 1982). Since these jobs are a significant source of poverty, employment and training interventions focused on high-risk youth have the potential to significantly reduce the poverty rate.

Responding to the above issues, Congress in 1977 established four employment and training programs for youth under the Youth Employment and Demonstration Projects Act (YEDPA). In addition, the two major youth programs already in existence at that time (the Job Corps and summer employment) were expanded. Neither YEDPA nor the four programs it authorized are currently in existence. Nevertheless, evaluations of these efforts and selected demonstration projects have greatly increased our understanding of the effectiveness of employment and training interventions for youth. This knowledge can be of great value in designing JTPA youth programs.

The Job Corps has survived, although the executive branch has proposed that it be terminated. This program, established in 1964 under the Economic Opportunity Act, focuses on youth whose employment prospects are especially bleak, even when compared with those of other persistently unemployed youth. The program provides basic education, vocational skill training, work experience, counseling, and health services. Unlike other youth programs, the Job Corps is largely administered in a full-time residential setting, with Corps members usually leaving their home communities to participate in the program.

Summer jobs for low-income youth also continue to receive federal funding. Federal initiatives in this area began with the summer component of the Neighborhood Youth Corps (NYC), a program established by the 1964 Economic Opportunity Act. The main purposes of NYC were to help poor youth at the secondary school level continue their education and/or obtain work training, either of which could be expected to enhance their future employability. It soon became clear that the summer NYC was achieving neither its educational nor its skill-training objectives, with the majority of summer jobs being low-level in nature (maintenance, clerical, etc.). Over time the program came to be primarily seen as a means of transferring income to needy youth and keeping neighborhoods peaceful during the summer.

When CETA was established in 1973, the Summer Program for Disadvantaged Youth was enacted, a program whose major components were very similar to those of the summer NYC. Since 1977, this program has been known as the Summer Youth Employment Program, with the provision of part-time employment to low income youth remaining the basic objective. In addition, a variety of demonstration projects have been conducted to enrich participants' experiences in the program. In essence, these projects represent a return to the educational and training goals that originally characterized the summer NYC. The Summer Training and Education Program (STEP), for example, includes basic skills instruction, a life-planning curriculum, and social support services in addition to the fundamental work experience provided to all summer program participants (Branch, 1985).

The overall design of employment and training strategies for youth parallels in many ways the design of comparable programs for adults (see Hahn and Lerman, 1985). Thus, we should not be surprised to find parallels in the performance of the programs as well (for reviews of this research see Anderson, 1980; Butler and Mangum, 1983; Congressional Budget Office, 1982c; Hahn and Lerman, 1985; Stromsdorfer, 1980; and Taggart, 1981). Strategies that focus on intensive skill training appear to be the most effective at increasing the employment levels of low-income youth, although in some cases the positive effects diminish rather rapidly over time (Hahn and Lerman, 1985; Public/Private Ventures, 1982; Stromsdorfer, 1980). It also appears that in many cases substantial remedial work in basic academic skills is necessary for program success.

The most extensively studied youth training program has been the Job Corps (e.g., Levitan and Johnston, 1975; Long, Mallar, and Thornton, 1981; Taggart, 1981). These evaluations have consistently shown that Job Corps graduates experience significant earnings gains as a result of their participation in the program. More comprehensive cost-benefit analyses suggest that the overall benefits society derives from the Job Corps substantially exceed the program's admittedly high cost. A major reason for this is the significant reduction in criminal activity associated with Job Corps participation. The executive branch has nevertheless proposed that the program be cut back, citing the fact that a majority of Job Corps entrants drop out before finishing their training.

Evaluations of one of the YEDPA programs, the Youth Incentive Entitlement Pilot Project (YIEPP), also also instructive (Farkas et al., 1984). YIEPP was a two-year experimental program that guaranteed participants a full year's employment (part-time during the school year) at the minimum wage in exchange for a commitment to return to, or stay in, high school. The program was effective at raising the post-program earnings of participants relative to nonparticipants, with the short term effects having been estimated at over $700 per year. This difference was mainly caused by participants having a higher rate of post-program employment than nonparticipants.

YIEPP does not appear to have had a positive impact on the rates of high school enrollment, high school graduation, or college enrollment of participants. This is unfortunate, since high school graduates benefitted more from YIEPP (in terms of earnings) than nongraduates. This latter outcome is not surprising, given the greater mastery of basic educational skills that graduates probably possess. Indeed, the importance attributed to these skills was a major reason for the inclusion of YIEPP's school-enrollment requirement. Without this feature YIEPP would have closely resembled other work experience programs for youth, programs whose performance has not been impressive (Bassi, 1983a; Hahn and Lerman, 1985; Johnston, 1981; Stromsdorfer, 1980; Taggart, 1981). Most of the key provisions of YIEPP have been retained in the Exemplary Youth Programs component of JTPA, and a wide range of supportive services have been added.

Another type of program attempts to link youth with employers. These pre-employment assistance efforts usually include some subset of the following: career and personal counseling; labor market information and job-seeking skills; classroom vocational exploration or worksite visits; world-of-work orientation; and direct supervision in job seeking. Programs for out-of-school youth tend to be more intensive, short-term, and directed toward specific job finding than those aimed at students.

Pre-employment interventions can be effective at increasing youth employment rates in the short run, although the quality of jobs obtained does not seem to be greatly affected (*Employment and Training Report*, 1983; Hahn and Lerman, 1985; Lefkowitz, 1982; Newitt et al., 1984). Moreover, in the long run it does not appear that these services have a significant employment or earnings impact on participants (Hahn and Lerman, 1985). For example, a carefully designed evaluation of one nationally known program found that the levels of employment, occupational status, and earnings achieved by participants two to three years after enrollment did not significantly differ from those of nonparticipants (Public/Private Ventures, 1983). Overall, it is hard to escape the conclusion that these services do little more than shorten the job search period for teenagers.

Finally, recent studies of the regular and enriched summer work programs suggest that they are doing a somewhat better job of achieving educational and employment goals than their predecessors. The basic academic skills, school enrollment, and part-time employment of participants generally exceed those of nonparticipants, though differences on the second and third dimensions are usually small (Branch, 1985; Hahn and Lerman, 1985).

Minimum Wage Legislation

Created by the Fair Labor Standards Act of 1935, the minimum wage was designed to improve the health, efficiency, and general well-being of workers through the elimination of substandard wages. Over the years amendments to the act have raised the level of the minimum wage and extended coverage of the act to new groups of workers. Originally set at 25¢ per hour, the federal minimum wage was $3.35 in 1985. Over 90% of all nonsupervisory wage earners are covered by minimum wage legislation, with most noncovered workers being in the nonagricultural service and retail areas (*Report of the Minimum Wage Study Commission*, 1981).

Whether the benefits of the minimum wage justify its costs has been the subject of considerable debate among economists and others (see U.S. General Accounting Office, 1983b). Employees who would have been paid less than the minimum wage in the absence of the legislation clearly benefit economically. On the other hand, in some cases an employer would rather offer no job at all, than offer one that pays as much as the minimum wage. Thus, unemployed persons who would have been hired for these jobs are worse off financially, at least in the short run, than they would have been without minimum wage legislation. This process results in the national employment rate being lower than it otherwise would be.

Overall, teenagers appear to be the group most negatively affected by the minimum wage. Brown, Gilroy, and Kohen (1982, 1983) estimate that a 10% increase in the federal minimum wage would reduce employment of sixteen to nineteen year olds by approximately 1% (see also Solon, 1985). Greater impacts have been estimated for out-of-school youth (Meyer and Wise, 1981). Whether these figures are viewed as unacceptably high or not is basically a question of social and political values. In absolute terms, however, it appears that the minimum wage plays a relatively small role in accounting for the labor market difficulties experienced by teenagers and other low-wage workers (Chaikin and Comstock, 1983; Hahn and Lerman, 1985; Mills and Frobes, 1981).

As an antipoverty policy the minimum wage also appears to

have a quite limited impact. In 1984, a family of four with one full-time minimum wage earner would have had an income which was 66% of the official poverty line. Kohen and Gilroy (1981) conclude, on the basis of their review of the relevant literature, that the minimum wage has had a small but significant positive economic impact on those at the bottom of the income distribution. Increases in the coverage or level of the minimum wage would benefit a significant segment of the working poor, though some of these benefits would be offset by a small reduction in the number of jobs available to this group.

In recent years the executive branch has repeatedly proposed that the minimum wage for teenagers be reduced during the summer in order to increase the employment level of this group. The fact that Congress has not enacted such legislation seems well advised. It is not at all clear that the positive impact of this measure on teenagers would outweigh its negative side effects (Chaikin and Comstock, 1983).

U.S. Employment Service

The Employment Service, known as the Job Service in most states, was created by the 1933 Wagner-Peyser Act. Its major purpose is to serve as a labor exchange in which the skills and interests of job applicants are matched with the job openings listed by employers using the service (U.S. General Accounting Office, 1982b). The Job Service is available free of charge to any individual eligible to work in the United States, and in 1982 its local offices placed approximately three million individuals in jobs (Levitan, 1985). The services provided to applicants include counseling; proficiency, aptitude, and interest testing; access to a variety of job listings within and outside of the United States; and job development contacts and referrals to potential employers. Additional services are provided to those entering the job market for the first time, those reentering after a period of absence, and those with limited job experience and skills.

In addition to serving as a labor exchange, the Job Service is involved in administering a variety of laws, executive orders, and agreements with other federal agencies pertaining to employment. For example, certain participants in the Unemployment Insurance, AFDC, and Food Stamp programs are required to register for job placement with the Job Service. State and local Job Service officials, as well as many employers, view these non-labor-exchange functions negatively, claiming that they conflict with the Job Service's labor exchange activities (U.S. General Accounting Office, 1982b).

The 1982 Job Training and Partnership Act revised the Wagner-Peyser Act with the intention of giving states greater flexibility in the planning and administration of the Job Service. The changes were also designed to foster greater coordination of Job Service efforts with federal training activities in employment. Overall, however, funding for the Job Service has been significantly reduced in recent years.

Since the era of the War on Poverty, policy guidelines have required that the Job Service focus much of its effort on the poor and disadvantaged. Because many employers are reluctant to hire these individuals, the Job Service receives fewer job listings than it would in the absence of such policies. Listings are usually for nonprofessional, low-skill, short-duration jobs. Not surprisingly, the Job Service is more successful in filling these openings than those which require higher skills and provide longer term employment (U.S. General Accounting Office, 1982b). Consistent with this pattern, the age and educational level of applicants are negatively associated with the chances of their finding employment through the Job Service (Director, Englander, and Moeller, 1984; U.S. General Accounting Office, 1982b). Overall, the Job Service's annual placement rate has ranged from 22% to 25% in recent years.

The Job Service appears to have a significant economic impact on females but not males. Johnson, Dickinson, and West (1985) found that females who received a job referral from the program achieved greater earnings than did female clients who did not receive a referral. This was primarily due to the fact that referred females were more likely to find employment, and to find it sooner, than non-referred females. There was no significant difference in the average wages earned by those who found jobs in the two groups.

These results resemble those for the training programs we

reviewed earlier, which showed that female participants derived greater economic benefits than males. The extent to which poor females are actually raised above the poverty line by these interventions remains unclear, however. Certainly the earnings achieved by most female job service participants are not sufficient, in and of themselves, to achieve such a goal. Neither the hours worked nor the wage rates received are substantial enough (Johnson, Dickinson, and West, 1985).

Work Incentive Program and Related Efforts

The Work Incentive Program (WIN) provides employment, training, job-search assistance, and employment-related social services to certain categories of AFDC recipients who are legally required to register with the program. The fundamental goal of WIN is to minimize the use of AFDC by individuals who could be economically self-supporting.

All AFDC recipients sixteen years of age or older are required to register with WIN unless they fall into an exempt category (e.g., mothers caring for children under six years old). At the end of 1984 there were 1.5 million WIN registrants (Committee on Ways and Means, 1985a). The majority of registrants in the regular WIN program were female (71%), between the ages of twenty-two and forty-four (76%), and lacking a high school diploma (51%).

The WIN program has been revised several times since it was enacted in 1967 as an amendment to the Social Security Act. These revisions have shifted the focus of the program from education and classroom training to on-the-job training and direct job placement. Consistent with this trend, there has been increased emphasis in recent years on intensive individual and group job-search activities. Moreover, in 1985 there were WIN demonstration projects operating in twenty-two states in place of the regular WIN program. Authorized by the 1981 Omnibus Budget Reconciliation Act, these projects are solely administered by state welfare departments and represent an attempt to develop innovative programming for the employable AFDC population (Committee on Ways and Means, 1985a).

WIN has been the subject of continuing criticism and controversy since its inception. Indeed, in recent years the executive branch has proposed that the program be eliminated because of its poor cost-effectiveness, and replaced with Community Work Experience Programs that would be mandatory in all states. Evaluations of WIN indicate that it has not been very effective as a work requirement, as a means of significantly reducing the AFDC rolls, or as an avenue for upward economic mobility for the majority of employable AFDC recipients (AuClaire, 1979; Ehrenberg and Hewlett, 1976; Goodwin, 1983; Levy, 1979; Lurie, 1978; Ozawa, 1982; Rein, 1982; Rodgers, 1981; Schiller, 1978; Smith, Fortune, and Reid, 1975; U.S. General Accounting Office, 1982d).

With respect to the first objective it is important to recognize that participation in WIN need not, and usually does not, entail enrollment in work or training activities. Participation in the program simply means that one has been evaluated by a WIN staffer and is following whatever course of action the staffer prescribes. In many cases this may mean no action at all, since a recipient may be declared unemployable or put in a holding category in which there is minimal involvement with WIN activities. Thus, a major reason WIN does not function as a stringent work test for AFDC recipients is that its structure does not require it to do so. Against this background it is noteworthy that local WIN offices that take an aggressive stance in declaring registrants suitable for work or training apparently perform better than those which do not (Mead, 1983).

Other reasons for WIN's poor performance include difficulties in monitoring the extent to which participants comply with WIN regulations, lack of adequate employment and training resources, funding limitations, poorly coordinated control of the program by different organizational units, and the failure to provide incentives to staff to enforce existing work requirements (Rodgers, 1981).

Given the relatively small proportion of AFDC recipients who receive training and job-related services from WIN, it is not surprising that the program's impact on the welfare rolls has been minimal. Moreover, those WIN participants who do obtain full-time unsubsidized jobs frequently do not make enough to support their families without continued AFDC assistance. In relative terms, they do gain some measure of economic independence (Goodwin, 1983). Nevertheless, it is probable that many of these individuals would have found jobs even in the absence of WIN (U.S. General Accounting Office, 1982d).

Finally, significant upward mobility for participants cannot be expected from a program that emphasizes immediate job search and placement as much as WIN does. Nor does the basic education and classroom training that characterized the earlier WIN program appear to be sufficient for this purpose. More intensive skill training directed at well-paying job markets would seem to be required.

In recent years the executive branch has repeatedly proposed that WIN be terminated, citing its ineffectiveness at substantially reducing welfare dependency. Although WIN has survived, the 1981 Omnibus Budget Reconciliation Act (OBRA) permits states to modify the program through the use of demonstration projects. The act also established a number of other work-oriented programs directed at AFDC recipients which states can adopt. In the Community Work Experience Program (CWEP), certain recipients can be required to work in public service jobs for the number of hours equal to their AFDC benefits divided by the minimum wage. States can also require AFDC applicants and recipients to engage in a job search program. Finally, AFDC benefits may be used to subsidize wages and jobs for recipients through work supplementation and grant diversion projects. Participation in these projects varies widely. The most popular option is CWEP, with nearly half of the states participating. In contrast, only one state has implemented a work supplementation program (Committee on Ways and Means, 1985a).

Whether any or all of these optional projects can improve upon WIN's performance has yet to be determined. Given their overall design, however, there is reason to be skeptical. CWEP, for example, has thus far not even performed well as a basic work requirement (U.S. General Accounting Office, 1984a). Most employable adult AFDC recipients in participating states are not in CWEP because (1) most CWEP programs are not statewide; (2) many recipients are exempt from participation in the first place; and (3) states tend not to require participation on the part of those who would be costly to place. Of those who do participate in the program, most do not have to work off the full cost of their AFDC checks, and most states do not expect participants to work in CWEP for as long as they are on AFDC. Indeed, in an attempt to increase the employability of CWEP participants, many states allow them to substitute job training or search activities for time at the work site. To the extent that these activities can truly upgrade the skills of participants, they may have a significant antipoverty effect. At this point, however, it is not clear that these approaches differ from the more traditional WIN activities they are supposed to replace.

Vocational Education

Though most vocational education programs are based in schools of one sort or another (especially high schools and technical schools), this is basically an employment and training intervention rather than an educational one. Indeed, in historical terms vocational education can be regarded as the nation's first federal employment and training effort, having been initially funded in 1917. Its major purpose is to prepare non–college bound youth and adults for work by providing education and skill development directly related to occupational requirements. Vocational education programs encompass training in a wide variety of occupations, with the student's exposure ranging from a single course in a specific field to a well-integrated program leading to a licensed occupation (National Commission for Employment Policy, 1981).

In most studies of vocational education programs serving high school students, male participants do not appear to derive any net economic benefits from vocational education when their earnings are compared with those of nonparticipants (Desy, Mertens, and Gardner, 1984; National Commission for Employment Policy, 1981; National Institute of Education, 1981; Rumberger and Daymont, 1984). In contrast, the earnings of females in the business and office training curricula of vocational education are positively affected, but only in the short run. Several years after high school graduation the differences in earnings between female participants and nonparticipants virtually disappear. A major reason for these diminishing benefits is that the commercial training provided to females in vocational education usually leads to jobs with relatively little opportunity for upward mobility.

It is important to recognize that the comparison groups in these evaluations are students enrolled in other high school curricula. Thus, the finding of no economic impact does not mean that vocational education is worthless to participants. Rather, it is just that its economic value is no greater than that of other courses of study (Rumberger and Daymont, 1984). It is the *amount* of schooling one obtains at the high school level that is important economically, not the *type* of schooling.

Few evaluations of postsecondary vocational education programs have been conducted. The results of these studies suggest that postsecondary programs, especially those providing on-the-job training, may be more economically beneficial to participants than secondary ones (Desy et al., 1984; National Commission for Employment Policy, 1981; National Institute of Education, 1981; Tannen, 1983). More outcome data are needed, however, before definitive conclusions can be drawn concerning the effectiveness of these programs.

Continuing Issues in Employment and Training Policy

On the basis of the preceding review it would appear that the overall antipoverty impact of employment and training programs is, at best, quite modest. Certainly their demonstrated effectiveness is much less than that of the more successful direct income strategies. The employment and training approach is nonetheless very popular with policymakers and the public (e.g., Lewis and Schneider, 1985) since it emphasizes the goal of economic self-sufficiency. This popularity makes it all the more important that the factors which limit the effectiveness of these programs be fully understood.

First of all, it must be noted that only potentially employable persons and their dependents can benefit from such a strategy. Those who are too old, too ill, too demoralized, or too burdened with the care of young children to be labor force participants will not be helped by this approach, and a significant percentage of the poor fall into these categories. Indeed, Grinker (1984, p. 5) estimates that approximately 40% of the structurally unemployed are probably "no longer employable at a reasonable cost level."

Being potentially employable, however, is no guarantee that one will be helped by employment and training policy. For one thing, limited resources prevent many of these programs from serving all those who are eligible for them. Of far greater importance, however, is the fact that employment and training strategies can only eliminate poverty to the extent that they directly or indirectly enable participants to obtain jobs at non-poverty wages. Overall, they have not been notably successful at achieving this goal. A major reason is that the skill development that takes place in these programs is frequently minimal. Consequently, the jobs that participants can command upon "graduation" are necessarily entry-level positions near the bottom of the wage scale. As long as the wages associated with these jobs are as low as they are, employment and training programs that provide short-term, low-level skill training are likely to be relatively ineffective at reducing poverty.

It must be kept in mind, however, that the more ambitious a skill training program is, the more expensive it tends to be (Taggart, 1981). Not only are longer training periods involved, but the resources required—staff, instructional materials, and support services—are much greater. This is problematical for policymakers who wish to provide services to as many constituents as possible. Unless spending for these efforts is increased substantially, the development and expansion of higher-level training programs necessitates that the number of people being assisted be reduced. In this context it is significant that the funds provided for employment and training activities under JTPA are less than those available under CETA.

One should not conclude from the preceding discussion that those trained for low-level jobs are always successful at obtaining even this level of employment. Especially during recessionary periods, there may be a shortage of these jobs. While job creation strategies represent one way of dealing with this problem (e.g., Palmer, 1978; Schiller, 1984; Taggart, 1977), they tend to be less popular than training approaches, especially when focused upon structural unemployment. Indeed, to the extent that PSE wages are more attractive than those in the secondary labor market, businesses that rely on that labor market are jeopardized. Moreover, the job creation approach is subject to the adequacy versus affordability trade-off that characterizes poverty policy in general. These factors generate pressures to keep wages low and the length of employment short in PSE, thereby diminishing the strategy's antipoverty impact.

It should be clear from this discussion that the assumptions that most employment and training programs must satisfy in order to be effective are both numerous and demanding. In the case of training strategies, for example, participants must possess a minimum threshold of motivation and ability if they are to learn what is taught. The training itself must be at an appropriate level, which in turn is a reflection of difficult decisions concerning the allocation of scarce program funds. Finally, the economy itself must be vigorous enough to ensure a demand for the skills developed. Given all of these requirements, it is little wonder that the achievements of employment and training policy have been so modest.

This analysis reinforces the position that employment and training policy has multiple purposes, with the elimination of poverty being only one of them. Indeed, the most fundamental justification for this strategy is the notion that it is better for people to work than not to work, even if that work nets them little more economically than they could derive from direct income strategies. To be sure, there are important noneconomic benefits (e.g., self-esteem, family stability) that steady employment may provide to individuals and their families, although the nonpoor probably overestimate the extent to which these benefits are available to the holders of menial, poorly paid jobs. In the present context, however, the more relevant point is that this Protestant ethic orientation toward the value of work contributes to the legitimation of employment and training interventions whose antipoverty impact is likely to be minimal. Many of these programs help to maintain an unattractive low-wage labor market in which there is little opportunity for upward mobility (Hasenfeld, 1975). It is instructive to recall Gans's (1973) claim that one function of poverty is to insure that individuals are available to do society's poorly paid dirty work. From this perspective, the low-level emphasis of many employment and training programs is an approach that is more consistent with the *perpetuation* of a low-income strata in society than with the *elimination* of it.

To the extent that this is the case, it is certainly an open question whether JTPA can be implemented in a way that alters the traditional thrust of employment and training policy. While the increased involvement of the private sector under JTPA is a potentially promising sign, this involvement does not represent a panacea for the problems that have characterized past policy efforts (Bernick, 1984; Ripley and Franklin, 1983). Indeed, the available evidence has not established that programs that rely heavily on the private sector are inherently superior to those that do not (U.S. General Accounting Office, 1983a).

JTPA's performance thus far has done little to allay the fears of skeptics (Walker, Feldstein, and Solow, 1985; Walker et al., 1984). In most locations there has been little attempt to target services to those most in need. Instead, the emphasis has been on providing short-term training to those who are deemed "job ready." While this approach has yielded high job placement rates, at least in the short term, many of these individuals would probably have found employment without JTPA's assistance. There is also little indication that JTPA graduates are obtaining more skilled employment than that routinely achieved under CETA. To the extent that JTPA policy is not redirected at the federal level, it is likely that these trends will continue.

EDUCATION

In American society education has traditionally been viewed as crucial to the achievement of upward economic mobility. Indeed, free public education at the elementary and secondary levels has served as one of the most important symbols of our society's commitment to equality of opportunity.

In theory, the educational system provides individuals with the chance to develop and demonstrate their motivation and cognitive abilities in a variety of contexts. It is furthermore assumed that these qualities are rewarded by the labor market in both the short and the long run, but especially the latter. Thus, individuals of high motivation and ability are viewed as being in a favorable position to obtain the sorts of jobs that offer the greatest protection against poverty.

As was the case with employment and training policy, federal support for education began to focus on the low-income population during the 1960s. Indeed, President Johnson regarded the educational strategy as the cornerstone of War on Poverty programs (Jeffrey, 1978). This should not be surprising, given that it is the approach most consistent with an individualistic model of economic stratification. From this perspective, other types of interventions would be much less necessary if the educational system fulfilled its potential. Within this framework most educational strategies can be categorized according to where they attempt to intervene in the educational life of the individual: preschool; elementary and/or secondary school; college and/or graduate school.

Preschool Programs

The major preschool program aimed at the poor is Head Start, which served nearly 450,000 children in 1985. Established by the Economic Opportunity Act of 1965, Head Start operates on the premise that poor children enter the elementary school system disadvantaged in a variety of ways. Accordingly, the overall objective of the program is to provide these children with experiences and resources that will enable them to compete on a more equal basis with other students when they begin their formal education. More specifically, the multiple goals of Head Start focus on physical and emotional health, cognitive skills, and social and interpersonal competence. Extensive parental involvement is a key feature of the program.

In order to achieve this ambitious set of objectives Head Start has evolved over the years into a network of programs (Valentine, 1979). This network supplements and extends many of the services provided by the basic program in its summer and year-long versions. Perhaps the best known of these programs is Follow Through, which is essentially the basic Head Start program extended through the kindergarten and elementary school years (Rhine, 1981).

Evaluations of Head Start and other preschool programs indicate that these interventions have a positive, but time-limited, impact on participants' performance on both intelligence and achievement tests (for reviews see Berrueta-Clement, et. al., 1984: Consortium for Longitudinal Studies, 1983; Datta, 1979; Glazer, 1985; Palmer and Anderson, 1979; and U.S. General Accounting Office, 1981; see also Jordan, Grallo, Deutsch, and Deutsch, 1985). That is, the differences between participants and controls on these dimensions tend to fade to insignificance after several years of schooling have passed.

Of perhaps greater importance, however, is the fact that preschool participants are less likely than controls to be placed in special education or remedial classes, and are more likely to graduate from high school. Because high school graduation is positively related to later employment, preschool experience has an *indirect* effect on labor market participation in late adolescence and early adulthood (Consortium for Longitudinal Studies, 1983).

In this context it is instructive that one longitudinal study has found that preschool participants are more likely to be employed, in college, or in vocational training at age nineteen, and less likely to be receiving welfare assistance, than nonparticipants (Berrueta-Clement et al., 1984). It appears, however, that participants' earnings only exceed by a very modest amount what they would have received if they had been eligible for welfare assistance (Gramlich, 1984). Thus, definitive conclusions concerning the antipoverty impact of preschool programs would seem premature at this point. It may be that such programs are much more effective at increasing self-sufficiency than at eliminating poverty.

Elementary and Secondary School Programs

Like preschool programs, a major goal of elementary and secondary school interventions is the enhancement of cognitive skills and academic achievement. Most federal support for these efforts is provided through Chapter 1 of the 1981 Educational

Consolidation and Improvement Act. This chapter continues
the basic intent of Title 1 of the 1965 Elementary and Secondary Education Act, which focused on compensatory education.
Title 1 was enacted by Congress with three purposes in mind
(National Institute of Education, 1978):

1. to provide financial aid to school districts with large numbers of low-income students and to specific schools with the high-
est concentrations of these students;

2. to support special services for low-achieving children in
schools having low revenues; and

3. to contribute to the cognitive, social, and emotional development of poor children.

Compensatory education programs typically involve small
classes of students receiving special instruction in basic areas
such as reading and mathematics from teachers and other staff
having specific training for this purpose. Frequently there are
attempts to provide students with individualized instruction.

Recent evaluations of compensatory education programs have
generally been positive. Fiscal assistance appears to be targeted fairly well, with school districts having large numbers
of low-income students getting more aid than other districts.
Indeed, these funds represent a substantial portion of the overall education budget for many poor school districts. Central
cities, rural areas, and areas with high percentages of minorities receive the largest proportions of compensatory education
money (National Institute of Education, 1978; U.S. Department
of Education, 1982). It is also clear that, in general, these funds
have been used by school districts to supplement rather than
replace the educational services that would have been available
to disadvantaged students in the absence of federal support
(Feldstein, 1978; U. S. Department of Education, 1982).

Finally, and most importantly, compensatory education programs have been found to have a significant positive impact
on participants' school performance (Mullin and Summers, 1983;
U. S. Department of Education, 1983). Estimates of the magnitude of this impact vary, depending on the subject area (reading or math) and the grade in school examined. Overall,

however, the gains appear to be small. As was the case with preschool programs, beneficial impacts diminish as the child advances in school.

Postsecondary Programs

The primary aim of postsecondary interventions is to increase the rate of college attendance and completion by low-income youth and adults, with completion of high school frequently addressed as a subsidiary goal. Two major types of programs can be identified here: those that provide some combination of information, motivation, support, and guidance, and those that render direct financial assistance. Representing the former are several programs administered by the Department of Education: Upward Bound, Talent Search, Educational Opportunity Centers, and Special Services for Disadvantaged Students.

Upward Bound, for example, focuses on youth who display academic potential but whose high school preparation is inadequate to meet the requirements of postsecondary education. The program attempts to provide the needed skills and motivation through remedial instruction, altered curriculum, tutoring, cultural activities, and counseling. During the summer, Upward Bound participants usually spend a six-to-eight-week period at a college, university, or secondary school campus. Part-time involvement in program activities occurs during the rest of the year.

Talent Search also focuses on identifying and supporting youth who have the potential for postsecondary education. Services vary from site to site, but generally include information on educational opportunities and financial aid, as well as assistance in applying for admission and aid. Some sites also conduct follow-up activities dealing with enrollment and campus adjustment.

The services provided by Educational Opportunity Centers are similar to those of Talent Search, but are targeted to individuals who are at least nineteen years old. Finally, Special Services for Disadvantaged Students provides several types of assistance to students already enrolled in institutions of higher education. These services include remedial and bilingual education, guidance, and counseling. The goal of the program is to increase the retention and graduation rate of these students.

Meaningful evaluation data exist only for the Upward Bound and Special Services for Disadvantaged Students programs. The findings for Upward Bound are generally positive (U.S. Department of Education, 1983). The average participant is much more likely than a comparable nonparticipant to enroll in postsecondary education (91% vs. 70%), and also is more likely to attend a four-year college or university (66% vs. 35%). Participating in Upward Bound is also associated with staying in school longer and receiving a greater amount of financial aid.

The results for Special Services for Disadvantaged Students indicate that those who receive the full range of this program's services are two and one-fourth times more likely to complete their first year of college than those who do not receive them (U.S. Department of Education, 1983). On long-term measures of effectiveness, such as duration of enrollment, number of course units attempted and completed, and grade point average, recipients of moderate levels of services perform better than those receiving no services or intensive combinations of services. In this context, nonacademic services (orientation, cultural services, assessment, and referral) appear to be particularly beneficial.

Programs designed to provide financial assistance directly to students take a variety of forms, including grants, loans, and work-study arrangements. Grant programs include Basic Educational Opportunity Grants (Pell Grants), Supplemental Educational Opportunity Grants, and State Student Incentive Grants. The Pell Grant program is by far the largest of these. It was initially designed to provide a funding floor for low-income students, but in 1978 the Middle Income Assistance Act extended the reach of this and other direct assistance programs to higher income groups.

The two major loan programs are the Guaranteed Student Loan and National Direct Student Loan programs. In a manner similar to Pell Grants, the Guaranteed Student Loan program was greatly affected by the Middle Income Assistance Act.

Finally, the Work-Study program is designed to stimulate part-time employment, primarily on campus, of financially needy students attending postsecondary institutions. The federal government pays up to 80% of the student's earnings and also assists in paying administrative costs. Once again, the percentage of higher-income students in this program has increased since the passage of the Middle Income Assistance Act.

Evaluations of these direct assistance programs yield mixed results (Hansen, 1982; Hansen and Lampman, 1982; Robinson, 1983; U. S. Department of Education, 1983). It is clear that this strategy has transferred considerable amounts of money to low income students, which has helped support their attendance at postsecondary institutions. (And since 1978 many middle- and upper-income students have been helped as well.) It also appears that these programs are effective in terms of (1) having higher participation rates among students from lower income families than higher income ones, and (2) covering a greater portion of the total education costs for the former than the latter.

It is important to recognize, however, that the economic burden of college costs on low-income families remains substantial. On the average, grants and scholarships cover no more than 50% of the college expenses that these families must pay (Miller and Hexter, 1985).

There is no conclusive evidence that federal aid has brought about a significant change in the college enrollment rates of low-income youth relative to those of higher income youth. However, this assistance does seem to have enabled more low-income students to attend relatively expensive private institutions than would have otherwise been the case.

Education and Poverty Policy

Perhaps more than any other strategy, educational interventions illustrate the problems involved in trying to attack poverty through its individualistic causes rather than through its symptoms. The interrelated assumptions underlying the educational approach frequently extend over a period of many years. Moreover, some of these assumptions are very difficult to satisfy.

One major assumption is that these interventions have their immediate intended effects, i.e., an increase in cognitive ability and achievement and/or an increase in the rate of school enrollment and completion. We have seen, however, that the impact of educational programs on these variables is usually quite modest, especially where the ability and achievement dimensions are concerned. There are also assumptions regarding the relationship of educational outcomes to economic success. Enhanced cognitive skill, for example, is seen as increasing this success both directly, through factors such as high-quality job performance, and indirectly, by enabling the individual to obtain additional schooling. As we saw in Chapter 2, there is evidence in support of both parts of this assumption, though the education-income relationship appears to be much stronger than the cognitive ability–income one.

Another major assumption is that the economic benefits received by those who participate in educational interventions will not be obtained at the expense of those who do not participate. In other words, it is assumed that one person's escape from poverty due to increased ability and education does not cause another individual to fall into poverty because of the limited number of good jobs available (Schiller, 1984). It is debatable how justified this assumption is. It is unlikely that it is totally justified, especially during recessionary periods.

What should be clear from this discussion is that the overall antipoverty effectiveness of educational strategies is not simply a product of their most valid assumption, which is that education is positively related to income. Rather, it is the joint result of all assumptions operating in sequence. Consequently, the true impact of educational interventions on the poverty rate is probably significant but very modest. Quantitative estimates of this impact do not exist, in large part because of major methodological obstacles to assessing the long-term outcomes of such programs. It is highly unlikely, however, that educational interventions can reduce poverty to the extent implied by America's equality-of-opportunity ideology.

The limitations of the educational approach should not keep

us from appreciating its positive features. In those instances where it is successful, its effects are much more likely to be intergenerational than would be the case with direct income strategies. Children of well-educated, nonpoor parents stand a better chance of avoiding poverty themselves than do children of nonpoor parents with little education.

The educational strategy is also viewed favorably by the general public, since it is seen as helping the poor help themselves. Because of this popularity, the social stigma attached to enrollment in many poverty programs does not apply to most educational interventions. Successful participation in them is thus likely to have a positive effect on the self-image of the poor.

There is also a strong relationship between level of education and various forms of political participation and awareness. With increased education, then, the poor are more likely to engage in various forms of political activity on their own behalf.

The popularity of educational interventions is not so great that they are immune to the winds of political change, however. Commitment to achieving the objectives of the educational approach varies with political administrations, hence sufficient funding cannot always be counted upon. In recent years, for example, the executive branch has succeeded in reducing federal expenditures (in real terms) for a variety of educational programs (Doyle and Hartle, 1984; Kelley, 1984). Elementary and secondary school programs, which are frequently targeted to poor school districts, have been particularly hard hit. Given that these programs failed to reach many low-income children in need of them *prior* to the cutbacks, the horizontal inequities of educational policy have probably increased in recent years.

ECONOMIC DEVELOPMENT

The basic goal of economic development is to stimulate private-sector investment at the national, regional, and/or local levels. The underlying antipoverty premise is that the increased demand for labor associated with economic growth benefits the poor who might otherwise not be able to obtain jobs. Economic growth also contributes to wage and salary increases.

Finally, the increased tax revenues generated by such growth permits the government to establish more generous assistance programs than it could otherwise afford (Crawford and Jusenius, 1980).

National Economic Growth

This strategy calls for federal policies designed to foster the expansion of the national economy. Included here are measures such as consumer tax cuts, increased investment and depreciation allowances, easier access to low-cost credit, and decreased federal regulation of business (Congressional Budget Office, 1981; Schiller, 1984). In recent years this approach has received the strong support of the executive branch, and has been the foundation of its domestic economic policy. It is claimed that the number of jobs that this strategy will eventually generate for the poor will more than offset the negative effects of budget reductions in a wide range of other programs.

The available evidence indicates that the poor do in fact benefit substantially from the general prosperity associated with national economic growth (Bendick, 1982; Freeman, 1981; Gottschalk and Danziger, 1984, 1985). Indeed, Gottschalk and Danziger estimate that between 1967 and 1979, increases in mean market incomes were nearly as important as direct assistance programs (cash and in-kind) in reducing the poverty rate. Since 1979 market incomes have declined, and the antipoverty impact of direct assistance programs has decreased as well. Consequently, the poverty rate has increased.

In this context it is important to note that economic growth does not necessarily benefit all population subgroups equally. To the extent that lower income groups gain less than higher ones, the income distribution becomes more unequal and the antipoverty impact of growth is reduced. This is precisely what has occurred during the past two decades.

Targeted Development Programs

The remaining approaches are all place-oriented interventions; that is, they are designed to foster growth in specific geographical locales that are judged to be economically distressed. It is assumed that these areas are physically and economically isolated from the mainstream of American life, and that changes in their basic economic structures are necessary. The major targeted programs include the Economic Development Administration, Urban Development Action Grants, Community Development Block Grants, the Industrial Development Loan Program, and the Appalachian Regional Commission. In recent years the executive branch has proposed that all of these programs, with the exception of Community Development Block Grants, be terminated.

The measures used to achieve targeted development goals can be direct or indirect. In the former approach, private businesses are provided with credit. In some cases this credit would be unobtainable by the businesses without the presence of the economic development program. In others, the credit may lower the risks of doing business in a given area to a level that firms find acceptable (Congressional Budget Office, 1981).

Development can be encouraged indirectly through the funding of public works projects. Construction of basic facilities such as sewers, roads, and water mains is usually necessary for economic growth of any magnitude to occur. The provision of these facilities thus paves the way for private investment in the community or region (Congressional Budget Office, 1981).

The Economic Development Administration (EDA), administered by the Department of Commerce, provides funding for both direct and indirect economic development projects. Thus, grants and loans are available to local areas for public works and development facilities, along with loans and loan guarantees for business development. Funds for technical assistance, research, and planning relevant to local development are available as well (U.S. Department of Commerce, 1985).

Urban Development Action Grants (UDAGs) have been administered by the Department of Housing and Urban Development since 1977 (U.S. Department of Housing and Urban Development, 1985). This is a competitive grant program in which financial aid from the federal government is combined with private and local resources to carry out projects focusing on commercial, industrial, or housing revitalization that would not be realized otherwise. In 1981 the program was modified to emphasize projects that would generate the greatest impact in terms of new permanent jobs and local tax revenues. And in 1984 changes were introduced to allow more communities experiencing long-term, high levels of unemployment to apply for Action Grants.

Unlike EDA, the UDAG program can only provide grants to local governments, but these governments can use the funds to finance the activity of private firms. A more substantial difference between the two programs is that in order for a locality to receive UDAG funding, it must first demonstrate that the private sector has made a firm commitment to participate in the proposed project. Private investment must be at least two and one-half times the size of the grant.

The Community Development Block Grant (CDBG) program, as originally enacted in 1974, did not specifically focus on economic development. Accordingly, CDBG funds were not restricted to economically distressed areas. The wide range of community activities eligible for funding under this program, however, included several with a public works or economic development emphasis. In 1977, amendments to the Housing and Community Development Act added economic development as an explicit objective of the program. Grantees were permitted to purchase property and engage in a variety of projects involving commercial and/or industrial facilities. Economic development activity still consumes a relatively small percentage of CDBG funding in major population areas; expenditures for this activity in 1984 were just 13% of all CDBG spending. In the CDBG small cities program, which funds cities with populations of under 50,000, economic development represents about 20% of all spending (U.S. Department of Housing and Urban Development, 1985).

The Industrial Development Loan Program is administered by the Department of Agriculture's Farmers Home Administration. As the title suggests, its emphasis is on providing major business and industrial loans to private firms and local governments in rural areas. In making loan decisions the program emphasizes four objectives: preservation of existing jobs; expansion and improvement of existing businesses and industries; creation of new jobs; and stabilization of local economies (Crawford and Jusenius, 1980).

Finally, The Appalachian Regional Commission has functioned since 1960 as an independent, nonfederal agency providing grants to the thirteen-state Appalachian region for highway construction, economic development, and community development. Highway construction has received about two-thirds of the commission's funds. Over time the remaining monies have been increasingly used for the development of human resources (e.g., health, education) rather than physical resources (Appalachian Regional Commission, 1984).

Evaluation of Targeted Programs

The ultimate goal of most economic development programs is increased employment in the affected areas. Increases may come about directly through the construction and permanent jobs generated by the project, and indirectly through jobs with local suppliers and sellers of consumer goods.

Definitive studies of these impacts are few (for reviews see Bendick, 1982; Congressional Budget Office, 1981; Crawford and Jusenius, 1980; U. S. Department of Housing and Urban Development, 1982, 1985). Direct employment effects are typically measured using a dollars-per-job ratio, in which project expenditures or obligations are compared with the number of jobs created. On this criterion UDAG fares significantly better than EDA, with the latter's very expensive ratios for its public works projects being primarily responsible for the differences observed. Comparable data for other development programs are not available.

Where indirect employment effects are concerned, ratios are not available for specific programs. It has been estimated, however, that in large diversified locales seven to nine jobs may be indirectly generated for every ten that are created or maintained by a development project (Congressional Budget Office, 1981).

Do the poor actually obtain a high percentage of the jobs directly or indirectly produced by economic development policies? Though the quality and quantity of the data bearing on this question leave much to be desired, the answer appears to be a qualified "no" (Congressional Budget Office, 1981; Crawford and Jusenius, 1980). It is true that in programs such as UDAG a substantial proportion (about half in UDAG) of the new permanent jobs are intended for low and moderate income persons (U.S. Department of Housing and Urban Development, 1985). Nevertheless, low-income, unemployed individuals apparently account for a very small percentage, perhaps 10–15%, of those who actually obtain employment as a result of these projects. Consequently, the antipoverty effectiveness of the projects is uncertain.

At a more basic level, of course, is the question of how many of the jobs associated with economic development activities would have been generated in the absence of the projects. In other words, to what extent would state and local authorities and the private sector have invested in developing these areas, had federal money not been available? Though estimates of the magnitude of this federal substitution effect vary, there is little doubt that some substitution does occur. The UDAG program, however, appears to perform quite well on this dimension. In an evaluation of eighty UDAG projects nationwide, evidence of total or partial substitution was found in only 21% of the cases (8% total, 13% partial). In nearly two-thirds (64%) of the projects no evidence of substitution was found (U.S. Department of Housing and Urban Development, 1982).

A major reason for substitution is that many firms do not regard financial incentives as a particularly important factor when making decisions about where to locate or expand. Indeed, because so many areas across the country are eligible for at least one economic development program, in some instances it appears that a firm will first decide where it wants to be, and then ascertain the specific program(s) for which it is eligible (Crawford and Jusenius, 1980). As a result, the net employment effects of economic development programs for the poor are probably less than the estimates we have presented.

Overall, the assumptions required for targeted economic development programs to be highly effective have some weak links, just as was the case for employment and education. First, at least some of these programs stimulate little development that would not have otherwise occurred. Second, while jobs are generated by these projects, they are often generated at a high administrative cost. Indeed, in certain cases, it appears that jobs are generated in one project locale at the expense of jobs that would have been created elsewhere in the absence of the program. Thus, the net result is redistribution of employment rather than expansion of it. Third, only a small percentage of the created or redistributed jobs are obtained by the poor. The overall antipoverty impact of this strategy is thus quite limited.

Recent attempts to strengthen targeted economic development programs have focused on three issues: private sector commitment, linkages between economic development and training, and the deregulation of development in certain areas.

The emphasis on private sector commitment derives largely from the implementation experience of UDAG and EDA. One reason UDAG appears to have been more successful than EDA in stimulating investment and jobs is that UDAG grants are only awarded if private firms have already committed their participation to the development project. The absence of such a requirement in EDA has sometimes resulted in a lack of private tenants for the industrial parks and other facilities constructed with EDA funds (Congressional Budget Office, 1981). To the extent that targeted economic development efforts survive the attempts of the executive branch to terminate them, it is likely that future programs will embody commitment requirements similar to those of UDAG.

Where training is concerned, it is probably safe to assume that as long as economic development projects do not involve a substantial training component they are not likely to provide significant long-term benefits to many of the poor. Admittedly, there are major obstacles to incorporating training into these projects, not the least of which is the reluctance of employers to hire high-risk individuals. Several experimental attempts to establish training-development linkages have been conducted, with mixed results (Crawford and Jusenius, 1980). The future will probably see increased efforts in this area, especially if policymakers become convinced that economic development efforts should have a significant antipoverty impact.

Finally, the notion of deregulated development areas is embodied in recent proposals by the executive branch to establish a small number of enterprise zones. A distinguishing characteristic of enterprise zones is the relative absence of federal intervention with respect to the locales in question. Firms locating in the zones would be exempt from a variety of federal regulations that, in theory, can hinder growth. In addition, businesses would be eligible for several federal income tax credits. State and local governments would also be expected to provide these firms with regulatory and tax relief and would be responsible for making the zones more attractive to business in other ways (improved public services, increased job training, etc.).

The overall philosophy guiding this approach is one that places great faith in the ability of unfettered market forces to generate economic development. How justified this faith is remains to be seen. Preliminary analyses of proposals for the federal portion of the enterprise zone legislation suggest that the impact of such a program on development would be modest. This is because it is very questionable whether the federal government can offer inducements to business that are great enough to offset the latter's reluctance to locate in economically depressed areas (Bendick, 1982; U.S. General Accounting Office, 1982e).

The executive branch's support of enterprise zones sharply contrasts with its attempt to terminate most of the other targeted development efforts we have reviewed. While the evaluative evidence certainly justifies questioning the efficacy of current targeted policies, they also raise serious doubts concerning the potential viability of enterprise zones. It is the strong emphasis of enterprise zones on reducing federal constraints on the marketplace that imbues this strategy with an ideological appeal for conservatives that other targeted programs are hard pressed to match. Indeed, for many conservatives enterprise zones undoubtedly represent a policy approach they would like to see applied on as wide a scale as possible.

CONCLUSIONS

For most Americans, the programs addressed in this chapter undoubtedly represent highly desirable ways of responding to the plight of the able-bodied poor. It is particularly trouble-some, therefore, to find that the antipoverty effectiveness of most of these efforts is so limited. To be sure, incremental improvements are possible and perhaps even likely. There is little reason to believe, however, that any dramatic increase in the impact of these policies is forthcoming.

These findings and conclusions are inconsistent with some of the basic tenets of American ideology concerning how society should function. The long-term persistence of structural un-employment, for example, calls into question the belief that interventions that focus directly or indirectly on the labor mar-ket can substantially reduce poverty in America (Levin, 1977). In many instances the assumptions that must be fulfilled in order for a major impact to occur are simply too great, in either number or difficulty, for the interventions (and our economic system) to sustain.

In short, no matter how much policymakers and the public may wish otherwise, the ability of most of these approaches to reduce poverty appears to be severely constrained. Increased recognition of this fact would be a major step toward relieving these programs of the burden of unrealistically high expecta-tions, and would foster greater appreciation of the actual and potential accomplishments of other approaches. There is no guarantee, of course, that this recognition will lead to the de-velopment of more effective poverty policy. At the very least, however, there is likely to emerge a more sophisticated un-derstanding of the dynamics of poverty in American society.

6

Poverty Policy: Stability and Change

What policymaking lessons and conclusions emerge from the analyses we have presented in the preceding chapters? What are the chances that poverty policy will be more effective in the future than it has been in the past? To the extent that increases in effectiveness occur, are they more likely to result from incremental reform or the fundamental redesign of policy? What do these issues tell us about the fundamental functions of poverty policy in American society? These are some of the key questions to be addressed in this final chapter.

EVALUATING ACCOMPLISHMENTS AND TRENDS IN POVERTY POLICY

On the basis of the evidence we have reviewed, it would appear that the importance of national economic growth and direct cash and in-kind assistance for reducing poverty in the United States cannot be stressed too greatly. In contrast, the antipoverty impact of most of the other approaches we have examined has been modest at best and nonexistent at worst. Moreover, we are not optimistic that most of these latter strategies can be strengthened to the point where they have a major economic impact on the poor. The assumptions involved are simply too demanding, in terms of their number and/or quality, to permit such an achievement. Thus, if poverty is to be eliminated or reduced to negligible levels (say, 1% to 3%) in the United States, economic growth and direct assistance programs must be the means through which the bulk of this accomplishment occurs.

This view, insofar as it emphasizes direct assistance programs, it not a popular one. Not only is it anathema to conservative analysts (e.g., Gilder, 1981; Murray, 1984), it is rejected by many liberals as well. Schiller (1984, p. 191), for example, asserts that:

> Simply providing money to the poor has little potential for stimulating financial independence. The only possible lasting solution to the problem of poverty is to assume that decent jobs are available to all who seek them. Under such circumstances, poverty and the need for income maintenance will be at a minimum.

In a similar vein, Levitan (1985, p. 138), claims that "a lasting response to the problems of the poor must emphasize those efforts that attack the causes of poverty rather than those that merely mitigate the symptoms."

For these authors and a host of others, increased self-sufficiency is the key to eliminating poverty. Our analysis suggests, however, that it is simply not possible to increase self-sufficiency in a manner that will result in this goal being achieved. Put another way, if the problem of poverty is defined such that the only way to solve it is through greatly increased self-sufficiency, we believe that there is no realistic solution to poverty in the United States. We wish this were not the case. Self-sufficiency is certainly a worthwhile social goal. But it is not the ultimate solution to poverty.

Against this background it is important to reiterate that we are not claiming that poverty programs oriented toward self-sufficiency are totally without value. Many of these efforts have had some positive impact, and there is clearly a role for them within the overall framework of federal poverty policy. Society's expectations concerning what these measures can accomplish, however, need to become more realistic.

In concluding that economic growth and straightforward economic redistribution are the only processes with the potential to eliminate poverty on a national scale, we recognize that the realization of this potential is an exceedingly difficult task. Undoubtedly, there are limits to society's ability to achieve and maintain high levels of growth and redistribution (Page, 1983; Spivey, 1985). Cross-national evidence suggests, however, that the United States could redistribute much more income to the lower class than it currently does without substantially decreasing its economic growth (Burtless, 1985).

A much more important obstacle, in our view, is the basic orientation of policymakers and the public toward high levels of redistribution. The major tax increases required by such redistribution would threaten the material interests and living standards of the nonpoor, and it is this group whose preferences are most likely to be translated into policy. The nature of these priorities, at least as they involve redistribution, is perhaps best summarized by Plattner's (1979, p. 29) observation that a policy "*explicitly* aimed at reducing inequality in incomes ... has never been endorsed by the American people or their representatives." Economic inequality per se, while troubling to some Americans, is generally viewed as not sufficiently problematical to warrant policies that would dramatically alter the income distribution (e.g., Hochschild, 1981; Lane, 1962; Rainwater, 1974; Verba and Orren, 1985). Consequently, the ideological mandate for such an alteration does not currently exist in America, nor is it likely to develop in the forseeable future.

Given this background, the lack of interest displayed by policymakers in *relative* poverty is understandable. This indifference has major implications for evaluating the success of poverty policy, since economic growth and direct assistance programs have had very little impact on the incidence of relative poverty. Indeed, there is a lesson here for those who would like to see public discussion of poverty evolve into a broader examination of the problematical nature of economic inequality (e.g., Haveman, 1977; Jencks et al., 1972; Miller and Roby, 1970; Page, 1983; Ryan, 1981). In the absence of large-scale events that would focus attention on the latter issue, there is little reason to expect that concern over inequality will grow in the United States.

It is probable, then, that redistribution of resources to low-income groups will continue to take place within a policy framework which explicitly defines the issue as one of poverty, and absolute poverty at that. This framework is conducive to poverty being viewed as just one of the many problems competing for the attention of policymakers and the public (Levitan, 1985). The poor, however, are not in a strong position to press for such attention on their own behalf. In addition, poverty does not appear to be a salient issue for the public-at-large (Morris, 1985). Consequently, the government sector ends up being particularly influential in establishing the parameters within which poverty is discussed.

In recent years, of course, the executive branch has attempted to define these parameters in a way that greatly reduces federal support for antipoverty efforts. Even so, it is important to recognize that the fundamental structure of most poverty programs has remained intact. Quantitative reduction, rather than qualitative change, has been the primary achievement. This is a significant indicator of the programmatic stability that the welfare state has attained in the United States (Glazer, 1984; Piven and Cloward, 1982). Recent attempts at comprehensive reform, such as the Family Assistance Plan and the Program for Better Jobs and Income, have been conspicuously unsuccessful. Indeed, a growing number of analysts have taken the position that fundamental reform of federal poverty policy is simply not politically possible, and perhaps not even desirable (e.g., Albrecht, 1982; Doolittle, Levy, and Wiseman, 1977; Ellwood and Summers, 1985; Schiller, 1981). They argue that, at most, certain incremental changes are feasible. In general, these commentators appear to believe that the current array of policies and programs accomplishes about as much as can be reasonably expected in view of the constraints imposed by both the nature of poverty and the policymaking process.

Not everyone, of course, accepts the status quo quite so readily. The more basic point, however, is that the fundamental character and mix of American poverty programs is likely to remain constant for some time to come, regardless of one's evaluation of the efficacy of those programs. Policies of the future will be shaped more by major social, economic, and demographic trends than by the exhortations of poverty researchers and analysts, whatever their political persuasion (Spivey, 1985; Zald, 1977). Among these trends are changes in the nature of work, an increase in the percentage of the population which is elderly, the huge federal deficit, and the continued disproportionate percentage of female-headed families within the poverty population. With respect to female-headed families, the overall increase in labor force participation among women will continue to erode the norm that mothers with young children should not be expected to work.

Those advocating large-scale change are almost certain to be disappointed by the policy consequences of these trends. The days of viewing a guaranteed annual income, national health insurance, and guaranteed jobs as meaningful policy options would appear to be past. And while there is no shortage of more recent policy proposals that are nearly as ambitious as these (e.g., Blaustein, 1981; Celebrezze et al., 1982; Garfinkel, 1985; Greene, 1981; Harrington, 1984; Joe, 1984; Ozawa, 1982; Rodgers, 1982; Stanback, 1984; Worcester, 1980), in an era of record-breaking federal deficits the prospects for their adoption are virtually nil.

In all probability, then, the future of poverty policy will be one of incremental change. We believe that the most significant changes will focus on three major issues: children, education, and employment.

Children

In recent years the high poverty rate among children, as well as the high welfare dependency rate of children in female-headed families, have received increasing attention (Committee on Ways and Means, 1985b). The policymaking consequences of this concern have taken several forms. The most prominent has been the growing emphasis on using child support payments from absent parents as a vehicle for reducing the cost of the AFDC program (Garfinkel, 1985). Only 42% of all female-headed families below the poverty line in 1983 had child support awards. Moreover, of those who were actually supposed to receive child support payments during that year, only 62% did. And many of these families received less than the full amount due them. Overall, the mean annual amount received by these low-income families was just $1,430 (U.S. Bureau of the Census, 1985e).

Clearly, then, there is room for substantial improvement in the performance of the American child support system, especially as it relates to low-income families. Federal legislation in this area has existed since 1950, and a major Child Support Enforcement Program (CSEP) was established in 1975 as an amendment to the Social Security Act. Most child support collected by CSEP on behalf of AFDC children is kept by the government to offset the cost of AFDC. In some cases, however, the payments are large enough to allow a family to leave the welfare rolls, in which case the family receives the payments directly. In 1984, 40,000 families left AFDC by this route. CSEP collections grew by 112% from 1978 to 1984, from $471 million to over $1 billion. Still, the latter figure represented less than 10% of all AFDC assistance granted that year (Committee on Ways and Means, 1985a).

A major obstacle to CSEP effectiveness is the judicial nature of the support process. Legally enforceable court orders must be obtained, adequate support levels established, and payments of these levels by absent parents enforced. In recent years the greatest attention has focused on the third step in this process. In 1981, for example, the Omnibus Budget Reconciliation Act authorized the Internal Revenue Service to deduct delinquent support payments from federal income tax refunds. Numerous changes also occurred in 1984 under the Child Support Enforcement Amendments. Included here were such measures as mandatory wage withholding of child support for delinquent parents, expansion of federal and state tax intercept programs, and increased federal incentives to states for their collection efforts.

The evidence indicates that changes such as these are much more effective at reducing AFDC costs than they are at reducing welfare dependency or lowering the poverty rate among

AFDC families (Oellerich, 1984; Robins, 1984). Major modifications in the other two steps of the child support process need to occur if the dependency and poverty of these families are to be greatly affected (McDonald, Moran, and Garfinkel, 1983; Oellerich and Garfinkel, 1983). Whether such changes will occur in the foreseeable future is unclear. While there is a great desire on the part of policymakers and the public to reduce welfare dependency among AFDC families, achieving significant poverty reduction among this group is an expensive undertaking and has not traditionally been a high-priority concern. This ambivalence is evident in the 1984 legislation. States are required to develop overall standards for child support benefits, for example, but local judges are not required to abide by these standards in setting award amounts.

Perhaps the most promising recent sign in this regard is the federal government's sponsorship of a major child support demonstration project in Wisconsin. Children in participating families receive a benefit that is equal to the child support tax paid by the absent parent or a socially insured minimum benefit, whichever is higher (Garfinkel, 1985). If the absent parent cannot contribute an amount equal to the minimum benefit, the difference is paid out of AFDC funds. The results of this demonstration should greatly increase our understanding of the antipoverty potential of child support policy.

An improved child support system is not the only means of providing financial assistance to needy children that would be less stigmatizing than AFDC. For example, from time to time it is suggested that the United States establish a universal system of children's allowances (e.g., Ozawa, 1982; Piccione, 1983). These allowances would be regular cash payments to *all* families having children, with the children being specified as the beneficiaries. Because the program would assist all children, female-headed families would not be singled out for negative attention. Moreover, making these payments subject to taxation would result in much (but not all) of the assistance rendered to the nonpoor being recouped.

The United States is the only industrialized nation without a child allowance system. The possibility that one will be enacted here in the foreseeable future is very slim, however. The expenditures involved would represent a substantial increase over current AFDC costs, even when taking into account taxed benefits (Committee on Ways and Means, 1985b). Moreover, most Americans are likely to regard as inefficient an assistance program that taxes away a significant portion of the benefits that most (i.e., nonpoor) participants receive. A children's allowance would also represent a qualitative change of major proportions in American social policy. Such change is difficult to achieve under any circumstances, but is especially improbable in the absence of compelling external events or vigorous program sponsorship by the government's executive branch. Neither of these conditions currently applies in the United States. Finally, it should be noted that the well-being of children in our society has traditionally been viewed as primarily the private responsibility of the family rather than the public responsibility of the state. For this reason many Americans would object to a children's allowance policy on ideological grounds, regardless of the economic issues involved.

It is much more likely that increased aid to poor children will come in the form of changes in the AFDC program. If such changes occur, they will probably involve one or more of the following steps (Committee on Ways and Means, 1985b):

1. Establishing a *national* minimum benefit which would increase over time at the same rate as the poverty line;

2. Extending AFDC benefits to all low-income two-parent families;

3. Increasing monthly deductions from income, so that families with outside income would have higher AFDC benefits;

4. Liberalizing the asset restrictions that apply to AFDC families; and

5. Reducing the extent to which states have to share the burden of financing increases in AFDC benefits.

Taken together, these changes could have a substantial antipoverty impact on families affected by them (Committee on Ways and Means, 1985b). While it is highly unlikely that all of these proposals will be enacted in the near future, the chances that a subset of them will be adopted by policymakers appear good.

Finally, in the coming years federal funding of demonstration projects aimed at reducing teenage pregnancy will probably increase markedly (Gilchrist and Schinke, 1983). Since government intervention in the domain of birth control and family planning currently exists, increased efforts in this regard do not represent a dramatic shift in poverty policy. Unfortunately, the most effective programs in this area, i.e., those that provide contraceptive services to sexually active teenagers, also tend to be the most controversial in ideological terms. To the extent that this controversy results in family planning initiatives being expanded in a way that does not include increased access to contraceptive services, it is unlikely that teenage pregnancy will be substantially reduced. This would indeed be ironic, since these are the only social services (other than legal services) that have demonstrated a significant antipoverty impact.

Education

The publication of *A Nation at Risk* in 1983 by the National Commission on Excellence in Education has ushered in a new era of public concern over the quality of elementary and secondary education in the United States (see Peterson, 1983). While this concern is not primarily focused on the education of the poor, the poor are likely to be affected by whatever education reforms emerge. Given the decentralized nature of American public education, it is inevitable that specific reforms will vary from community to community and state to state. Even so, it is probable that a common denominator of many of these changes will be an increase in the rigor of academic programs, in terms of both program content and expectations for student performance. Whether this emphasis will have a positive or negative impact on the poor will depend on the school and community contexts within which it is established. Increasing the academic demands placed upon students, without providing additional supportive resources for those who are ill-prepared to meet them, is unlikely to yield benefits. In the presence of such resources, however, an increase in the academic achievements of many low-income students might take place. As we have seen, however, the translation of these achievements into nonpoverty incomes involves a set of assumptions that are by no means automatically fulfilled, especially if the academic performance of nonpoor students is also improving (Schiller, 1984).

Attempts to strengthen the relationship between secondary schools and the workplace could turn out to be the educational reform with the greatest direct impact on the poor (e.g., Barton, 1983; Lacey, 1983). There are an increasing number of models being developed to structure these partnerships. They range from adopt-a-school programs, in which one or more businesses focus their resources on a particular school, to community-wide councils, which typically consist of employers, educators, and union personnel, as well as representatives from the voluntary and private sectors. These collaborative ventures have resulted in a wide variety of activities, including job placement assistance, occupational site visits, apprenticeship and on-the-job training, coordination of youth training programs, and skill-oriented curriculum development.

To the extent that these efforts enable disadvantaged youth to obtain more highly skilled employment than they otherwise could, their antipoverty impact could be substantial. At this point, however, it is not clear whether the mix of programs that has evolved reflects the knowledge that has been developed in recent years concerning the relative efficacy of various youth-oriented strategies. Failure to incorporate this knowledge base would probably result in these newly developed partnerships between business and education representing little improvement over traditional vocational education, at least where the poor are concerned.

Employment

Society-wide changes in the nature of work can be expected to have a major impact on the poor's chances for upward mobility in the years ahead. A significant influence here has been the rise of high-technology industries rooted in the development and application of computers (National Commission for Employment Policy, 1982). While these industries are generating a variety of well-paying jobs, many of them require a higher level of skill than the entry-level positions traditionally associated with blue-collar work. Moreover, many traditional positions (as well as the jobs they lead to) are being eliminated by high technology, either directly through automation or indirectly through the diminished competitiveness of industries that fail to adapt to foreign competition and/or the changing technological environment. Thus, those who enter the labor market with few skills are likely to have a more difficult time achieving economic security via blue-collar occupations than did the semi-skilled of previous generations. It is true that the number of service-oriented jobs is expected to expand in the coming decade, absorbing some of these individuals. Unfortunately, many of these occupations—custodial jobs, for instance—are characterized by relatively low pay.

A major implication of these trends is that, at least for the duration of a transitional period in the American industrial economy, the ranks of the structurally unemployed may increase. Unless countered by other trends, this increase would result in an increase in the poverty rate. How long this transitional period is likely to last is difficult to predict. Its ultimate importance, however, resides less in its length than in the new equilibrium that may be established for the level of structural unemployment. To the extent that this level significantly exceeds the present one, poverty policy relevant to employment is almost certain to be subjected to strong pressures for change.

Whether JTPA can respond to these pressures in a productive fashion remains to be seen, though the early evidence reported in Chapter 5 does not encourage great optimism. Neither does the fact that the United States lacks a comprehensive national employment policy (National Commission for Employment Policy, 1983). Such a policy, to the extent that it included a guaranteed jobs component, could have a substantial antipoverty impact. This is because guaranteed jobs represent a direct income approach to employment policy. This is also the reason, however, that such jobs are very unlikely to be utilized by American policymakers when attempting to design a permanent solution to poverty.

The chances are greater, though perhaps not high in absolute terms, that policymakers will eventually reorient job *training* programs in ways that will enhance their antipoverty impact. A consensus has clearly developed among policy analysts concerning the characteristics of the more successful training efforts (Bassi and Ashenfelter, 1985; Bernick, 1984; Bresnick, 1984; Burtless, 1984; Hahn and Lerman, 1985; National Council on Employment Policy, 1983; Taggart, 1981). These characteristics typically include:

1. Targeting of training to the hard-core unemployed, since they are the ones most likely to benefit;

2. Instruction in basic literacy skills for those who require it;

3. Extensive skill-training for jobs providing nonpoverty wages and/or reasonable chances for advancement;

4. Application of discipline and performance standards to participants throughout the entire instruction/training process;

5. Provision of supportive services (e.g., counseling) during and after training; and

6. Whenever possible, linking training to *specific* job openings in the private sector, through vehicles such as on-the-job training.

Developing programs which incorporate all or even most of these characteristics is an imposing task, which is a major reason why training efforts have had such modest impacts on participants. The challenge for the future is to establish an overall framework for employment policy that facilitates the accomplishment of these objectives in a routine fashion. Regrettably, JTPA does not appear to represent such a framework.

PLACING THE FUTURE IN PERSPECTIVE

On the basis of the analysis of poverty policy we have presented, it would not be unreasonable to conclude that to a significant degree "the poor will always be with us" in the

United States. While the historical justification for this prediction is strongest with respect to *relative* poverty, it applies
to *absolute* poverty as well. Where the latter is concerned, even
the counting of in-kind benefits as income does not reduce the
size of the poor population to negligible levels. And to the extent
that one agrees with those who argue that the official poverty
line has been set much too low, there is reason to believe that
absolute poverty will, as a matter of course, continue to affect
a substantial minority of the population at any given time.

One need not be a confirmed cynic to draw the conclusions
we have outlined. Social problems of the magnitude and complexity of poverty can resist even the most concerted efforts of
policymakers to solve them. In the case of poverty, of course,
something much less than the most concerted efforts has traditionally characterized the policymaking process, especially
in recent years. Poverty per se is not, and has never been, a
high-priority issue for the American public. Nor have there
been powerful constituencies that, over the years, could consistently be relied upon to place the elimination of poverty at
or near the top of their list of policy concerns.

In the absence of such constituencies, the main function of
poverty policy increasingly, and inevitably, becomes the management rather than the elimination of poverty. The current
era of management-oriented policy actually appears to have
begun during the winding down of the War on Poverty. For all
its rhetorical excess and commitment to questionable models
of poverty causation, the War on Poverty represented an explicit attempt to reduce poverty (Haveman, 1977; Patterson,
1981). Indeed, during that period the question "What does it
do for the poor?" represented a benchmark against which a
wide variety of social programs were evaluated (Lampman,
1974). Supporters of that benchmark wield much less influence
today (Glazer, 1984).

For those who are committed to bringing about progressive
change in poverty policy, the obstacles we have outlined need
not be regarded as insurmountable. To be sure, the evolution
of poverty policy has been subjected to conflicting historical
interpretations (Margolis, 1985; Rochefort, 1981). Some of these
interpretations, most notably that of Piven and Cloward (1971,

1977), have viewed civil disorder and disruption as key components of successful attempts to extract increased benefits from economic elites wishing to protect their vested interests. In such an analysis, the level of resistance encountered by progressive reformers is portrayed as exceedingly high.

Other commentators (e.g., Gronbjerg, 1977), view the establishment and expansion of poverty programs within a less conflict-ridden framework. The structural dislocations associated with the development of industrialized society inevitably place many individuals at economic risk. There is thus a need to develop large-scale assistance programs, a need to which society responds with the considerable resources at its disposal. In this model of poverty policy, society's response to need is seen as reflecting, at least in part, a humanitarian motivation which the conflict model claims not to find in the decision-making behavior of economic elites.

Our interpretation of the available evidence is that both models are useful for analyzing the development of poverty policy. The strongest support for the conflict model comes from analyses of the relationship between urban riots and welfare spending during the 1960s (Betz, 1974; Isaac and Kelly, 1981; Jennings, 1980, 1983. Attempts to apply this model to other periods have been less successful (Trattner, 1983), and convincing analyses exist that suggest that, even during the 1960s, riots were by no means the primary cause of welfare expansion (Albritton, 1979; Durman, 1973; Gronbjerg, 1977; Patterson, 1981). These unsuccessful attempts and alternative analyses typically conclude that a need-based model fits the data better than a conflict-oriented one.

Regardless of the model one finds more persuasive, it is clear that change is much easier to achieve when it is presented as being supportive of, rather than in opposition to, society's dominant value system. Even activists within the conflict school tend to develop strategies that focus attention on the failure of policymakers to design programs that embody key societal values. Consequently, we believe that the principle of value congruence has numerous applications within the context of striving for progressive change in poverty policy.

Foremost, perhaps, is its relevance to the adequacy-of-benefits issue. It is very difficult to use this value in arguing for *substantially* increased assistance to groups other than the elderly and disabled. Policymakers and the public tend to view recipients such as female-headed families with too much suspicion to be greatly moved by appeals that these households are suffering because their benefits are not high enough. Focusing upon horizontal equity—that is, fairness—is likely to be a more productive strategy. As we have seen, there is clearly a need for a nationally uniform AFDC benefit standard which should encompass unemployed parents in all states. Fairness would also be served by setting this national standard high enough so that those currently residing in high-benefit states would not be penalized. Applying automatic cost-of-living increases to AFDC benefits, another progressive objective, is also more effectively argued for from a fairness perspective. In this case the relevant comparison would be SSI, a major public assistance program whose benefits are indexed.

Our analysis also suggests that advocacy of a national supported work program for AFDC mothers makes both antipoverty and strategic sense. Supported work is clearly effective at increasing the income, work effort, and financial independence of poor women. Though the program may be an expensive one, at least initially, its work-ethic appeal is powerful. Indeed, a supported work proposal might even be useful as a bargaining chip in lobbying for AFDC reforms that focus more directly on benefit levels. A work-ethic rationale could also be employed in striving for an increase in the Earned Income Tax Credit, a program of potentially great benefit to the nonwelfare working poor (Center on Budget and Policy Priorities, 1984; Joe, 1984; Levitan, 1985).

Where the elderly, blind, and disabled are concerned, emphasizing adequacy of assistance has much to recommend it from a value perspective. To be sure, there are signs that the aged are no longer viewed as compassionately as they were prior to the controversy over the Social Security crisis (Binstock, 1983). Nevertheless, there would still appear to be strong support for the notion that the elderly should not have to live

in poverty. Thus, a concerted effort on the part of key constituencies to raise SSI benefits to the poverty level would appear
to have a reasonable chance of success.

Achievement of this objective would, in turn, make possible
an equity argument in favor of increasing AFDC and Food
Stamp assistance so that the combined benefits equaled the
poverty line. Given the negative reputation of AFDC families,
it would probably be futile to pursue this goal for AFDC recipients prior to doing so for the SSI population.

Finally, activists would be wise to phrase their policy objectives in terms of reducing absolute poverty rather than reducing relative poverty or economic inequality per se. As we have
indicated, the latter two phenomena are not likely to mobilize
the policymaking sentiments of most Americans. In fact, it
might even be argued that whatever potency these concepts
may have in the United States is only likely to emerge after
absolute poverty has been reduced to negligible levels. This is
not to say that analyses of the dynamics of relative poverty
and inequality cannot be useful in *formulating* policy proposals
focusing on absolute poverty. Using such a framework to *present* these proposals, however, would probably do little to enhance, and might even hurt, their chances of being accepted.

There are those who maintain, of course, that the failure to
link poverty to the more general phenomenon of economic inequality does an injustice to both issues. That is a possibility
that must be acknowledged. Indeed, at a more basic level this
possibility should remind us that whether one views the performance of poverty policy as a glass half empty or half filled
depends on the ideological predispositions one brings to the
problem. Even so, what is clear from our review of the evidence
is that there is no reason to expect that straightforward redistribution, in conjunction with economic growth, can ever be
replaced as the primary vehicle through which poverty policy
operates. Most other approaches, however desirable they may
be in certain respects, are by nature very limited methods for
achieving explicit antipoverty goals.

We have already indicated that American policymakers and
the public are unlikely to look favorably upon this conclusion.
In public discourse, "throwing money at problems" has increas-

ingly become synonymous with "intervening ineffectively." Where poverty is concerned, however, that charge is simply not true with respect to direct transfer programs, since the problem involved is precisely one of lack of money. This is the reality that poverty policy must face. Consequently, any attempt to substantially curtail such programs is destined to increase the ranks of the poor (Danziger, Gottschalk, and Smolensky, 1984; Joe and Rogers, 1985; Moon and Sawhill, 1984; U.S. General Accounting Office, 1984b). To be sure, decision makers may believe that such an increase in poverty is a necessary side effect of achieving other desirable policy objectives. But to not expect such a consequence, to not believe that the redistribution of sizable amounts of income is needed to significantly reduce poverty, represents a fundamental misunderstanding of the relationship between the American economy, the poor, and poverty policy.

Unfortunately, this is a misunderstanding that our ideological heritage facilitates. It is also one that must be overcome if we are to emerge from the current era of simply managing poverty to one of substantially reducing it.

Notes

CHAPTER 1

1. Much of the analysis in this section is drawn from Morris and Williamson (1982).

CHAPTER 2

1. Much of the discussion in this and the following section is drawn from Morris and Williamson (1982).

CHAPTER 3

1. This figure overestimates the impact of direct income programs to a certain extent since, in the absence of government transfers, income redistribution through *private* channels (e.g., between families) would be greater than it currently is (Lampman and Smeeding, 1983). The negative impact of direct income programs on work effort has also been cited by those who claim that the antipoverty impact of this strategy tends to be overestimated (Plotnick, 1984). It should be noted, however, that decreased work effort would also accompany any increase in private redistribution.

2. A third direct income strategy is the refundable tax credit, which pays a subsidy to low-income workers in families with children. The impact of this approach, as represented by the Earned Income Tax

Credit, is miniscule in comparison with public assistance and social insurance.

3. The urban disorders of the 1960s also appear to have contributed to changes in welfare policies and regulations (Betz, 1974; Isaac and Kelly, 1981; Jennings, 1980, 1983; Piven and Cloward, 1971).

4. Pretransfer income is census income minus government cash transfers (social insurance, public assistance, etc.). Thus, the pretransfer poor are those with market incomes below the official poverty line.

CHAPTER 4

1. A fourth category is energy assistance, represented by the Low-Income Home Energy Assistance Program (Rigby and Scott, 1983). LIHEAP is a hybrid program, combining the features of a direct income strategy and an in-kind approach. It is a small program, with only $2 billion in federal appropriations in 1985.

References

Aaron, H. J. *Shelter and subsidies: Who benefits from federal housing policies?* Washington, D.C.: Brookings Institution, 1972.

Aaron, H. J. Policy implications: A progress report. In K. L. Bradbury and A. Downs (eds.), *Do housing allowances work?* Washington, D.C.: Brookings Institution, 1981.

Aaron, H. J. *Economic effects of Social Security.* Washington, D.C.: Brookings Institution, 1982.

Aday, L. A., Anderson, R., and Fleming, G. *Health care in the U.S.: Equitable for whom?* Beverly Hills, CA: Sage, 1980.

Akin, J., Guilkey, D. K., Popkin, B. M., and Smith, K. M. The impact of federal transfer programs on the nutrient intake of elderly individuals. *Journal of Human Resources,* 1985, *20,* 383–404.

Albrecht, W. P. Welfare reform: An idea whose time has come and gone. In P. M. Sommers (ed.), *Welfare reform in America: Perspectives and prospects.* Boston: Kluwer-Nijhoff, 1982.

Albritton, R. B. Social amelioration through mass insurgency? A reexamination of the Piven and Cloward thesis. *American Political Science Review,* 1979, *73,* 1003–1011.

Allen, J. T. The concept of vertical equity and its application to social program design. In P. C. Brown, C. Johnson, and P. Vernier (eds.), *Income support: Conceptual and policy issues.* Totowa, NJ: Rowman and Littlefield, 1981.

Allen, V. L. Personality correlates of poverty. In V. L. Allen (ed.), *Psychological factors in poverty.* Chicago: Markham, 1970.

Alston, J. P., and Dean, K. I. Socioeconomic factors associated with attitudes toward welfare recipients and the causes of poverty. *Social Service Review*, 1972, *46*, 13–23.

Altman, D. Health care for the poor. *Annals of the American Academy of Political and Social Science*, 1983, *468*, 103–121.

American Assembly. *Youth employment and public policy*. Englewood Cliffs, NJ: Prentice-Hall, 1980.

Anderson, B. E. How much did the programs help minorities and youth? In E. Ginzberg (ed.), *Employing the unemployed*. New York: Basic Books, 1980.

Anderson, M. The objectives of the Reagan administration's social welfare policy. In D. L. Bawden (ed.), *The social contract revisited: Aims and outcomes of President Reagan's social welfare policy*. Washington, D.C.: Urban Institute, 1984.

Andrisani, P. J. Internal-external attitudes, personal initiative, and the labor market experience of black and white men. *Journal of Human Resources*, 1977, *12*, 308–328.

Andrisani, P. J. *Work attitudes and labor market experience*. New York: Praeger, 1978.

Andrisani, P. J. Internal-external attitudes, sense of efficacy, and labor market experiences: A reply to Duncan and Morgan. *Journal of Human Resources*, 1981, *16*, 658–666.

Appalachian Regional Commission. *1983 annual report*. Washington, D.C.: Author, 1984.

AuClaire, P. A., The mix of work and welfare among long-term AFDC recipients. *Social Service Review*, 1979, *53*, 586–605.

Auletta, K. *The underclass*. New York: Random House, 1982.

Bane, M. J. *Household composition and poverty* (IRP Conference Paper). Madison, WI: Institute for Research on Poverty, 1985.

Bane, M. J. and Ellwood, D. *The dynamics of dependence: The routes to self-sufficiency*. Cambridge, MA: Urban Systems Research and Engineering, 1983. (a)

Bane, M. J. and Ellwood, D. *Slipping into and out of poverty: The dynamics of spells* (Working paper No. 1199). Cambridge, MA: National Bureau of Economic Research, 1983. (b)

Banfield, E. C. *The unheavenly city revisited*. Boston: Little, Brown, 1974.

Bannister, R. C. *Social Darwinism: Science and myth in Anglo-American social thought*. Philadelphia: Temple University Press, 1979.

Barmack, J. A. The case against in-kind transfers: The Food Stamp program. *Policy Analysis*, 1977, *3*, 509–530.

Baron, J. M., and Mellow, W. Interstate differences in Unemployment Insurance. *National Tax Journal*, 1981, *34*, 105–113.

Barton, P. E. *Partnerships between corporations and schools.* Washington, D.C.: National Commission for Employment Policy, 1983.

Bassi, L. J. CETA: Did it work? *Policy Studies Journal*, 1983, *12*, 106–118. (a)

Bassi, L. J. The effect of CETA on the postprogram earnings of participants. *Journal of Human Resources*, 1983, *18*, 539–556. (b)

Bassi, L. J. *AFDC: An examination of the growing caseload* (Discussion Paper 748–84). Madison, WI: Institute for Research on Poverty, 1984. (a)

Bassi, L. J. Estimating the effect of training programs with nonrandom selections. *Review of Economics and Statistics*, 1984, *66*, 36–43. (b)

Bassi, L. J., and Ashenfelter, O. The effect of direct job creation and training programs on low-skilled workers (IRP Conference Paper). Madison, WI: Institute for Research on Poverty, 1985.

Bawden, D. L. (ed.). *The social contract revisited: Aims and outcomes of President Reagan's social welfare policy.* Washington, D.C.: Urban Institute, 1984.

Becker, G. S. *Human capital.* New York: Columbia University Press, 1964.

Beeghley, L. *Living poorly in America*, New York: Praeger, 1983.

Beeghley, L. Illusion and reality in the measurement of poverty. *Social Problems*, 1984, *31*, 322–333.

Bendick, M., Jr. Employment, training, and economic development. In J. L. Palmer and I. V. Sawhill (eds.), *The Reagan experiment.* Washington, D.C.: Urban Institute, 1982.

Benham, L., and Benham, A. The impact of incremental health services on health status, 1963–1970. In R. Andersen, J. Kravits, and O. W. Anderson (eds.), *Equity in health services.* Cambridge, MA: Ballinger, 1975.

Bernick, M. The truth about job-training programs. *Journal of Contemporary Studies*, 1984, 7 (1), 37–43.

Berrueta-Clement, J. R., Schweinhart, L., Barrett, W., Epstein, A., and Weikart, D. *Changed lives: The effects on the Perry Preschool program on youths through age 19.* Ypsilanti, MI: High/Scope Press, 1984.

Betz, M. Riots and welfare: Are they related? *Social Problems*, 1974, *21*, 345–355.

Binstock, R. M. The aged as scapegoat. *The Gerontologist*, 1983, *23*, 136–143.

Bird, F. B. *The poor be damned: An analysis of how Americans have perceived and responded to the problem of poverty, 1885–1970.* Unpublished doctoral dissertation, Graduate Theological Union, 1973.

Birdsall, W. C., and Hankins, J. L. The future of Social Security. *Annals of the American Academy of Political and Social Science*, 1985, *479*, 82-100.

Bishop, J. H. Jobs, cash transfers and marital instability: A review and synthesis of the evidence. *Journal of Human Resources*, 1980, *15*, 301–334.

Bishop, J. H., and Haveman, R. H. *Targeted employment subsidies: Issues of structure and design* (Special Report 24). Madison, WI: Institute for Research on Poverty, 1978.

Blank, R. M., and Blinder, A. S. *Macroeconomics, income distribution, and poverty* (IRP Conference Paper). Madison, WI: Institute for Research on Poverty, 1985.

Blaustein, S. J. *Job and income security for unemployed workers: Some new directions*. Kalamazoo, MI: W. E. Upjohn Institute for Employment Research, 1981.

Blendon, R., and Moloney, T. W. (eds.). *New approaches to the Medicaid crisis*. New York: Frost and Sullivan, 1983.

Blum, Z. D., and Rossi, P. H. Social class research and images of the poor: A bibliographic review. In D. P. Moynihan (ed.), *On understanding poverty: Perspectives from the social sciences*. New York: Basic Books, 1969.

Blumenthal, D., and Calkins, D. Health care and the poor. In M. Carballo and M. J. Bane (eds.), *The state and the poor in the 1980s*. Boston: Auburn House, 1984.

Borus, M. E. Assessing the impact of training programs. In E. Ginzberg (ed.), *Employing the unemployed*. New York: Basic Books, 1980.

Borus, M. E. (ed.). *Youth and the labor market*. Kalamazoo, MI: W. E. Upjohn Institute for Employment Research, 1984.

Boskin, M. J., and Nold, F. C. A Markov model of turnover in Aid to Families with Dependent Children. *Journal of Human Resources*, 1975, *10*, 467–481.

Bovard, J. Busy doing nothing: The story of government job creation. *Policy Review*, 1983, Spring, 87–102. (a)

Bovard, J. Feeding everybody: How federal food programs grew and grew. *Policy Review*, 1983, Fall, 42–51. (b)

Bovbjerg, R. R., and Holahan, J. *Medicaid in the Reagan era: Federal policy and state choices*. Washington, D.C.: Urban Institute, 1982.

Bradbury, K. L., and Downs, A. (eds.). *Do housing allowances work?* Washington, D.C.: Brookings Institution, 1981.

Branch, A. Y. *Summer Training and Education Program: Report of the pilot experience*. Philadelphia: Public/Private Ventures, 1985.

Bremner, R. H. *From the depths: The discovery of poverty in the United States.* New York: New York University Press, 1956.

Bresnick, D. *Youthjobs: Toward a private/public partnership.* Westport, CT: Quorum Books, 1984.

Brinker, P. A., Klos, J. J.,. and Kesselring, R. (2nd ed.). *Poverty, manpower, and Social Security.* Austin, TX: Austin Press, 1982.

Brown, C., Gilroy, C., and Kohen, A. The effect of the minimum wage on employment and unemployment. *Journal of Economic Literature,* 1982, *20,* 487–528.

Brown, C., Gilroy, C., and Kohen, A. Time-series evidence of the effect of the minimum wage on youth employment and unemployment. *Journal of Human Resources,* 1983, *18,* 3–31.

Brown, E. R. Medicare and Medicaid: Band-aids for the old and poor. In V. W. Sidel and R. Sidel (eds.), *Reforming medicine: Lessons of the last quarter century.* New York: Pantheon, 1984.

Buchele, R. Economic achievement and the power of positive thinking. *Journal of Human Resources,* 1983, *13,* 441–449.

Budget of the United States government, fiscal year 1986—Appendix. Washington, D.C.: U.S. Government Printing Office, 1985.

Burkhauser, R. V., and Warlick, J. L. Disentangling the annuity from the redistributive aspects of Social Security. *Review of Income and Wealth,* 1981, *27,* 401–421.

Burtless, G. *Unemployment Insurance and poverty: Testimony for the Committee on Ways and Means, U.S. House of Representatives.* Washington, D.C.: Brookings Institution, 1983. (a)

Burtless, G. Why is insured unemployment so low? *Brookings Papers on Economic Activity,* 1983, #1, 225–249. (b)

Burtless, G. Manpower policies for the disadvantaged: What works? *Brookings Review,* 1984, *3* (1), 18–22.

Burtless, G. Are targeted wage subsidies harmful? Evidence from a wage voucher experiment. *Industrial and Labor Relations Review,* 1985, *39,* 105–114.

Burtless, G. *Public spending for the poor: Trends, prospects, and economic limits* (IRP Conference Paper). Madison, WI: Institute for Research on Poverty, 1985.

Burtless, G., and Haveman, R. *Taxes, transfers, and labor supply: The evolving views of U.S. economists* (Discussion Paper 778–85). Madison, WI: Institute for Research on Poverty, 1985.

Burtless, G., and Saks, D. H. *The decline in insured unemployment during the 1980s.* Washington, D.C.: Brookings Institution, 1984.

Butler, E., and Mangum, G. *Applying the lessons of youth programs.* Salt Lake City: Olympus Publishing Company, 1983.

Butler, J. S., Ohls, J. C., and Posner, B. The effect of the Food Stamp program on the nutrient intake of the eligible elderly. *Journal of Human Resources*, 1985, *20*, 405–420.

Cain, G. C. Welfare economics of policies toward women. *Journal of Labor Economics*, 1985, *3* (1, pt. 2), S375-S396.

Cannon, N. An evaluation of the Early and Periodic Screening, Diagnosis and Treatment program. In S. H. Altman and H. M. Sapolsky (eds.), *Federal health programs: Problems and prospects*. Lexington, MA: Lexington Books, 1981.

Carter, G. M., Coleman, S. B., and Wendt, J. C. Participation under open enrollment. In J. Friedman and D. H. Weinberg (eds.), *The great housing experiment*. Beverly Hills, CA: Sage, 1983.

Celebrezze, A., Cohen, W., Finch, R., Flemming, A., Harris, P. H., Mathews, P., Ribicoff, A., and Richardson, E. *Welfare policy in the United States*. Racine, WI: Johnson Foundation, 1982.

Center for Community Change. *Beyond the numbers: The failure of the official measure of poverty*. Washington, D.C.: Author, 1979.

Center on Budget and Policy Priorities. *Taxing the poor*. Washington, D.C.: Author, 1984.

Chaikin, S. C., and Comstock, P. Subminimum wage: Sub-par idea. *Journal of the Institute for Socioeconomic Studies*, 1983, *8* (2), 74–89.

Chamie, M., and Henshaw, S. K. The costs and benefits of government expenditures for family planning programs. *Family Planning Perspectives*, 1981, *13*, 117–134.

Champagne, A. Legal services: A program in need of assistance. In A. Champagne and E. J. Harpham (eds.), *The attack on the welfare state*, Prospect Heights, IL: Waveland Press, 1984.

Champagne, A., and Harpham, E. J. (eds.). *The attack on the welfare state*. Prospect Heights, IL: Waveland Press, 1984.

Champagne, A., and Nagel, S. S. Law and social change. In E. Seidman (ed.), *Handbook of social intervention. Beverly Hills, CA: Sage, 1983.*

Chief, E. Need determination in AFDC program. *Social Security Bulletin*, 1979, *42* (9), 11–21.

Chirikos, T. N., and Nestel, G. Further evidence on the economic effects of poor health. *Review of Economics and Statistics*, 1985, *67*, 61–69.

Citizen's Commission on Hunger in New England. *American hunger crisis: Poverty and health in New England*. Boston: Author, 1984.

Clague, E., and Kramer, L. *Manpower policies and programs: A review, 1935–75*. Kalamazoo, MI: W. E. Upjohn Institute for Employment Research, 1976.

Coe, R. D. A preliminary empirical examination of the dynamics of welfare use. In M. S. Hill and J. N. Morgan (eds.), *Five thousand American families—Patterns of economic progress* (vol. 9). Ann Arbor, MI: Institute for Social Research, 1981.

Coe, R. D. Nonparticipation in welfare programs by eligible households: The case of the Food Stamp program. *Journal of Economic Issues*, 1983, *17*, 1035–1056.

Coe, R. D. *A longitudinal analysis of nonparticipation in the Food Stamp program by eligible households* (Discussion Paper 773–85). Madison, WI: Institute for Research on Poverty, 1985. (a)

Coe, R. D. Nonparticipation in the SSI program by the eligible elderly. *Southern Economic Journal*, 1985, *51*, 891–897. (b)

Coe, R. D., Duncan, G. J., and Hill, M. S. *Dynamic aspects of poverty and welfare use in the United States.* Paper presented at the Clark-Luxembourg Conference on Anti-Poverty Programs, Worcester, MA, August 1982.

Colasanto, D., Kapteyn, A., and van der Gaag, J. Two subjective definitions of poverty: Results from the Wisconsin Basic Needs Study. *Journal of Human Resources*, 1984, *19*, 127–138.

Coleman, R. P., Rainwater, L., and McClelland, K. A. *Social standing in America: New dimensions of class.* New York: Basic Books, 1978.

Coll, B. D. *Perspectives in public welfare: A history.* Washington, D.C.: U.S. Government Printing Office, 1969.

Collins, R. *The credential society: An historical sociology of education and stratification.* New York: Academic Press, 1979.

Committee on Ways and Means, U.S. House of Representatives. *Background material on poverty.* Washington, D.C.: U.S. Government Printing Office, 1983.

Committee on Ways and Means, U.S. House of Representatives. *Background material and data on programs within the jurisdiction of the Committee on Ways and Means.* Washington, D.C.: U.S. Government Printing Office, 1985. (a)

Committee on Ways and Means, U.S. House of Representatives. *Children in poverty.* Washington, D.C.: U.S. Government Printing Office, 1985. (b)

Congressional Budget Office. *Feeding children: Federal child nutrition policies in the 1980's.* Washington, D.C.: U.S. Government Printing Office, 1980.

Congressional Budget Office. *Local economic development: Current programs and alternative strategies.* Washington, D.C.: Author, 1981.

Congressional Budget Office. *Containing medical care costs through market forces.* Washington, D.C.: U.S. Government Printing Office, 1982. (a)

Congressional Budget Office. *Federal housing assistance: Alternative approaches.* Washington, D.C.: U.S. Government Printing Office, 1982. (b)

Congressional Budget Office. *Improving youth employment prospects: Issues and options.* Washington, D.C.: U.S. Government Printing Office, 1982. (c)

Congressional Budget Office. *Changing the structure of Medicare benefits: Issues and options.* Washington, D.C.: U.S. Government Printing Office, 1983. (a)

Congressional Budget Office. *Federal subsidies for public housing: Issues and options.* Washington, D.C.: U.S. Government Printing Office, 1983. (b)

Congressional Budget Office. *The combined effects of major changes in federal taxes and spending programs since 1981.* Washington, D.C.: Author, 1984. (a)

Congressional Budget Office. *The Targeted Jobs Tax Credit.* Washington, D.C.: Author, 1984. (b)

Congressional Budget Office. *Promoting employment and maintaining incomes with unemployment insurance.* Washington, D.C.: U.S. Government Printing Office, 1985.

Congressional Budget Office and National Commission for Employment Policy. *CETA training programs: Do they work for adults?* Washington, D.C.: U.S. Government Printing Office, 1982.

Consortium for Longitudinal Studies. *As the twig is bent: Lasting effects of preschool programs.* Hillsdale, NJ: Lawrence Erlbaum Associates, 1983.

Corbett, T., Masters, S., and Moran, J. *Tax credits to stimulate the employment of disadvantaged workers: A report on Phase I of the Wisconsin Wage Bill Subsidy Research Project* (Special Report 31). Madison, WI: Institute for Research on Poverty, 1981.

Corcoran, M., and Datcher, L. P., Intergenerational status transmission and the process of individual attainment. In M. S. Hill, D. H. Hill, and J. N. Morgan (eds.), *Five thousand American families—Patterns of economic progress* (vol. 9). Ann Arbor, MI: Institute for Social Research, 1981.

Corcoran, M., and Hill, M. S. Unemployment and poverty. *Social Service Review*, 1980, *54*, 407–413.

Corson, W., and Nicholson, W. *The Federal Supplemental Benefits program: An appraisal of Emergency Extended Unemployment Insurance Benefits.* Kalamazoo, MI: W. E. Upjohn Institute for Employment Research, 1982.

Coughlin, R. M. *Ideology, public opinion and welfare policy: Attitudes toward taxes and spending in industrialized societies.* Berkeley:

Institute of International Studies, University of California, 1980.

Crawford, E., and Jusenius, C. Economic development policies to reduce structural unemployment. In National Commission for Employment Policy, *Sixth annual report*. Washington, D.C.: U.S. Government Printing Office, 1980.

Cronin, F. J. Participation in the Experimental Housing Allowance Program. In R. J. Struyk and M. Bendick, Jr. (eds.), *Housing vouchers for the poor: Lessons from a national experiment*. Washington, D.C.: Urban Institute, 1981.

Cronin, F. J. The efficiency of demand-oriented housing programs: Generalizing from experimental findings. *Journal of Human Resources*, 1983, *18*, 100–125.

Danziger, S., and Gottschalk, P. The measurement of poverty: Implications for antipoverty policy. *American Behavioral Scientist*, 1983, *26*, 739–756.

Danziger, S., Gottschalk, P., and Smolensky, E. *The effects of unemployment and policy changes on America's poor* (Discussion Paper 770–84). Madison, WI: Institute for Research on Poverty, 1984.

Danziger, S., Haveman, R., and Plotnick, R. How income transfer programs affect work, savings, and the income distribution: A critical review. *Journal of Economic Literature*, 1981, *19*, 975–1028.

Danziger, S., Haveman, R., and Plotnick, R. *Antipoverty policy: Effects on the poor and the nonpoor* (IRP Conference Paper). Madison, WI: Institute for Research on Poverty, 1985.

Danziger, S., and Jakubson, G. The distributional impact of targeted public employment programs. In R. H. Haveman (ed.), *Public finance and public employment*. Detroit, MI: Wayne State University Press, 1982.

Danziger, S., Jakubson, G., Schwartz, S., and Smolensky, E. Work and welfare as determinants of female poverty and household headship. *The Quarterly Journal of Economics*, 1982, *97*, 519–534.

Danziger, S., van der Gaag, J., Smolensky, E., and Taussig, M. Implications of the relative economic status of the elderly for transfer policy. In H. Aaron and G. Burtless (eds.), *Retirement and economic behavior*. Washington, D.C.: Brookings Institution, 1984.

Danziger, S., van der Gaag, J., Taussig, M. K., and Smolensky, E. The direct measurement of welfare levels: How much does it cost to make ends meet? *Review of Economics and Statistics*, 1984, *66*, 500–505.

Datta, Lois-ellin. Another spring and other hopes: Some findings from national evaluations of Project Head Start. In E. Zigler and J. Valentine (eds.), *Project Head Start: A legacy of the War on Poverty*. New York: Free Press, 1979.

Davidson, C., and Gaitz, C. M. "Are the poor different?" A comparison of work behavior and attitudes among the urban poor and non-poor. *Social Problems*, 1974, *22*, 229–245.

Davidson, S. M. The status of aid to the medically needy. *Social Service Review*, 1979, *53*, 92–105.

Davis, E. M., and Millman, M. L. *Health care for the urban poor: Directions for policy*. Totowa, NJ: Rowman and Allanheld, 1983.

Davis, K. A decade of policy developments in providing health care for low-income families. In R. H. Haveman (ed.), *A decade of federal antipoverty programs: Achievements, failures, and lessons*. New York: Academic Press, 1977.

Davis, K., and Schoen, C. *Health and the War on Poverty: A ten-year appraisal*. Washington, D.C.: Brookings Institution, 1978.

Davis, R. *The relationship of health status to welfare dependency* (Discussion Paper 672–81). Madison, WI: Institute for Research on Poverty, 1981.

Daymont, T.N., and Andrisani, P. J. Job preferences, college major, and the gender gap in earnings. *Journal of Human Resources*, 1984, *19*, 408–428.

Della Fave, L. R. Success values: Are they universal or class-differentiated? *American Journal of Sociology*, 1974, *80*, 153–169.

Della Fave, L. R. Aspirations through four years of high school: An inquiry into the value-stretching process. *Pacific Sociological Review*, 1977, *20*, 371–388.

Della Fave, L. R., and Klobus, P. A., Success values and the value stretch: A biracial comparison. *Sociological Quarterly*, 1976, *17*, 491–502.

Desy, J., Mertens, D. M., and Gardner, J. A. *The long-term effects of vocational education: Earnings, employment, education, and aspirations*. Columbus, OH: National Center for Research in Vocational Education, 1984.

Dickinson, K. Transfer income. In J. N. Morgan, K. Dickinson, J. Dickinson, J. Benus, and G. J. Duncan, *Five thousand American families—Patterns of economic progress* (vol. 1). Ann Arbor, MI: Institute for Social Research, 1975.

Dillingham, C. L. The value stretch: An empirical test. *Sociology and Social Research*, 1980, *64*, 249–262.

Director, S. M., Englander, F., and Moeller, P. V. The probability of placement by the Public Employment Service. *Policy Studies Review*, 1984, *3*, 417–425.

Dolbeare, C. N. The low-income housing crisis. In C. Hartman (ed.), *America's housing crisis: What is to be done?* Boston: Routledge and Kegan Paul, 1983.

Doolittle, F., Levy, F., and Wiseman, M. The mirage of welfare reform. *Public Interest*, 1977, Spring, 62–87.

Doyle, D. D., and Hartle, T. W. Ideology, pragmatic politics, and the education budget. In J. C. Weicher (ed.), *Maintaining the safety net: Income redistribution programs in the Reagan administration.* Washington, D.C.: American Enterprise Institute, 1984.

Drazga, L., Upp, M., and Reno, V. Low-income aged: Eligibility and participation in SSI. *Social Security Bulletin*, 1982, *45* (5), 28–35.

Dubnoff, S. How much income is enough? Measuring public judgments. *Public Opinion Quarterly*, 1985, *49*, 285–299.

Duncan, G. J. *Years of poverty, years of plenty: The changing economic fortunes of American workers and families.* Ann Arbor, MI: Institute for Social Research, 1984.

Duncan, G. J., and Liker, J. K. Disentangling the efficacy-earnings relationship among white men. In G. J. Duncan and J. N. Morgan (eds.), *Five thousand American families—Patterns of economic progress* (vol. 10). Ann Arbor, MI: Institute for Social Research, 1983.

Duncan, G. J., and Morgan, J. N. Persistence and change in economic status and the role of changing family composition. In M. S. Hill, D. H. Hill, and J. N. Morgan (eds.), *Five thousand American families—Patterns of economic progress* (vol. 9). Ann Arbor, MI: Institute for Social Research, 1981. (a)

Duncan, G. J., and Morgan, J. N. Sense of efficacy and subsequent change in earnings: A replication. *Journal of Human Resources*, 1981, *16*, 649–657. (b)

Dunn, P. The Reagan solution for aiding families with dependent children: Reflections of an earlier era. In A. Champagne and E. J. Harpham (eds.), *The attack on the welfare state.* Prospect Heights, IL: Waveland Press, 1984.

Durman, E. Have the poor been regulated? Toward a multivariate understanding of welfare growth. *Social Service Review*, 1973, *47*, 339–359.

Ehrenberg, R. G., and Hewlett, J. G. The impact of the WIN 2 program on welfare costs and recipient rates. *Journal of Human Resources*, 1976, *11*, 219–232.

Ellwood, D., and Bane, M. J. *The impact of AFDC on family structure and living arrangements.* Unpublished manuscript. Cambridge, MA: Harvard University, 1984.

Ellwood, D., and Summers, L. *Poverty in America: Is welfare the answer or the problem?* (IRP Conference Paper). Madison, WI: Institute for Research on Poverty, 1985.

Employment and training report of the President. Washington, D.C.: U.S. Government Printing Office, 1983.

Farkas, G., Olsen, R., Stromsdorfer, E. W., Sharpe, L. C., Skidmore, F., Smith, D. A., and Merrill, S. *Post-program impacts of the Youth Incentive Entitlement Pilot Projects.* New York: Manpower Demonstration Research Corporation, 1984.

Farrell, W., Parent, R., and Tenney, M. Administration and service delivery in the SSI program: The first 10 years. *Social Security Bulletin*, 1984, *47* (8), 3–22.

Feagin, J. R. *Subordinating the poor: Welfare and American beliefs.* Englewood Cliffs, NJ: Prentice-Hall, 1975.

Featherman, D. L. Achievement orientations and socioeconomic career attainments. *American Sociological Review*, 1972, *37*, 131–143.

Feder, J., Holahan, J., Bovbjerg, R. R., and Hadley, J. Health. In J. L. Palmer and I. V. Sawhill (eds.), *The Reagan experiment.* Washington, D.C.: Urban Institute, 1982.

Feldstein, M. Facing the Social Security crisis. *Public Interest*, 1977, Spring, 88–100.

Feldstein, M. The effect of a differential add-on grant: Title I and local education spending. *Journal of Human Resources*, 1978, *13*, 443–458.

Fendler, C., and Orshansky, M. Improving the poverty definition. *Proceedings of the Social Statistics section.* Washington, D.C.: American Statistical Association, 1979.

Filer, R. K. Male-female wage differences: The importance of compensating differentials. *Industrial and Labor Relations Review*, 1985, *38*, 426–437.

Flaim, P. O. Discouraged workers: How strong are their links to the job market? *Monthly Labor Review*, 1984, *107* (8), 8–11.

Foltz, A. *An ounce of prevention: Child health politics under Medicaid.* Cambridge, MA: MIT Press, 1982.

Food Research and Action Center. *Food and nutrition issues in the Food Stamp program.* Washington, D.C.: Author 1981.

Food Research and Action Center. *Hunger in the eighties: A primer.* Washington, D.C.: Author, 1984.

Forrest, J. D., Hermalin, A. I., and Henshaw, S. K. The impact of family planning clinic programs on adolescent pregnancy. *Family Planning Perspectives*, 1981, *13*, 109–116.

Freeland, M. S., and Schendler, C. E. National health expenditure growth in the 1980's: An aging population, new technologies, and increasing competition. *Health Care Financing Review*, 1983, *4* (3), 1–58.

Freeman, R. B. Troubled workers in the labor market. In National Commission for Employment Policy, *Seventh annual report*. Washington, D.C.: U.S. Government Printing Office, 1981.

Freeman, R. B., and Wise, D. A. The youth labor market problem: Its nature, causes, and consequences. In R. B. Freeman and D. A. Wise (eds.), *The youth labor market problem: Its nature, causes, and consequences*. Chicago: University of Chicago Press, 1982.

Friedman, J., and Weinberg, D. H. (eds.). *The great housing experiment*. Beverly Hills, CA: Sage, 1983. (a)

Friedman, J., and Weinberg, D. H. Rent rebates and housing standards. In J. Friedman and D. H. Weinberg (eds.), *The great housing experiment*. Beverly Hills, CA: Sage, 1983. (b)

Friedman, L. M. The social and political context of the War on Poverty: An overview. In R. H. Haveman (ed.), *A decade of federal antipoverty programs: Achievements, failures, and lessons*. New York: Academic Press, 1977.

Fuchs, V. R. Redefining poverty and redistributing income. *Public Interest*, 1967, Summer, 89–94.

Gallup Report, 1983, May, p. 12.

Gallup Report, 1985, March, pp. 21–24.

Gans, H. J. Culture and class in the study of poverty: An approach to anti-poverty research. In D. P. Moynihan (ed.), *On understanding poverty: Perspectives from the social sciences*. New York: Basic Books, 1969.

Gans, H. J. *More equality*. New York: Pantheon Books, 1973.

Garfinkel, I. Conclusion. In I. Garfinkel (ed.), *Income-tested transfer programs: The case for and against*. New York: Academic Press, 1982.

Garfinkel, I. The role of child support insurance in antipoverty policy. *Annals of the American Academy of Political and Social Science*, 1985, *479*, 119–131.

Garfinkel, I., and McLanahan, S. *The feminization of poverty: Nature, causes, and a partial cure* (Discussion Paper 776–85). Madison, WI: Institute for Research on Poverty, 1985.

Geiger, H. J. Community health centers: Health care as an instrument of social change. In V. W. Sidel and R. Sidel (eds.), *Reforming medicine: Lessons of the last quarter century*. New York: Pantheon, 1984.

Giertz, J. F., and Sullivan, D. H. The role of food stamps in welfare reform. In P. M. Sommers (ed.), *Welfare reform in America: Perspectives and prospects*. Boston: Kluwer-Nijhoff, 1982.

Gilbert, N. *Capitalism and the welfare state: Dilemmas of social benevolence*. New Haven: Yale University Press, 1983.

Gilchrist, L. D., and Schinke, S. P. Teenage pregnancy and public policy. *Social Service Review*, 1983, *57*, 307–322.

Gilder, G. *Wealth and poverty*. New York: Basic Books, 1981.

Ginsburg, P. B., and Moon, M. An introduction to the Medicare financing problem. In *Proceedings of the Conference on the Future of Medicare*. Washington, D.C.: U.S. Government Printing Office, 1984.

Girschick, L. B., and Williamson, J. B. The politics of measuring poverty among the elderly. In R. Goldstein and S. M. Sachs (eds.), *Applied poverty research*. Totowa, NJ: Rowman and Allanheld, 1984.

Glazer, N. Beyond income maintenance—A note on welfare in New York City. *Public Interest*, 1969, Summer, 102–119.

Glazer, N. The social policy of the Reagan administration. In D. L. Bawden (ed.), *The social contract revisited: Aims and outcomes of President Reagan's social welfare policy*. Washington, D.C.: Urban Institute, 1984.

Glazer, N. *Education and training programs and poverty: Or, opening the black box* (IRP Conference Paper). Madison, WI: Institute for Research on Poverty, 1985.

Goggin, M. L. Reagan's revival: Turning back the clock in the health care debate. In A. Champagne and E. J. Harpham (eds.), *The attack on the welfare state*. Prospect Heights, IL: Waveland Press, 1984.

Goodban, N. *Historical and contemporary aspects of the welfare system and the effects on clients*. Unpublished manuscript, Harvard University, 1977.

Goodban, N. The psychological impact of being on welfare. *Social Service Review*, 1985, *59*, 403–422.

Goodwin, L. *Do the poor want to work? A social-psychological study of work orientations*. Washington, D.C.: Brookings Institution, 1972.

Goodwin, L. Middle-class misperceptions of the high life aspirations and strong work ethic held by the welfare poor. *American Journal of Orthopsychiatry*, 1973, *43*, 554–564.

Goodwin, L. *Causes and cures of welfare*. Lexington, MA: Lexington Books, 1983.

Goodwin, L., and Tu, J. The social psychological basis for public acceptance of the Social Security system: The role for social research in public policy formation. *American Psychologist*, 1975, *30*, 875–883.

Gottschalk, P. *U.S. labor market policies since the 1960s: A survey of programs and their effectiveness*. (Discussion Paper 730–83). Madison, WI: Institute for Research on Poverty, 1983.

Gottschalk, P., and Danziger, S. Macroeconomic conditions, income transfers, and the trend in poverty. In D. L. Bawden (ed.), *The social contract revisited: Aims and outcomes of President Reagan's social welfare policy*. Washington, D.C.: Urban Institute, 1984.

Gottschalk, P., and Danziger, S. A framework for evaluating the effects of economic growth and transfers on poverty. *American Economic Review*, 1985, *75*, 153–161.

Graham, G. C. Searching for hunger in America. *Public Interest*, 1985, Winter, 3–17.

Gramlich, E. Commentary on *Changed Lives*. In J. R. Berrueta-Clement, L. Schweinhart, W. Barnett, A. Epstein, and D. Weikart, *Changed lives: The effects of the Perry Preschool program on youths through age 19*. Ypsilanti, MI: High/Scope Press, 1984.

Greene, L. M. *Free enterprise without poverty*. New York: W. W. Norton and Company, 1981.

Grinker, W. J. *Statement on structural unemployment to the Urban Unemployment Task Force of the National League of Cities*. New York: Grinker, Walker and Associates, 1984.

Gronbjerg, K. *Mass society and the extension of welfare: 1960–1970*. Chicago: University of Chicago Press, 1977.

Grosse, S., and Morgan, J. N. Intertemporal variability in income and the interpersonal distribution of economic welfare. In M. S. Hill, D. H. Hill, and J. N. Morgan (eds.), *Five thousand American families—Patterns of economic progress* (vol. 9). Ann Arbor, MI: Institute for Social Research, 1981.

Grubb, W. N. The price of local discretion: Inequalities in welfare spending within Texas. *Journal of Policy Analysis and Management*, 1984, *3*, 359–372.

Gutowski, M. F., and Koshel, J. J. Social services. In J. L. Palmer and I. V. Sawhill (eds.), *The Reagan experiment*. Washington, D.C.: Urban Institute, 1982.

Guttman, R. Job Training Partnership Act: New help for the unemployed. *Monthly Labor Review*, 1983, *106* (3), 3–10.

Hadley, J. *More medical care, better health? An economic analysis of mortality rates*. Washington, D.C.: Urban Institute, 1982.

Hahn, A. and Lerman, R. *What works in youth employment policy?* Washington, D.C.: National Planning Association, 1985.

Hamermesh, D. S. What is an appropriate benefit level for the unemployed? In P. M. Sommers (ed.), *Welfare reform in America: Perspectives and prospects*. Boston: Kluwer-Nijhoff, 1982.

Hamilton, W. L. Economic and racial/ethnic concentration. In J. Friedman and D. H. Weinberg (eds.), *The great housing experiment*. Beverly Hills, CA: Sage, 1983.

Handler, J. F. *Reforming the poor: Welfare policy, federalism, and morality*. New York: Basic Books, 1972.

Handler, J. F., and Hollingsworth, E. J. *How obnoxious is the "obnoxious means test"? The views of AFDC recipients* (Discussion Paper 31–68). Madison, WI: Institute for Research on Poverty, 1968.

Handler, J. F., and Sosin, M. *Last resorts: Emergency assistance and special needs programs in public welfare*. New York: Academic Press, 1983.

Hansen, W. L. *Economic growth and equal opportunity: Conflicting or complementary goals in higher education?* (Discussion Paper 706–82). Madison, WI: Institute for Research on Poverty, 1982.

Hansen, W. L., and Lampman, R. J. *Good intentions and mixed results: An update on the Basic Educational Opportunity Grants* (Discussion Paper 705–82). Madison, WI: Institute for Research on Poverty, 1982.

Harpham, E. J. Fiscal crisis and the politics of Social Security reform. In A. Champagne and E. J. Harpham (eds.), *The attack on the welfare state*. Prospect Heights, IL: Waveland Press, 1984.

Harrington, M. *The new American poverty*. New York: Holt, Rinehart, and Winston, 1984.

Harris Survey reports that one in eleven American families suffer from hunger. *Foodlines*, April 1984, p. 8.

Hartman, C. Housing allowances: A bad idea whose time has come. *Working Papers*, 1982, *9* (6), 55–58.

Hasenfeld, Y. The role of employment placement services in maintaining poverty. *Social Service Review*, 1975, *49*, 569–587.

Hasenfeld, Y. The administration of human services. *Annals of the American Academy of Political and Social Science, 1985, 479*, 67–81.

Haveman, R. H. Introduction: Poverty and social policy in the 1960s and 1970s—An overview and some speculations. In R. H. Haveman (ed.), *A decade of federal antipoverty programs: Achievements, failures, and lessons*. New York: Academic Press, 1977.

Haveman, R. H., and Palmer, J. L. (eds). *Jobs for disadvantaged workers: The economics of employment subsidies*. Washington, D.C.: Brookings Institution, 1982.

Haveman, R. H., and Wolfe, B. L. Disability transfers and early retirement: A causal relationship? *Journal of Public Economics*, 1984, *24*, 47–66.

Hawkins, S. C. SSI: Trends in state supplementation, 1979–81. *Social Security Bulletin*, 1983, *46* (6), 3–8.

Hayghe, H. Working mothers reach record numbers in 1984. *Monthly Labor Review*, 1984, *107* (12), 31–34.

Heclo, H. *The political foundations of antipoverty policy* (IRP Conference Paper). Madison, WI: Institute for Research on Poverty, 1984.

Hetherington, E. M., Camara, K. A., and Featherman, D. L. Achievement and intellectual functioning of children in one-parent households. In J. Spence (ed.), *Achievement and achievement motives*. San Francisco: W. H. Freeman, 1983.

Hill, M. S. Some dynamic aspects of poverty. In M. S. Hill, D. H. Hill, and J. N. Morgan (eds.), *Five thousand American families— Patterns of economic progress* (vol. 9). Ann Arbor, MI: Institute for Social Research, 1981.

Hill, M. S., Augustyniak, S., Duncan, G. J., Gurin, G., Gurin, P., Liker, J. K., Morgan, J. N., and Ponza, M. *Motivation and economic mobility*. Ann Arbor, MI: Institute for Social Research, 1985.

Hoagland, G. W. The effectiveness of current transfer programs in reducing poverty. In P. M. Sommers (ed.), *Welfare reform in America: Perspectives and prospects*. Boston: Kluwer-Nijhoff, 1982.

Hoagland, G. W. Perception and reality in nutrition programs. In J. C. Weicher (ed.), *Maintaining the safety net: Income redistribution in the Reagan administration*. Washington, D.C.: American Enterprise Institute, 1984.

Hochschild, J. L. *What's fair? American beliefs about distributive justice*. Cambridge, MA: Harvard University Press, 1981.

Hofferth, S. L., and Moore, K. A. Early childbearing and later economic well-being. *American Sociological Review*, 1979, *44*, 784–815.

Hofstadter, R. *Social Darwinism in American thought* (rev. ed.). Boston: Beacon Press, 1955.

Hollingsworth, E. J. Ten years of legal services for the poor. In R. H. Havemen (ed.), *A decade of federal antipoverty programs: Achievements, failures, and lessons*. New York: Academic Press, 1977.

Hollister, R. G., Jr., Kemper, P., and Maynard, R. A. (eds). *The National Supported Work Demonstration*. Madison: University of Wisconsin Press, 1984.

Horan, P. M., and Austin, P. L. The social bases of welfare stigma. *Social Problems*, 1974, *21*, 648–657.

Inkeles, A. Industrial man: The relation of status to experience, perception, and value. *American Journal of Sociology*, 1960, *66*, 1–31.

Isaac, L., and Kelly, W. R. Racial insurgency, the state, and welfare expansion: Local and national level evidence from the postwar United States. *American Journal of Sociology*, 1981, *86*, 1348–1386.

Isserman, A. M. Food Stamps: An economic analysis. *Social Service Review*, 1975, *49*, 588–607.

Jeffrey, J. R. *Education for children of the poor: A study of the origin and implementation of the Elementary and Secondary Education Act of 1965*. Columbus, OH: Ohio State University Press, 1978.

Jencks, C. Heredity, environment, and public policy reconsidered. *American Sociological Review*, 1980, *45*, 723–736.

Jencks, C., Bartlett, S., Corcoran, M., Crouse, J., Eaglesfield, D., Jackson, G., McClelland, K., Mueser, P., Olneck, M., Schwartz, J., Ward, S., and Williams, J. *Who gets ahead? The determinants of economic success in America*. New York: Basic Books, 1979.

Jencks, C., Smith, M., Acland, H., Bane, M. J., Cohen, D., Gintis, H., Heyns, B., and Michelson, S. *Inequality: A reassessment of the effect of family and schooling in America*. New York: Basic Books, 1972.

Jennings, E. T., Jr. Urban riots and welfare policy change: A test of the Piven-Cloward theory. In H. M. Ingram and D. E. Mann (eds). *Why policies succeed or fail*. Beverly Hills, CA: Sage, 1980.

Jennings, E. T., Jr. Racial insurgency, the state, and welfare expansion: A critical comment and reanalysis. *American Journal of Sociology*, 1983, *88*, 1220–1236.

Joe, T. The case for income support. In A. Gartner, C. Greer, and F. Riessman (eds.), *Beyond Reagan: Alternatives for the '80s*. New York: Harper and Row, 1984.

Joe, T., and Rogers, C. *By the few for the few: The Reagan welfare legacy*. Lexington, MA: Lexington Books, 1985.

Johnson, T. R., Dickinson, K. P., and West, R. W. An evaluation of the impact of ES referrals on applicant earnings. *Journal of Human Resources*, 1985, *20*, 117–137.

Johnston, J. W. An overview of federal employment and training programs. In National Commission for Employment Policy, *Sixth annual report*. Washington, D.C.: U.S. Government Printing Office, 1980.

Johnston, J. W. The national employment and training "system." In National Commission for Employment Policy, *Seventh annual report*. Washington, D.C.: U.S. Government Printing Office, 1981.

Jones, R., Kaminsky, D., and Roanhouse, M. *Problems affecting low-rent public housing projects.* Washington, D.C.: U.S. Department of Housing and Urban Development, 1979.

Jordan, T. J., Grallo, R., Deutsch, M., and Deutsch, C. P. Long-term effects of early enrichment: A 20-year perspective on persistence and change. *American Journal of Community Psychology*, 1985, *13*, 393–415.

Kamalich, R. F., and Polachek, S. W. Discrimination: Fact or fiction? An examination using an alternative approach. *Southern Economic Journal*, 1982, *49*, 450–461.

Kaplan, H. R., and Tausky, C. Work and the welfare Cadillac: The function of and commitment to work among the hard-core unemployed. *Social Problems*, 1972, *19*, 469–483.

Kaplan, H. R., and Tausky, C. The meaning of work among the hard-core unemployed. *Pacific Sociological Review*, 1974, *17*, 185–198.

Kaufman, A. S., and Doppelt, J. E. Analysis of WISC-R standardization data in terms of the stratification variables. *Child Development*, 1976, *47*, 165–171.

Kaufman, R. L. A structural decomposition of black-white earnings differentials. *American Journal of Sociology*, 1983, *89*, 585–611.

Keefe, D. E. Governor Reagan, welfare reform, and AFDC fertility. *Social Service Review*, 1983, *57*, 234–253.

Kelley, E. W. Defederalization of education. In A. Champagne and E. J. Harpham (eds.), *The attack on the welfare state.* Prospect Heights, IL: Waveland Press, 1984.

Kennedy, S. D., and MacMillan, J. E. Participation under random assignment. In J. Friedman and D. H. Weinberg (eds.), *The great housing experiment.* Beverly Hills, CA: Sage, 1983.

Kerbo, H. R. The stigma of welfare and a passive poor. *Sociology and Social Research*, 1976, *60*, 173–187.

Kerckhoff, A. C. *Socialization and social class.* Englewood Cliffs, NJ: Prentice-Hall, 1972.

Khadduri, J., and Struyk, R. J. Housing vouchers for the poor. *Journal of Policy Analysis and Management*, 1982, *1*, 196–208.

Kiker, B. F., and Condon, C. M. The influence of socioeconomic background on the earnings of young men. *Journal of Human Resources*, 1981, *16*, 94–105.

Kohen, A. I., and Gilroy, C. L. The minimum wage, income distribution and poverty. In *Report of the Minimum Wage Study Commission* (vol. 7). Washington, D.C.: U.S. Government Printing Office, 1981.

Krauze, T., and Slomczynski, K. M. How far to meritocracy? Empirical tests of a controversial thesis. *Social Forces*, 1985, *63*, 623–642.

Lacey, R. A. *Becoming partners: How schools and companies meet mutual needs.* Washington, D.C.: National Commission for Employment Policy, 1983.

Lampman, R. J. What does it do for the poor? A new test for national policy. *Public Interest*, 1974, Winter, 66–82.

Lampman, R., and Smeeding, T. Interfamily transfers as alternatives to government transfers to persons. *Review of Income and Wealth*, 1983, Series 29 (1), 45–66.

Lane, R. E. *Political ideology: Why the American common man believes what he does.* New York: Free Press, 1962.

Lefkowitz, B. *Jobs for youth: What we have learned.* New York: The Edna McConnell Clark Foundation, 1982.

Leimer, D. R., and Petri, P. A. Cohort specific effects of Social Security policy. *National Tax Journal*, 1981, *34*, 9–28.

Leman, C. *The challenge of welfare reform: Political institutions, policy, and the poor in Canada and the United States.* Cambridge, MA: MIT Press, 1980.

Lesnoy, S. D., and Leimer, D. R. Social Security and private saving: Theory and historical evidence. *Social Security Bulletin*, 1985, *48* (1), 14–30.

Levin, H. M. A decade of policy developments in improving education and training for low-income populations. In R. H. Haveman (ed.), *A decade of federal antipoverty programs: Achievements, failures, and lessons.* New York: Academic Press, 1977.

Levitan, S. A. *Programs in aid of the poor* (5th ed.). Baltimore: Johns Hopkins University Press, 1985.

Levitan, S. A., and Johnson, C. M. *Beyond the safety net: Reviving the promise of opportunity in America.* Cambridge, MA: Ballinger, 1984.

Levitan, S. A., and Johnston, B. H. *The Job Corps: A social experiment that works.* Baltimore: Johns Hopkins University Press, 1975.

Levitan, S. A., and Taggart, R. (eds.). *Emergency Employment Act: The PEP generation.* Salt Lake City: Olympus Publishing Company, 1974.

Levy, F. *How big is the American underclass?* (Working Paper 0090–1). Washington, D.C.: Urban Institute, 1977.

Levy, F. The labor supply of female household heads, or AFDC work incentives don't work too well. *Journal of Human Resources*, 1979, *14*, 76–97.

Levy, F. *The intergenerational transfer of poverty: Final project report* (Working Paper 1241–02). Washington, D.C.: Urban Institute, 1980.

Lewis, I. A., and Schneider, W. Hard times: The public on poverty. *Public Opinion*, 1985, *8* (3), 1–7, 59–60.

Lewis, O. *La Vida: A Puerto Rican family in the culture of poverty.* New York: Random House, 1966.

Lewis, O. The culture of poverty. In D. P. Moynihan (ed.), *On understanding poverty: Perspectives from the social sciences.* New York: Basic Books, 1969.

Lindeman, D. The concept of horizontal equity and its application to social program design. In P. G. Brown, C. Johnson, and P. Vernier (eds.), *Income support: Conceptual and policy issues.* Totowa, NJ: Rowman and Littlefield, 1981.

Long, D. A., Mallar, C. D., and Thornton, C. V. D. Evaluating the benefits and costs of the Job Corps. *Journal of Policy Analysis and Management,* 1981, *1,* 55–76.

Lowenberg, F. M. The destigmatization of public dependency. *Social Service Review,* 1981, *55,* 434–452.

Luft, H. S. *Poverty and health: Economic causes and consequences of health problems.* Cambridge, MA: Ballinger, 1978.

Lundberg, M. J. *The incomplete adult: Social class constraints on personality development.* Westport, CT: Greenwood Press, 1974.

Lurie, I. Integrating income maintenance programs: Problems and solutions. In I. Lurie (ed.), *Integrating income maintenance programs.* New York: Academic Press, 1975.

Lurie, I. Work requirements in income-conditioned transfer programs. *Social Service Review,* 1978, *52,* 551–566.

Lynn, L. E., Jr. *The state and human services: Organizational change in a political context.* Cambridge, MA: MIT Press, 1980.

MacDonald, M. *Food, stamps, and income maintenance.* New York: Academic Press, 1977.

MacDonald, M., and Sawhill, I. V. Welfare policy and the family. *Public Policy,* 1978, *26,* 89–119.

Magill, R. S. *Community decision making for social welfare: Federalism, city government, and the poor.* New York: Human Sciences Press, 1979.

Mallan, L. B. Labor force participation, work experience, and the pay gap between men and women. *Journal of Human Resources,* 1982, *17,* 437–448.

Margolis, D. R. *From our hearts or against our wills: The two faces of social welfare.* Paper presented at the annual meeting of the Society for the Study of Social Problems, Washington, D.C., August, 1985.

Marx, K., and Engels, F. *Manifesto of the Communist Party.* New York: International Publishers, 1932 (original work published 1848).

Mayo, S. K. The household composition effects of income transfer programs. *Public Policy,* 1976, *24,* 395–422.

Mayo, S. K. Benefits from subsidized housing. In J. Friedman and D. H. Weinberg (eds.), *The great housing experiment*. Beverly Hills, CA: Sage, 1983.

McDonald, T., Moran, J., and Garfinkel, I. *Wisconsin study of absent fathers' ability to pay more child support* (Special Report 34). Madison, WI: Institute for Research on Poverty, 1983.

McKay, S. F. Long-range projection of average benefits under OASDI. *Social Security Bulletin*, 1982, *45* (1), 15–20.

McLanahan, S. Family structure and the reproduction of poverty. *American Journal of Sociology*, 1985, *90*, 873–901.

McLanahan, S., Cain, G., Olneck, M., Piliavin, I., Danziger, S., and Gottschalk, P. *Losing ground: A critique* (Special Report 38). Madison, WI: Institute for Research on Poverty, 1985.

Mead, L. M. Social programs and social obligations. *Public Interest*, 1982, Fall, 17–32.

Mead, L. M. Expectations and welfare work: WIN in New York City. *Policy Studies Review*, 1983, *2*, 648–662.

Menefee, J. A., Edwards, B., and Schieber, S. J. Analysis of nonparticipation in the SSI program. *Social Security Bulletin*, 1981, *44* (6), 3–21.

Mercy, J. A., and Steelman, L. C. Familial influence on the intellectual attainment of children. *American Sociological Review*, 1982, *47*, 532–542.

Meyer, J. A. The unfinished agenda in health policy. In J. C. Weicher (ed.), *Maintaining the safety net: Income redistribution programs in the Reagan administration*. Washington, D.C.: American Enterprise Institute, 1984.

Meyer, R., and Wise, D. *The effects of the minimum wage on the employment and earnings of youth* (Working Paper No. 849). Cambridge, MA: National Bureau of Economic Research, 1981.

Miller, S. E., and Hexter, H. *How low-income families pay for college*. Washington, D.C.: American Council on Education, 1985.

Miller, S. M., and Roby, P. A. *The future of inequality*. New York: Basic Books, 1970.

Miller, W. B. Lower class culture as a generating milieu of gang delinquency. *Journal of Social Issues*, 1958, *14* (3), 5–19.

Mills, D. Q., and Frobes, S. Impact of increases in the federal minimum wage on target groups in urban areas. *Public Policy*, 1981, *29*, 277–297.

Mirengoff, W., Rindler, L., Greenspan, H., and Harris, C. *CETA: Accomplishments, problems, solutions*. Kalamazoo, MI: W. E. Upjohn Institute for Employment Research, 1982.

Moffitt, R. An economic model of welfare stigma. *American Economic Review*, 1983, *73*, 1023–1035.

Moffitt, R. The effects of Grants-in-Aid on state and local expenditures: The case of AFDC. *Journal of Public Economics*, 1984, *23*, 279–305. (a)

Moffitt, R. Trends in Social Security wealth by cohort. In M. Moon (ed.), *Economic transfers in the United States*. Cambridge, MA: National Bureau of Economic Research, 1984. (b)

Moffitt, R., and Nicholson, W. The effect of Unemployment Insurance on unemployment: The case of Federal Supplemental Benefits. *Review of Economics and Statistics*, 1983, *64*, 1–11.

Moon, M., and Sawhill, I. V. Family incomes: Gainers and losers. In J. L. Palmer and I. V. Sawhill (eds.), *The Reagan Record*. Cambridge, MA: Ballinger, 1984.

Moon, M., and Smolensky, E. Introduction. In M. Moon and E. Smolensky (eds.), *Improving measures of economic well-being*. New York: Academic Press, 1977.

Morris, M. Are poverty and unemployment social problems? The dynamics of public definitions. *Sociology and Social Research*, 1985, *69*, 396–411.

Morris, M., and Williamson, J. B. Stereotypes and social class: A focus on poverty. In A. G. Miller (ed.), *In the eye of the beholder: Contemporary issues in stereotyping*. New York: Praeger, 1982.

Moscovice, I., and Craig, W. The Omnibus Budget Reconciliation Act and the working poor. *Social Service Review*, 1984, *58*, 49–62.

Moynihan, D. P. *The politics of a guaranteed income*. New York: Free Press, 1973.

Mullin, S. P., and Summers, A. A. Is more better? The effectiveness of spending on compensatory education. *Phi Delta Kappan*, 1983, *64*, 339–347.

Murray, C. The two wars against poverty: Economic growth and the Great Society. *Public Interest*, 1982, Fall, 3–16.

Murray, C. *Losing ground: American social policy, 1950–1980*. New York: Basic Books, 1984.

Nathan, R. P., Cook, R. F., and Rawlins, V. L. *Public service employment: A field evaluation*. Washington, D.C.: Brookings Institution, 1981.

National Commission for Employment Policy. *The federal role in vocational education*. Washington, D.C.: Author, 1981.

National Commission for Employment Policy. *Eighth annual report: The work revolution*. Washington, D.C.: Author, 1982.

National Commission for Employment Policy. *An employment policy for America's future*. Washington, D.C.: Author, 1983.

National Commission on Excellence in Education. *A nation at risk: The imperative for educational reform*. Washington, D.C.: U.S. Government Printing Office, 1983.

214   References

National Commission on Social Security Reform. *Report*. Washington, D.C.: U.S. Government Printing Office, 1983.

National Commission on Unemployment Compensation. *Unemployment Compensation: Final Report*. Washington, D.C.: U.S. Government Printing Office, 1980.

National Council on Employment Policy. *Back to basics under JTPA*. Washington, D.C.: Author, 1983.

National Institute of Education. *The Compensatory Education study: Executive summary*. Washington, D.C.: Author, 1978.

National Institute of Education. *The Vocational Education Study: The final report*. Washington, D.C.: U.S. Government Printing Office, 1981.

National Study Group on State Medicaid Strategies. *Reconstructing Medicaid: An agenda for change: Summary report*. Washington, D.C.: Center for the Study of Social Policy, 1983.

Nelson, W. J., Jr. Employment covered under the Social Security program, 1935–84. *Social Security Bulletin*, 1985, *48* (4), 33–39.

Nenno, M. K. Housing allowances are not enough. *Society*, 1984, *21* (3), 54–57.

Newitt, J., Armbruster, F. E., Deluty, P., Leveson, I., Melnick, R., and Yokelson, D. *School-to-work transition programs: A policy analysis*. Croton-on-Hudson, NY: Hudson Institute, 1984.

Newman, S. J., and Struyk, R. Housing and poverty. *Review of Economics and Statistics*, 1983, *65*, 243–253.

Oellerich, D. *The effects of potential child support transfers on Wisconsin AFDC costs, caseloads and recipient well-being* (Special Report 35). Madison, WI: Institute for Research on Poverty, 1984.

Oellerich, D., and Garfinkel, I. Distributional impacts of existing and alternative child support systems. *Policy Studies Journal*, 1983, *12*, 119–129.

O'Neill, D. M. Employment tax credit programs: The effects of socioeconomic targeting provisions. *Journal of Human Resources*, 1982, *17*, 449–459.

Orshansky, M. Counting he poor: Another look at the poverty profile. *Social Security Bulletin*, 1965, *28* (1), 3–29.

Otto, L. B., and Haller, A. O. Evidence for a social psychological view of the status attainment process: Four studies compared. *Social Forces*, 1979, *57*, 887–914.

Ozawa, M. N. *Income maintenance and work incentives: Toward a synthesis*. New York: Praeger, 1982.

Ozawa, M. N., and Alpert, W. T. Distributive effects of Survivors

Insurance benefits and public assistance. *Social Service Review*, 1984, *58*, 603–621.

Page, B. I. *Who gets what from government*. Berkeley: University of California Press, 1983.

Paglin, M. *Poverty and transfers in-kind*. Palo Alto, CA: Hoover Institution Press, 1980.

Paglin, M. How effective is our multiple-benefit antipoverty program? In P. M. Sommers (ed.), *Welfare reform in America: Perspectives and prospects*. Boston: Kluwer-Nijhoff, 1982.

Palmer, F. H., and Anderson, L. W. Long-term gains from early intervention: Findings from longitudinal studies. In E. Zigler and J. Valentine (eds.), *Project Head Start: A legacy of the War on Poverty*. New York: Free Press, 1979.

Palmer, J. L. (ed.). *Creating jobs: Public employment programs and wage subsidies*. Washington, D.C.: Brookings Institution, 1978.

Parsons, D. O. The decline in male labor force participation. *Journal of Political Economy*, 1980, *88*, 117–134.

Parsons, D. O. Disability insurance and male labor force participation: A response to Haveman and Wolfe. *Journal of Political Economy*, 1984, *92*, 542–549.

Patterson, J. T. *America's struggle against poverty 1900–1980*. Cambridge, MA: Harvard University Press, 1981.

Pechman, J. A., Aaron, H. J., and Taussig, M. K., *Social Security: Perspectives for reform*. Washington, D.C.: Brookings Institution, 1968.

Perry, C. R., Anderson, B. E., Rowan, R. L., and Northrup, H. R. *The impact of government manpower programs: In general, and on minorities and women*. Philadelphia: University of Pennsylvania Press, 1975.

Peterson, P. E. Did the education commissions say anything? *Brookings Review*, 1983, *2* (2), 3–11.

Phillips, M. H. Favorable family impact as an objective of income support policy. In P. G. Brown, C. Johnson, and P. Vernier (eds.), *Income support: Conceptual and policy issues*. Totowa, NJ: Rowman and Littlefield, 1981.

Piccione, J. *Help for families on the front lines: The theory and practice of family allowances*. Washington, D.C.: The Free Congress Research and Education Foundation, 1983.

Piliavin, I., Masters, S., and Corbett, T. *Administration and organizational influences on AFDC case decision errors: An empirical analysis* (Discussion Paper 542–79). Madison, WI: Institute for Research on Poverty, 1979.

Piven, F. F., and Cloward, R. A. *Regulating the poor: The functions of public welfare*. New York: Pantheon Books, 1971.

Piven, F. F., and Cloward, R. A. *Poor people's movements: Why they succeed, how they fail*. New York: Pantheon Books, 1977.

Piven, F. F., and Cloward, R. A. *The new class war: Reagan's attack on the welfare state and its consequences*. New York: Pantheon Books, 1982.

Placek, P. J., and Hendershot, G. E. Public welfare and family planning: An empirical study of the "Brood Sow" myth. *Social Problems*, 1974, *21*, 658–673.

Plattner, M. F. The welfare state vs. the redistributive state. *Public Interest*, 1979, Spring, 28–48.

Plotnick, R. The redistributive impact of cash transfers. *Public Finance Quarterly*, 1984, *12*, 27–50.

Plotnick, R. D., and Skidmore, F. *Progress against poverty: A review of the 1964–1974 decade*. New York: Academic Press, 1975.

Polit, D. F., and Kahn, J. R. Project Redirection: Evaluation of a comprehensive program for disadvantaged teenage mothers. *Family Planning Perspectives*, 1985, *17*, 150–155.

Poverty in America. *Public Opinion*, 1985, *8* (3), 25–31.

President's Task Force on Food Assistance. *Final Report*. Washington, D.C.: U.S. Government Printing Office, 1984.

Presser, H. B., and Salsberg, L. S. Public assistance and early family formation: Is there a pronatalist effect? *Social Problems*, 1975, *23*, 226–241.

Price, D. N. Workers' Compensation: 1978 program update. *Social Security Bulletin*, 1980, *43* (10), 3–10.

Price, D. N. Workers' Compensation: Coverage, benefits, and costs, 1982. *Social Security Bulletin*, 1984, *47* (12), 7–13.

Proceedings of the Conference on the Future of Medicare. Washington, D.C.: U.S. Government Printing Office, 1984.

Public/Private Ventures. *Ventures in Community Improvement: Final Report of the Demonstration*. Philadelphia: Author, 1982.

Public/Private Ventures. *Longer term impacts of pre-employment services on the employment and earnings of disadvantaged youth*. Philadelphia: Author, 1983.

Rainwater, L. *Behind ghetto walls*. Chicago: Aldine, 1970.

Rainwater, L. *What money buys: Inequality and the social meanings of income*. New York: Basic Books, 1974.

Rainwater, L. *Persistent and transitory poverty: A new look*. Cambridge, MA: Joint Center for Urban Studies, 1980.

Rainwater, L. Stigma in income-tested programs. In I. Garfinkel (ed.), *Income-tested transfer programs: The case for and against*. New York: Academic Press, 1982.

Rein, M. *Dilemmas of welfare policy: Why work strategies haven't worked*. New York: Praeger, 1982.

Rein, M., and Rainwater, L. Patterns of welfare use. *Social Service Review*, 1978, *52*, 511–534.

Rence, C., and Wiseman, M. The California Welfare Reform Act and participation in AFDC. *Journal of Human Resources*, 1978, *13*, 37–59.

Report of the Minimum Wage Study Commission (vol. 1). Washington, D.C.: U.S. Government Printing Office, 1981.

Report of the President's Commission on Housing. Washington, D.C.: U.S. Government Printing Office, 1982.

Reynolds, R. A. Improving access to health care among the poor—The neighborhood health center experience. *Millbank Memorial Fund Quarterly: Health and Society*, 1976, *54*, 47–82.

Rhine, W. R. (ed.). *Making schools more effective: New directions from Follow Through*. New York: Academic Press, 1981.

Rigby, D. E., and Scott, C. Low-Income Energy Assistance Program. *Social Security Bulletin*, 1983, *46* (1), 11–32.

Ripley, R. B. *The implementation of the Targeted Jobs Tax Credit: Final report*. Washington, D.C.: U.S. Department of Labor, 1981.

Ripley, R. B., and Franklin, G. A. The private sector in employment and training programs. *Policy Studies Review*, 1983, *2*, 695–714.

Ritti, R. R., and Hyman, D. W. The administration of poverty: Lessons from the welfare explosion 1967–1973. *Social Problems*, 1977, *25*, 157–175.

Robins, P. K. *Child support enforcement as a means of reducing welfare dependency and poverty*. (Discussion Paper 758–84). Madison, WI: Institute for Research on Poverty, 1984.

Robinson, R. V. Reproducing class relations in industrial capitalism. *American Sociological Review*, 1984, *49*, 182–196.

Robinson, W. C. Educational disinvestment. *Policy Review*, 1983, Fall, 59–64.

Rochefort, D. A. Progressive and social control perspectives on social welfare. *Social Service Review*, 1981, *55*, 568–592.

Rodgers, C. S. Work tests for welfare recipients: The gap between the goal and the reality. *Journal of Policy Analysis and Management*, 1981, *1*, 5–17.

Rodgers, H. R., Jr. *The cost of human neglect: America's welfare failure*. Armonk, NY: M. E. Sharpe, 1982.

Rodgers, H. R., Jr. Limiting poverty by design: The official measure of poverty. In R. Goldstein and S. M. Sachs (eds.), *Applied poverty research*. Totowa, NJ: Rowman and Allanheld, 1984.

Rodman, H., and Voydanoff, P. Social class and parents' range of aspirations for their children. *Social Problems*, 1978, *25*, 333–344.

Rodman, H., Voydanoff, P., and Lovejoy, A. E. The range of aspirations: A new approach. *Social Problems*, 1974, *22*, 184–198.

Ross, C. *Income transfers and the relative economic status of the elderly, 1967, 1974, and 1981* (Discussion Paper 760–84). Madison, WI: Institute for Research on Poverty, 1984.

Rossi, P. Residential mobility. In K. L. Bradbury and A. Downs (eds.), *Do housing allowances work?* Washington, D.C.: Brookings Institution, 1981.

Rubin, R. J. Statement before The Subcommittee on Oversight and Subcommittee on Public Assistance and Unemployment Compensation, November 3, 1983. In S. Danziger, P. Gottschalk, R. J. Rubin, and T. M. Smeeding, *Recent increases in poverty: Testimony before the House Ways and Means Committee* (Discussion Paper 740–83). Madison, WI: Institute for Research on Poverty, 1983.

Rumberger, R. W., and Daymont, T. N. The economic value of academic and vocational training acquired in high school. In M. E. Borus (ed.), *Youth and the labor market*. Kalamazoo, MI: W. E. Upjohn Institute for Employment Research, 1984.

Russell, L. B. *The baby boom generation and the economy*. Washington, D.C.: Brookings Institution, 1982.

Russell, L. B. Medical care. In J. A. Pechman (ed.), *Setting national priorities: The 1984 budget*. Washington, D.C.: Brookings Institution, 1983.

Ryan, W. *Blaming the victim* (rev. ed). New York: Vintage Books, 1976.

Ryan, W. *Equality*. New York: Pantheon Books, 1981.

Rydell, C., Palmerio, T., Blais, G., and Brown, D. *Welfare caseload dynamics in New York City*. New York: Rand Institute, 1974.

Sandefur, G. S., and Scott, W. J. *A sociological analysis of white, black, and American Indian male labor force activities* (Discussion Paper 765–84). Madison, WI: Institute for Research on Poverty, 1984.

Sanger, M. B. *Welfare of the poor*. New York: Academic Press, 1979.

Sardell, A. The mobilization of bias in primary care policy: The case of neighborhood health centers. *Policy Studies Journal*, 1980–81, *9*, 206–212.

Sarri, R. C., Beisel, N., Boulet, J., Butler, A., Churchill, S., Lambert, S., Ray, A., Russell, C., and Weber, J. *The impact of federal policy change on AFDC recipients and their families: An evaluation of 1981 OBRA policies in Michigan*. Ann Arbor, MI: Institute for Social Research, 1984.

Scarr, S., and Weinberg, R. A. Influence of "family background" on intellectual attainment. *American Sociological Review*, 1978, *43*, 674–692.

Schiller, B. R. Lessons from WIN: A manpower evaluation. *Journal of Human Resources*, 1978, *13*, 502–523.

Schiller, B. R. Welfare: Reforming our expectations. *Public Interest*, 1981, Winter, 55–65.

Schiller, B. R. *The economics of poverty and discrimination* (4th ed.). Englewood Cliffs, NJ: Prentice Hall, 1984.

Schwartz, N. H. Reagan's housing policies. In A. Champagne and E. J. Harpham (eds.), *The attack on the welfare state*. Prospect Heights, IL: Waveland Press, 1984.

Segalman, R. *The interaction of social policy and welfare dependency*. Paper presented at the Clark-Luxembourg Conference on Anti-Poverty Programs, Worcester, MA, August 1982.

Segalman, R., and Basu, A. *Poverty in America: The welfare dilemma*. Westport, CT: Greenwood Press, 1981.

Sewell, W. H., and Hauser, R. M. *Education, occupation, and earnings: Achievement in the early career*. New York: Academic Press, 1975.

Sloan, F., Mitchell, J., and Cromwell, J. Physician participation in state Medicaid programs. *Journal of Human Resources*, 1978, *13* (Supplement), 211–245.

Smeeding, T. M. The anti-poverty effectiveness of in-kind transfers. *Journal of Human Resources*, 1977, *12*, 360–378.

Smeeding, T. M. *Alternative methods for valuing selected in-kind transfer benefits and measuring their effect on poverty* (Technical Paper No. 50). Washington, D.C.: U.S. Government Printing Office, 1982.

Smeeding, T. M. What the official estimates fail to show. In S. Danziger, P. Gottschalk, R. J. Rubin, and T. M. Smeeding, *Recent increases in poverty: Testimony before the House Ways and Means Committee* (Discussion Paper 740–83). Madison, WI: Institute for Research on Poverty, 1983.

Smeeding, T. M. Approaches to measuring and valuing in-kind subsidies and the distribution of their benefits. In M. Moon (ed.), *Economic transfers in the United States*. Cambridge, MA: National Bureau of Economic Research, 1984. (a)

Smeeding, T. M. Is the safety net still intact? In D. L. Bawden (ed.), *The social contract revisited: Aims and outcomes of President Reagan's social welfare policy*. Washington, D.C.: Urban Institute, 1984. (b)

Smith, A. D., Fortune, A. E., and Reid, W. J. WIN, work, and welfare. *Social Service Review*, 1975, *49*, 396–404.

Solon, G. Labor supply effects of extended unemployment benefits. *Journal of Human Resources*, 1979, *14*, 247–255.

Solon, G. The minimum wage and teenage employment: A reanalysis with attention to serial correlation and seasonality. *Journal of Human Resources*, 1985, *20*, 292–297.

Sosin, M. *Legal rights and welfare change: 1960–1980* (IRP Conference Paper). Madison, WI: Institute for Research on Poverty, 1985.

Spivey, W. A. Problems and paradoxes in economic and social policies of modern welfare states. *Annals of the American Academy of Political and Social Science*, 1985, *479*, 14–30.

Stanback, H. Attacking poverty with economic policy. In A. Gartner, C. Greer, and F. Riessman (eds.), *Beyond Reagan: Alternatives for the '80s*. New York: Harper and Row, 1984.

Starr, P. *Health care and the poor: The last twenty years* (IRP Conference Paper). Madison, WI: Institute for Research on Poverty, 1984.

Sternlieb, G., and Hughes, J. W. Housing the poor in a postshelter society. *Annals of the American Academy of Political and Social Science*, 1983, *465*, 109–122.

Stevens, R., and Stevens, R. *Welfare medicine in America: A case study of Medicaid*. New York: Free Press, 1974.

Straszheim, M. R. Participation. In K. L. Bradbury and A. Down (eds.), *Do housing allowances work?* Washington, D.C.: Brookings Institution, 1981.

Stromsdorfer, E. W. The effectiveness of youth programs: An analysis of the historical antecedents of current youth iniatives. In The American Assembly, *Youth employment and public policy*. Englewood Cliffs, NJ: Prentice-Hall, 1980.

Struyk, R. J., and Bendick, M., Jr. (eds.). *Housing vouchers for the poor: Lessons from a national experiment*. Washington, D.C.: Urban Institute, 1981.

Struyk, R. J., Mayer, N., and Tuccillo, J. A. *Federal housing policy at President Reagan's midterm*. Washington, D.C.: Urban Institute, 1983.

Struyk, R. J., Tuccillo, J. A., and Zais, J. P. Housing and community development. In J. L. Palmer and I. V. Sawhill (eds.), *The Reagan experiment*. Washington, D.C.: Urban Institute, 1982.

Svahn, J. A., and Ross, M. Social Security amendments of 1983: Legislative history and summary of provisions. *Social Security Bulletin*, 1983, *46* (7), 3–48.

Taggart, R. (ed.). *Job creation: What works?* Salt Lake City: Olympus Publishing Company, 1977.

Taggart, R. *A fisherman's guide: An assessment of training and re-*

mediation strategies. Kalamazoo, MI: W. E. Upjohn Institute for Employment Research, 1981.

Taggart, R. *Hardship: The welfare consequences of labor market problems*. Kalamazoo, MI: W. E. Upjohn Institute for Employment Research, 1982.

Tannen, M. B. Vocational education and earnings for white males: New evidence from longitudinal data. *Southern Economic Journal*, 1983, *50*, 369–384.

Terry, S. L. Work experience, earnings, and family income in 1981. *Monthly Labor Review*, 1983, *106* (4), 13–20.

Thompson, L. H. The Social Security reform debate. *Journal of Economic Literature*, 1983, *21*, 1425–1467.

Tissue, T. Response to recipiency under public assistance and SSI. *Social Security Bulletin*, 1978, *41* (11), 3–15.

Tolbert, C., Horan, P. M., and Beck, E. M. The structure of economic segmentation: A dual economy approach. *American Journal of Sociology*, 1980, *85*, 1095–1116.

Trattner, W. I. (ed.). *Social welfare or social control? Some historical reflections on "Regulating the poor."* Knoxville: University of Tennessee Press, 1983.

Trattner, W. I. *From Poor Law to welfare state: A history of social welfare in America* (3rd ed.). New York: Free Press, 1984.

Treiman, D. J., and Hartmann, H. I. (eds.). *Women, work, and wages: Equal pay for jobs of equal value*. Washington, D.C.: National Academy Press, 1981.

Treiman, D. J., and Roos, P. A. Sex and earnings in industrial society: A nine-nation comparison. *American Journal of Sociology*, 1983, *89*, 612–650.

Tussing, A. D. *Poverty in a dual economy*. New York: St. Martin's Press, 1975.

U.S. Bureau of the Census. *Characteristics of households and persons receiving selected noncash benefits: 1983* (Current Population Reports, Series P–60, No. 148). Washington, D.C.: U.S. Government Printing Office, 1985. (a)

U.S. Bureau of the Census. *Characteristics of the population below the poverty level: 1983* (Current Population Reports, Series P–60, No. 147). Washington, D.C.: U.S. Government Printing Office, 1985. (b)

U.S. Bureau of the Census. *Estimates of poverty including the value of noncash benefits: 1984*. (Technical Paper 55). Washington, D.C.: U.S. Government Printing Office, 1985. (c)

U.S. Bureau of the Census. *Money income and poverty status of families and persons in the United States: 1984* (Current Population

Reports, Series P–60, No. 149). Washington, D.C.: U.S. Government Printing Office, 1985. (d)

U. S. Bureau of the Census. *Child support and alimony: 1983* (Current Population Reports, Series P–23, No. 141). Washington, D.C.: U.S. Government Printing Office, 1985. (e)

U.S. Department of Commerce. *1984 annual report, Economic Development Administration.* Washington, D.C.: U.S. Government Printing Office, 1985.

U.S. Department of Education. *Annual evaluation report, fiscal year 1982* (vol. 1). Washington, D.C.: Author, 1982.

U.S. Department of Education. *Annual evaluation report, fiscal year 1983.* Washington, D.C.: Author, 1983.

U.S. Department of Health, Education, and Welfare. *The measure of poverty.* Washington, D.C.: Author, 1976.

U.S. Department of Housing and Urban Development. *An impact evaluation of the Urban Development Action Grant program.* Washington, D.C.: U.S. Government Printing Office, 1982.

U.S. Department of Housing and Urban Development. *Consolidated annual report to Congress on community development programs.* Washington, D.C.: U.S. Government Printing Office, 1985.

U.S. General Accounting Office. *Social services: Do they help welfare recipients achieve self-support or reduced dependency?* Washington, D.C.: Author, 1973.

U.S. General Accounting Office. *Rental housing: A national problem that needs immediate attention.* Washington, D.C.: Author, 1979.

U.S. General Accounting Office. *Section 8 subsidized housing—Some observations on its high rents.* Washington, D.C.: Author, 1980.

U.S. General Accounting Office. *Head Start: An effective program but the fund distribution formula needs revision and management controls need improvement.* Washington, D.C.: Author, 1981.

U.S. General Accounting Office. *HUD needs to better determine extent of community block grants' lower income benefits.* Washington, D.C.: Author, 1982. (a)

U.S. General Accounting Office. *Information on the U.S. Employment Service's programs, activities, and functions.* Washington, D.C.: Author, 1982. (b)

U.S. General Accounting Office. *Insights into CETA's in-school youth programs.* Washington, D.C.: Author, 1982. (c)

U.S. General Accounting Office. *An overview of the WIN program: Its objectives, accomplishments, and problems.* Washington, D.C.: Author, 1982. (d)

U.S. General Accounting Office. *Revitalizing distressed areas through enterprise zones: Many uncertanties exist.* Washington, D.C.: Author, 1982. (e)

U.S. General Accounting Office. *Federal job training: A comparison of public and private sector performance.* Washington, D.C.: Author, 1983. (a)

U.S. General Accounting Office. *Minimum wage policy questions persist.* Washington, D.C.: Author, 1983. (b)

U.S. General Accounting Office. *Public and private efforts to feed America's poor.* Washington, D.C.: Author, 1983. (c)

U.S. General Accounting Office. *States are making good progress in implementing The Small Cities Community Development Block Grant Program.* Washington, D.C.: Author, 1983. (d)

U.S. General Accounting Office. *CWEP's implementation results to date raise questions about the administration's proposed mandatory workfare program.* Washington, D.C.: Author, 1984. (a)

U.S. General Accounting Office. *An evaluation of the 1981 AFDC changes: Initial analyses.* Washington, D.C.: Author, 1984. (b)

U.S. General Accounting Office. *Participation in the National School Lunch Program.* Washington, D.C.: Author, 1984. (c)

U.S. General Accounting Office. *WIC evaluations provide some favorable but no conclusive evidence on the effects expected for the Special Supplemental Program for Women, Infants, and Children.* Washington, D.C.: Author, 1984. (d)

Urquhart, M. A., and Hewson, M. A. Unemployment continued to rise in 1982 as recession deepened. *Monthly Labor Review*, 1983, *106* (2), 3–12.

Vachon, J. M. School lunch wins customers... and praise. *Food and Nutrition*, 1983, *13* (4), 2–5.

Valentine, C. A. *Culture and poverty: Critique and counter-proposals.* Chicago: University of Chicago Press, 1968.

Valentine, J. Program development in Head Start: A multifaceted approach to meeting the needs of families with children. In E. Zigler and J. Valentine (eds.), *Project Head Start: A legacy of the War on Poverty.* New York: Free Press, 1979.

Verba, S. and Orren, G. R. *Equality in America: The view from the top.* Cambridge, MA: Harvard University Press, 1985.

Villemez, W. J. Ability vs. effort: Ideological correlates of occupational grading. *Social Forces*, 1974, *53*, 45–52.

Vroman, W. *The Reagan administration and unemployment insurance.* (Working Paper). Washington, D.C.: Urban Institute, 1984.

Walker, G., Feldstein, H., and Solow, K. *An independent sector assessment of the Job Training Partnership Act—Phase II: Initial implementation.* New York: Grinker, Walker and Associates, 1985.

Walker, G., Grinker, W., Seessel, T., Smith, R. C., and Cama, V. *An independent sector assessment of the Job Training Partnership Act.* New York: Grinker, Walker and Associates, 1984.

Warlick, J. L. Participation of the aged in SSI. *Journal of Human Resources*, 1982, *17*, 236–260.

Warlick, J. Aged women in poverty: A problem without a solution? In W. P. Brown and L. K. Olson (eds.), *Aging and public policy: The politics of growing old in America.* Westport, CT: Greenwood Press, 1983.

Warlick, J. *How effectively does SSI guarantee minimum income for the low-income aged?* (Discussion Paper 751–84). Madison, WI: Institute for Research on Poverty, 1984.

Watson, H. Saving, Social Security, and uncertainty. *Southern Economic Journal*, 1982, *49*, 330–341.

Waxman, C. I. *The stigma of poverty: A critique of poverty theories and policies* (2nd ed.). New York: Pergamon Press, 1983.

Weicher, J. C. Halfway to a housing allowance? In J. C. Weicher (ed.), *Maintaining the safety net: Income redistribution programs in the Reagan administration.* Washington, D.C.: American Enterprise Institute, 1984. (a)

Weicher, J. C. (ed.). *Maintaining the safety net: Income redistribution programs in the Reagan administration.* Washington, D.C.: American Enterprise Institute, 1984. (b)

Williamson, J. B. The stigma of public dependency: A comparison of alternative forms of public aid to the poor. *Social Problems*, 1974, *22*, 213–228.

Wohlenberg, E. H. A regional approach to public attitudes and public assistance. *Social Service Review*, 1976, *50*, 491–505.

Worcester, D. A., Jr. Blueprint for a welfare state that contributes to economic efficiency. *Social Service Review*, 1980, *54*, 165–183.

Yando, R., Seitz, V., and Zigler, E. *Intellectual and personality characteristics of children: Social-class and ethnic-group differences.* Hillsdale, NJ: Lawrence Erlbaum Associates, 1979.

Zais, J. P. Repairs and maintenance on the units occupied by allowance recipients. In R. J. Struyk and M. Bendick, Jr. (eds.), *Housing vouchers for the poor: Lessons from a national experiment.* Washington, D.C.: Urban Institute, 1981.

Zald, M. N. Demographics, politics, and the future of the welfare state. *Social Service Review*, 1977, *51*, 110–124.

Index

About the Authors

MICHAEL MORRIS, Associate Professor of Psychology, University of New Haven, has contributed to *In the Eye of the Beholder* (Praeger, 1982). His articles have appeared in *Sociology and Social Research* and *Journal of Community Psychology*.

JOHN B. WILLIAMSON, Professor of Sociology, Boston College, is the author of *Strategies against Poverty in America*, *Aging and Public Policy: Social Control or Social Justice?*, and other books, as well as more than 30 journal articles dealing with poverty, inequality, and related issues.